The Veil Unveiled

Florida A&M University, Tallahassee
Florida Atlantic University, Boca Raton
Florida Gulf Coast University, Fort Myers
Florida International University, Miami
Florida State University, Tallahassee
University of Central Florida, Orlando
University of Florida, Gainesville
University of North Florida, Jacksonville
University of South Florida, Tampa
University of West Florida, Pensacola

University Press of Florida

GAINESVILLE · TALLAHASSEE · TAMPA · BOCA RATON
PENSACOLA · ORLANDO · MIAMI · JACKSONVILLE · FT. MYERS

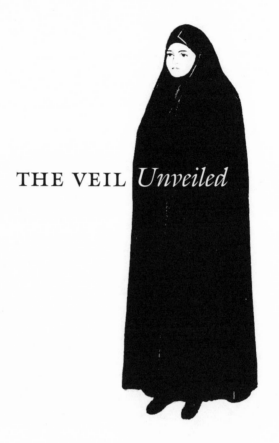

THE VEIL *Unveiled*

The Hijab in Modern Culture

Faegheh Shirazi

06 05 04 03 02 01 6 5 4 3 2 1

Library of Congress Cataloging-in-Publication Data
Shirazi, Faegheh, 1952–
The veil unveiled: the hijab in modern culture / Faegheh Shirazi.
p. cm.
Includes bibliographical references and index.
ISBN 0-8130-2084-0 (alk. paper)
1. Veils—Social aspects. 2. Muslim women—Costume.
3. Costume—Erotic aspects. 4. Muslim women in art. 5. Purdah.
6. Purdah in literature. I. Title.
GT2112 .S56 2001
391.4'3—dc21 00-053667

The University Press of Florida is the scholarly publishing agency for
the State University System of Florida, comprising Florida A&M
University, Florida Atlantic University, Florida Gulf Coast University,
Florida International University, Florida State University, University
of Central Florida, University of Florida, University of North
Florida, University of South Florida, and University of West Florida.

University Press of Florida
15 Northwest 15th Street
Gainesville, FL 32611–2079
http://www.upf.com

To my late father, Dr. Mahmood Shirazi,
whose dedication to and interest in the lives and
education of his children are truly admirable.

Contents

Figures

Note on Transliteration

In this book I have used a simplified transcription system in which long vowels are not indicated. The *ayn* ʿ and the *hamza* ʾ are represented by the conventional symbols. To facilitate greater ease in reading Arabic and Persian words and names, I have used the anglicized version of these when available.

Acknowledgments

This book is the product of more than six years of research. It took numerous trips to the Middle East and months of finding and reading various contemporary magazines from the Middle East and the Indian subcontinent. I spent countless hours at the law library at the University of Texas analyzing the representations of Muslim women in American erotica. After word spread about my project, students, colleagues, friends, friends of friends, and my family participated in my research. They shared their views and generously provided information. This book would not have been possible without their encouragement and support. In many ways, this book is truly a collaborative effort.

A University Cooperative Society Subvention Grant was awarded by the University of Texas at Austin to support my research.

I am grateful to the colleagues and friends who sacrificed their time to read parts of the manuscript: Kamran S. Aghaei, Yildiray Erdner, Mohammed Ghanoonparvar, Akel Kahera, and Esther Raizen. The book has only been improved by their careful reading and insightful comments. I owe a debt of gratitude to Hafez Farmayan. Hafez, thank you for your words of encouragement and reassurances when I had doubts about the whole project.

Thank you, Ian Hanks, for bringing to my attention representations of the veil in Ovid's *Metamorphoses*. The reaction of Chris Hofgren, former acquisitions editor at the University Press of Florida, to a paper I gave at a conference gave birth to the book in its present form. Moreover, he sent my manuscript to reviewers who not only carefully read it but made insightful comments and shared information. I want to extend my thanks to him as well as to the reviewers. I especially want to thank Farzaneh Milani, Shahla Haeri, and Virginia Wimberly for their careful and painstaking readings.

Dr. Abu Torabian, my work benefited greatly from your resources. You allowed me to make copies of rare articles in your private collection. My visits with you made me realize the plethora of primary sources available on the veil. Thank you for your time and generosity.

My two best friends, Shahla Hemati and Nahid Mirbagheri of Austin and Dallas, respectively, thank you both for your moral support and encouragement.

Robert (Rusty) Rush, you have helped me see the manuscript to its fruition. You listened patiently and asked intelligent questions when I talked once again about the subjects and chapters of the book. Thank you for the time you took helping me find the right contact persons to get copyright permissions. Without your help, I would have been wasting much precious time. I am also thankful for the time you spent helping me collate pages and prepare copies of the manuscript and shipping it. Thanks to Virginia Howell for sacrificing a weekend to make the manuscript comply with the press guidelines.

Many friends in Iran and Austin helped in various ways. Zahra Rahat sent me photographs, postcards, and articles. Kumkum Jain and Vandana Agarwal helped me identify songs and translate them from Hindi into English. Kum Kum, you put your own work aside to translate Yashpal's short story from Hindi into English. I appreciate your time and interest in my project.

Naima Boussofara, my dear friend from Tunisia, I benefited a lot from your knowledge of classical Arabic and Arab culture. Our discussions of Bedouin culture and its use in Saudi advertisements gave my analyses new perspectives.

I am thankful to Tanweer Aslam, who carefully and patiently translated a number of Urdu poems for me. Tanweer, you even watched those three-hour-long Hindi movies in order to compare my interpretation of the story plots with the songs in the movies. You confirmed that even though I am not from a Muslim South Asian culture I was able to understand the metaphors and significance of the veil in the Hindi movies under discussion. Thank you for the sleepless nights you spent polishing the translations when you had your own important deadlines to meet.

Many thanks to Diane Watts for allowing me to rely on her superb artistic talents, helpful suggestions, and patience in reproducing images. Diane, you have always done excellent work even when the deadlines were nearly impossible to meet. Your smile during those hard times meant more than I can say.

My highest regards to Renate Wise, my editor, who stood by me during the entire process of writing and researching the book. I benefited greatly from her professional expertise and suggestions. I have been blessed not only with an insightful editor but with a very good friend. Thank you, Renate.

I owe thanks to family members in India who have provided photographs and other materials that strengthened my analyses and argumentation. Thanks to Vijay Mahajan for his support and interest in my work. Vijay, you always gave me the opportunity to talk about my work. Your reactions to my material allowed me to gauge the prospective reactions of people from other fields of study. You were my sounding board for complex concepts and theories of the veil that proved difficult to support.

I want to thank my uncle Aboulghasem Shirazi for translating al-Azri's poem "Hijab" from Arabic into Persian. My Iraqi cousins Layla, Zaynab, Ala Kadhum, and Jamal Shirazi provided information and clippings from daily Iraqi newspapers and monthly publications on relevant topics. I appreciate your kindness and generosity, especially when considering the conditions under which Iraqi people are forced to live. Your regular mail and contact keep our family ties strong. My gratitude for what you have done cannot be expressed in words. I am sure that you feel it in your hearts.

I thank all my cousins in California for their support. Morteza, thank you for bringing the movie *The Sheltering Sky* to my attention.

My dear Mahmood Shirazi-Aslam, thank you for your careful responses to my inquiries. Your notes on different publications and special orders solved many problems. Thank you for staying up an entire night in order to read my manuscript when I was visiting you in Maryland. Your comments were important to me. Shabnam, your interest in my work enabled me to fathom how young college students may react to the issues I discuss here.

I am grateful to my brother Kamel Shirazi, my sister-in-law Fataneh, my niece Sougoul, and my nephew Samir for making me feel welcome in their home on the numerous occasions when I visited Iran. Kamel, you drove me to places and informed me about resources to which I would not have had access without your help. Samir and Sougoul, both of you told me about policies at your schools. Your routines at school are so different from those I experienced when I was a schoolgirl in Iran. Fataneh, thank you for collecting posters and brochures and information from the daily papers in Iran.

Mariam Shirazi-Aslam and Sharifeh Shirazi-Tarwand, you are my best friends. I could not ask for better sisters. Both of you helped me during the biggest crisis of my life when I was under so much pressure and still had to write my final chapters. Your many phone calls kept me going and made me feel proud to call you sisters.

Every summer when I made my trip to Iran, my late father, Dr. Mahmood Shirazi, was my research companion. He took me to all the hidden bookshops in downtown Tehran. He helped me with Arabic translations and, most of all, he helped me understand religious concepts. His study of the Qur'an, his fluency in Arabic, and his religious experience growing up in Najaf, Iraq, in a religious Shi"ite household with strong Islamic beliefs and training made him an expert on the religious aspects of my project. I wish you were here so you could enjoy the result of our collaboration. But I honestly believe you already know the result.

Many thanks to my beloved mother, Aghdas Shirazi (Simafar), who always provided great comfort to me and supported all my endeavors unconditionally. You always believed in me and my work and reminded me countless times of how proud you are of me. I am proud to have you as my mother.

My son, Ramin Shirazi-Mahajan, reminded me that I can get this project done and that it will be done. Thank you, Ramin, for your help. I am thankful to my daughter, Geeti Shirazi-Mahajan, my "junior" editor, for reading some of my chapters in their earliest stages. She gave me her honest opinion about my analyses of the representations of Middle Eastern women in advertisements. Thank you, Geeti, for being one of my earliest and strongest supporters. You greatly encouraged me by telling me how interesting my work was.

I consider myself blessed with Baraka and very lucky indeed to be surrounded by so many good and caring people who are always eager to lend a helping hand.

Alhamdulillah.

Introduction

Donning the Veil

It was long past midnight on the Lufthansa flight from Frankfurt to Tehran when a voice over the airplane's loudspeakers reminded me and fellow passengers that the Islamic Republic of Iran enforces the law of *hijab*.[1] Upon hearing this message, I knew that my plane had reached Iranian skies and that I had to put on my *rupush*, a loose outer garment that flows down past my knees and covers my arms, and my *rusari*, a large scarf that covers my hair, shoulders, and neck. Every year upon my visit home, for the last twenty years, I have chafed at the necessity of wearing this cumbersome attire but have complied with the dress code in order to avoid harassment and likely imprisonment upon arrival at Tehran's Mehrabad airport.

For the next few hours, I stood in line waiting to clear customs. Finally, it was my turn to be interrogated by a customs officer wearing white gloves. He asked me twice if I was carrying any videos, music tapes or CDs, magazines or books, or electronic equipment. After I answered twice in the negative, he demanded to know if I had illegal drugs, prescription medicine, or alcoholic beverages in my luggage. When I replied again that I did not, he wanted to know if I was sure that I wasn't in possession of any chocolate filled with liquor.[2] Eventually, I won my way free and was able to greet my brother, who had been waiting for hours behind a glass wall. Overjoyed, we hugged and kissed and he bustled me to his car. Breathing the cool crisp air of the early morning hours and looking at the snow-covered peak of Alburz Mountain, I gradually relaxed and began to enjoy the half-hour drive through nearly empty streets to my parents' house. Every now and then I read the graffiti that was plastered on the walls of houses and factories bordering the roadway. Slogans such as "the improperly veiled woman is a stain on the Islamic Republic of Iran who must be eliminated immediately" and "death to the improperly veiled woman!" jarred me from my solipsistic reverie. At these moments I adjusted my rupush and rusari, wiped my lips nervously to make sure that not a trace of lipstick was left, and looked furtively at my feet to ascertain that my thick black socks obscured the red polish on my toenails. I realized once again that for many of my compatriots the veil did not represent a cultural and religious artifact but had ideological proportions that continued to permeate every aspect of their daily lives.

But even this realization did not prepare me for an article in *Abrar* (July 19, 1997) that my fifteen-year-old niece, who is very interested in my research on the veil, urged me to read. A revolutionary guard from Tehran complains in this article that while the Iranian film industry complies with the laws of hijab, it does not actively promote the more severe form of hijab (chador) that Ayatollah Khomeini recommended as the best type of coverage for the female body.[3] I was aware that the Iranian clergy regards lipstick and nail polish as paraphernalia of the prostitute, but I was surprised to read that some Iranians are critical of the law of hijab because it does not enforce a specific form of hijab, namely the chador.[4] After skimming through the article, I glanced up at my niece, who sat across from me wearing jeans, a sweatshirt, and sneakers. She looked like an average American teenager and a world apart from the vision this revolutionary guard had of a properly veiled Iranian woman. Yet, later, when we left the house to visit my aunt in another part of Tehran, my niece donned the veil with a confidence that only years of experience could instill. She has worn the hijab outside the privacy of her home since the very first day she started school, when she was but seven years old.

During my three-week stay in Iran in 1997, I watched television programs that showed women wearing the proper hijab and listened to radio announcers extolling the virtues of the veil. Every newspaper and magazine I picked up explained the benefits of the veil and advised me on how to wear it properly. Even when buying a stamp to put on a letter I had written to my daughter back in the United States, I was reminded that the hijab is the only proper form of dress for the Iranian woman. This stamp, with the word *hijab* inscribed on the lower-left corner, depicts an eye whose pupil is a woman clad in a conservative black veil with the barrel of a gun reaching above her right shoulder (FIG 4.6). The Iranian woman is, of course, not allowed to actively participate in battle. As we shall see in chapter 4, Iranian women are depicted on stamps carrying guns in order to announce to the world that they lend their self-sacrificing support to Iran's male fighters.

Researching the Veil

Ever since the Islamic Revolution swept through my native country in 1979, I have been interested in issues related to the veil. Since 1994, when I started to teach courses on Middle Eastern culture at the University of Texas at Austin, I have collected visual and printed material that depicts veiled women and elaborates on the significance of the veil. At that time, I became aware that this unassuming piece of cloth has a history that antedates the Islamic Republic of Iran by thousands of years. Nikki Keddie informs us that the first known reference to veiling was made in an Assyrian legal text of the thirteenth century BCE. In this text, veiling is restricted to respectable women and prohibited for prostitutes.[5] The veil is also mentioned in the Middle-Assyrian Laws (750–612 BCE), more than twelve hundred years before the advent of Islam. Here, a harlot or slave girl found improperly wearing a veil in the street is ordered to be brought to the palace for punishment.[6] The Roman social commentator Ovid (43 BCE–17 CE) in Book IV of his *Metamorphoses* relies on the veil to carry a Babylonian love story.[7] Pyramus and Thisbe fall in love, but their parents disapprove of their relationship. The lovers agree to meet in secrecy at the tomb of the Babylonian King Ninus. Thisbe, who arrives early, sees a lioness and flees into a cave, leaving her veil behind. The lioness, whose muzzle is dripping with the blood of a fresh kill, rips Thisbe's veil. When Pyramus finds the torn and bloodstained veil, he concludes that the lioness has killed Thisbe and commits suicide with his sword. When Thisbe finds Pyramus's dead body, she throws herself on his blade.[8]

In the Assyrian, Greco-Roman, and Byzantine empires, as well as in pre-Islamic Iran, veiling and seclusion were marks of prestige and symbols of status.[9] Only wealthy families could afford to seclude their women. The veil was a sign of respectability but also of a lifestyle that did not require the performance of manual labor. Slaves and women who labored in the fields were not expected to wear the veil, which would have impeded their every movement. At the turn of the century, when the practice of veiling became associated with women's oppression under Islam, the veil was transformed into an object of political, social, and religious contention. As such, the veil quickly became a favorite subject for writers in the Muslim world. It suffices in this context to mention the Egyptian Qasim Amin, the Iraqi al-Azri, and the Iranians Iraj Mirza and Parvin E'tesami (chapter 6). In 1923, the Egyptian feminist Huda Shaarawi, who was returning from an international feminist meeting in Rome, drew the veil back from her face when she got off the train. Her daring act elicited loud applause from the waiting women and displeased frowns from the eunuchs who guarded the women.[10] Another important date in the history of the veil is 1936, when Reza Shah of Iran abolished the veil.

Moving forward to the present day, my investigations of American erotica (chapter 2) and the Hindi popular cinema (chapter 3) demonstrate that the veil has acquired cultural connotations that reach far beyond the borders and religious context of the Islamic Republic of Iran and even of the Muslim world itself. The veiled playmate in photographs in *Playboy* and *Penthouse* is without exception identified as an American or European woman posing as odalisque. The veiled heroine in the Hindi popular movie is as likely to be a Hindu as she is to be a Muslim. The fact that the veil possesses cultural significance not only for Muslims but for Hindus as well is also clearly revealed in a short story by the Indian writer Yashpal (chapter 6).

This historical and cultural near-omnipresence of the veil has shaped the focus of my research. The visual and printed material on the veil is so diverse and plentiful that to impose cultural or historical restrictions on my investigation seemed tantamount to a selective censoring of all that I had compiled over the last five years. In order to investigate fully the semantics of the veil, analyzing the meaning of the veil to Saudi advertisers of sanitary napkins proved just as relevant and revealing as exploring the poetic context in which Ayatollah Khomeini uses the veil. In addition to examining veiled images in television and magazine ads, I have utilized the collections of *Playboy, Penthouse,* and *Hustler* at the law library at The University of Texas at Austin and found more than 250 images of the Middle East in photographs and cartoons. These images have also played an important role in my research and have helped shape my understanding of the veil's significance and symbolic versatility. I was also surprised when, after spending one morning researching the veil, I found a picture of a veiled woman on the very can of couscous soup I was opening for lunch. Furthermore, when watching Iranian and Hindi films I realized that the veil has established a cinematics of its own.

But the veil appears not only in pictures. The words *hijab* or *muhajjibah* (veiled woman) are often used in the slogans plastered all over the whitewashed walls of houses, office buildings, and factories in Iran. On my most recent visits to the Islamic Republic of Iran, I have clandestinely, while riding on the bus, taken photographs of slogans praising the properly veiled woman and threatening the improperly veiled woman (chapter 4). My investigation of the semantics of the veil also focuses on poems, song lyrics, and short stories that are titled "The Veil." The Uzbeki *parandja,* the Arabic as well as Persian *hijab,* and the Urdu and Hindi *purdah* have provided the titles for works by authors from the former Soviet Union, Iraq, Iran, and India (chapter 6).

The large number of books whose cover designs or titles suggest a discussion of issues related to the veil aided as well as hindered the progress of my research. My work benefited from some books that use in their title the veil as metaphor, metonym, or synecdoche for the experiences of Muslim women. Books such as Mernissi's *Beyond the Veil* and *The Veil and the Male Elite;* Mabro's *Veiled Half-Truths: Western Travelers' Perception of Middle Eastern Women;* Abu-Lughod's *Veiled Sentiments: Honor and Poetry in a Bedouin Society;* Minces's *Veiled: Women in Islam;* and Goodwin's *Price of Honor: Muslim Women Lift the Veil of Silence on the Islamic World* have proven helpful to my research. Other books were too restricted in their subject matter to be of use in my effort to decipher the semantics of the veil. For example, Evelyne Accad in her groundbreaking *Veil of Shame* analyzes the role of women in the contemporary fiction of North Africa and the Arab world. Marianne Alireza in *At the Drop of a Veil* gives a grim account of her experiences in a harem in Saudi Arabia, while Cherry Mosteshar in *Unveiled: One Woman's Nightmare in Iran* describes her personal experiences in modern Iran. Unni Wikan's *Behind the Veil in Arabia: Women in Oman* describes the plight of women in Oman.

For every book whose title includes some form of the word "veil" and that addresses the practice of veiling in particular or women's issues in general, there is another utilizing similar language or imagery that has nothing to do with women's lives.[11] Both authors and publishers have a tendency to include "veil," "veiled," or "unveiled" as often as possible in the titles of books that discuss countries and regions in which women are known to veil, whether or not the work has anything to do with that particular article of clothing. The marketing departments at university presses have apparently discovered that using the word "veil" in the title or picturing a veiled woman on the cover sells books. This fact was brought home to me at the Middle East Studies Association (MESA) meeting in 1998. While there, I gave a paper on Muslim images in American erotica and was approached shortly thereafter by a representative of a university press who told me that his organization might be interested in my book if I were to include the term "veil" in the title. Taking his advice to heart, I decided not merely to use the word "veil" in the title but to make visual, political, and literary dynamics of the veil the focus of my entire work.

My research focuses particularly on the role of the veil in popular culture: the importance of the veil to advertisers of Western products; the exploitation of the veil in American erotica; the use of the veil in Iranian films, Indian popular films, and Bernardo Bertolucci's *The Sheltering Sky;* the utilization of the veil on posters and stamps promoted by the Iranian government; the chameleonlike quality of the veil that enables it to meet the requirements of the military forces of the United Arab Emirates, Iraq, and Iran; and the opinions of popular Iranian poets on the practice of veiling.

Defining the Semantics of the Veil

The large number of books of which the titles or subtitles include "veil," "veiled," or "unveiled" testifies to the semantic versatility of the garment. Once the veil is no longer perceived as a mere piece of cloth, a cultural or religious artifact, it quickly takes on semantic dimensions that can be fathomed only if we clearly define the parameters of our discourse. For example, we may be able to determine its meaning for the *Playboy* photographer who drapes a transparent veil over an otherwise nude model, thereby hoping to increase male interest in his subject. We may establish what significance a white veil has for the Saudi advertiser of sanitary napkins. We may deduce from the history and politics of the Mujahedin-e Khalq reasons that explain why their female combatants wear red veils. In all these examples we are able to determine the meaning of the veil because we know the specific context in which it is being used. The analyses of different visual, political, and literary representations of the veil demonstrate that its symbolic significance is being constantly defined and redefined, often to the point of ambiguity. Modern Iranian history may best exemplify the many possible alterations in the meaning of the veil: in 1936, Reza Shah abolished the veil because he saw it as a sign of backwardness; in 1979, the Islamic Republic of Iran forced women to adopt the veil because the Iranian clergy regards it as a sign of progress along the ideological path of Islam. In a period of less than fifty years, the rulers of Iran have allotted the veil diametrically opposed meanings.

This semantic versatility of the veil helps explain its enormous marketing potential. Not only university presses and academic authors have profited from the veil's marketability. Recent television ads for IBM computers and Jeep Cherokees have banked on the salability of the veiled woman. She is selling cigarettes, perfumes, and even soup to the American consumer. In *Sayidaty,* a Saudi magazine, veiled women promote sanitary napkins and Swiss watches. All these ads are tailored to appeal to a specific market, and thus almost all allot the veil a specific meaning. Interestingly, American advertisers rely on one particular connotation of the veil when marketing products to male consumers but on quite another when marketing products to women. Saudi advertisers exploit one meaning of the veil when selling sanitary napkins to average Saudi consumers and another when selling expensive Swiss watches to the wealthy (chapter 1).

The semantic versatility of the veil also manifests itself in American erotica. The garment's meaning varies from publication to publication. Since *Penthouse* and *Playboy* cater to different markets than *Hustler*, the photographers and cartoonists of these magazines portray the veil in disparate ways intended to appeal to their respective audiences. Furthermore, meanings of the veil also change within the pages of the same magazine, depending on whether photographs or cartoons are involved. While photographs of veiled women in *Playboy* and *Penthouse* aim at drawing the male gaze, cartoons of veiled women mock and ridicule Muslim society. The meaning of the veil when portrayed in a cartoon also depends on the overall state of political relations between the United States and the countries of the Middle East. For example, when the United States was at war with Iraq, cartoons, especially in *Hustler*, depicted veiling as a barbaric practice (chapter 2).

Once the veil is assigned a certain meaning, the veil itself acquires the power to dictate certain outcomes—the garment becomes a force in and of itself, and this force must be deferred to by many people. When the semantics of the veil are defined, they set a dynamics of the veil in motion that dictates context. The law of hijab that is enforced in the Islamic Republic of Iran provides a telling example. For the lawmakers in Iran, wearing the hijab is synonymous with obeying Islamic injunctions that define the proper behavior of the female believer. This law weighs on every aspect of daily life in Iran. It defines, for example, artistic expression: the Iranian film director is not allowed to show women in the privacy of their homes, where they would not veil. Iranian filmmakers have thus introduced ingenious techniques and subject matters in order to comply with government regulations (chapter 3). Iranian politics are also subject to the semantics of the veil. For Reza Shah, the veil was synonymous with backwardness, and thus he sought to promote progress by abolishing the veil. For Ayatollah Khomeini, unveiled women embodied Western values, and thus he sought to promote Islamic values by forcing women to veil (chapter 4). In countries that use the veil to segregate the sexes, women either are not allowed to join military forces (Iran), have limited access to certain branches (United Arab Emirates), or are permitted to join only if they wear loose-fitting uniforms and head scarves (Iraq) (chapter 5).

The female combatants of the NLA (National Liberation Army), the armed wing of the Mujahedin-e Khalq, demonstrate the difficulty of attempting to define the semantics of the veil. First, the Mujahedin-e Khalq, expatriate Iranians and Muslims, believe in sex segregation but allow women to participate actively in battle against the enemy Iran with the provision that the combatants stay celibate during their time of service. Second, this party, in order to survive politically, has to form alliances with nations willing to support it financially. Interestingly, the headgear of the female combatants changes with the party's attempts to forge alliances. The combatants wore red veils when support from the former Soviet Union was sought and green veils when the party was courting the Taliban in Afghanistan. In 1999, in a party demonstration in The Hague (The Netherlands) against the regime in Iran, the women were sporting American baseball caps (chapter 5).

Literary works on the veil expose the semantic versatility of the veil. Some writers endorse the veil, allotting a positive moral value to it. Others reject the veil, describing it as a sign of backwardness. Still other writers such as the Urdu poet Asadullah Khan Ghalib and Ayatollah Khomeini use the veil as metaphor to express their ontological anxieties. What cultural context makes it possible for a physical object to acquire metaphysical proportions? (chapter 6).

1 Veiled Images in Advertising

Images of Women in Advertising

American television commercials use images of veiled Muslim women in order to hawk products made in the United States. Pictures of these women are also plastered on printed advertisements peddling American products to the American consumer. In what roles do advertisers cast the Muslim woman in order to entice consumers into purchasing the advertised products? How flexible is her image and what image is used in what advertisement? Do advertisers focus on cultural differences between American and Middle Eastern women to sell their products? In order to find answers to these questions, it is necessary to look at ads for Western products that use images of veiled women.

The time when advertisers relied on slick imagery, exaggerated claims, and, often, deception to lure consumers into buying goods has long passed. Now, advertisers probe deep into the recesses of the subconscious minds of potential consumers and then construct ad campaigns that goad the unconscious mind and the body under its control into buying products that the conscious mind neither needs nor wants. Advertisers also no longer target a single mass market but tailor their ads to appeal to only a segment of a market that is divided along lines of age, class, gender, and race. For example, ads for skin products that claim to get rid of pimples target a teenage audience; ads for certain cars are aimed at the middle-class consumer; ads for the ever-burgeoning market of perfumes are directed toward women; and ads for certain hair products target the Afro-American market. By relying on hidden symbols to appeal to the subconscious mind of the consumer and by tailoring ads to appeal to certain segments of the market, advertisers perpetuate stereotypes and clichés. Ads for psychotropic drugs in medical journals are a telling example. Purchased mostly by male physicians, these journals run ads that recommend prescribing tranquilizers to female patients who have problems with the routine of their jobs in the household.[1] According to studies conducted by Alice E. Courtney and Thomas W. Whipple, "women are much more likely than men to be portrayed in advertising for psychotropic drugs."[2] These ads effectively perpetuate the notion that women are more hysterical than men but that men can control these women with the help of modern medicine.[3] In addition to the stereotype of the hysterical woman, advertising that targets the male market relies on the stereotype of the "reified" woman—alluring, decorative, and traditional. Woman is shown as a sex object, seducing man into buying the advertised product by promising that if he buys the product he will buy her. While some advertisements that target the female consumer also objectify women, others portray women in a wider range of roles. For example, while perfumes are sold by sexy, beautiful models, sanitary napkins are sold by more individualized images of women. In ads for diapers and cleaning agents, women are shown as mothers and housewives.[4]

In a market as large and fiercely competitive as advertising, selling products that the consumer often neither needs nor wants, the success of any advertising agency depends on the creativity of its artists—a creativity that often involves rehashing and revamping stereotypes presumably held by the targeted segment of the American population. It is not surprising, thus, that Western stereotypes of Middle Eastern women provide ample material for the advertising industry in the United States. Advertisers exploit "fixed" images of Muslim women—images that have been ingrained on

the Western mind: the concubine in the harem at the mercy of her tyranni-
cal master; the exotic but inaccessible veiled woman; and the suppressed
woman who is treated like chattel. These stereotypes are then tailored to
the segment of the market that is targeted by the advertiser. As we shall see,
advertisers have concluded, rightly or wrongly, that the reactions of American men to images of the veil are different from those of American women.
The extent to which advertising strategies are defined by cultural stereotypes and marketing by segments (age, class, gender, race) becomes tangible when we compare ads targeting the market in the United States to
those ads for the same products but targeting the market in Saudi Arabia.

The Veil Sells American-Made Products to American Consumers

Selling Jeep Cherokees

Recently, the veiled Muslim woman has been cast in television commercials
in the United States. She plays a part, albeit a supporting one, in the commercial for the Jeep Cherokee made by Chrysler in 1996. We see the Jeep
Cherokee speeding into a small town in Morocco. In the background we
notice a woman wearing a veil hanging clothes on a line and next to her a
few children playing soccer in the dusty road. As the Jeep maneuvers up
and down the road, a group of natives gathers looking at the car in awe.
The camera then swerves to the face of the veiled woman. She smiles. We
witness a brief conversation in Arabic between the woman and the children, and by their excited glances at the Jeep, we are led to believe that it is
a conversation expressing admiration for the car and its skilled driver.

What segment of the American population is the primary focus of this
commercial, and which stereotype is exploited? The type of show during
which a commercial is aired usually helps identify the target audience. For
example, a beer commercial will most likely be seen during a football, baseball, or basketball game, and not during a cartoon or soap opera. The Jeep
commercial was aired during the six o'clock news, a time slot usually reserved for commercials that are thought to appeal to the middle-class
worker or the elderly. The price of the Jeep Cherokee, about $30,000,
makes this sports utility vehicle unaffordable to people with below-average
incomes.[5] Furthermore, advertisers are aware of the fact that American
women earn on the average 25 percent less than American men and that the

majority of American women purchase cars in the $20,000 range.[6] Thus, we may safely conclude that the targeted consumers are middle-class, possibly middle-aged, men and that the commercial is tailored to appeal to this segment of the American population. We may also assume that the targeted consumer has a college degree, is interested in world affairs, and has traveled abroad to study other cultures and peoples. Car ads featuring Marilyn Monroe look-alikes in various states of undress and alluring poses may not meet this consumer's expectations of the new, the exciting, and the exotic that are missing in his daily life. This is, however, exactly what the Jeep commercial promises him. If he buys the Jeep, he will realize his dream of conquering terrain that is challenging and foreign. He may even win the admiration of the most inaccessible of women, the woman with the veil. The configuration of this commercial is based on the Western stereotype of the exoticism and otherness of the veiled Muslim woman. The consumer becomes subject to "homeopathic or sympathetic magic," a term coined by George Schoemaker.[7] "Homeopathic magic" operates on the principle that things that are alike will produce or experience the same effect. In this "magic," the Jeep is substituted for the woman, and by buying the Jeep, the consumer will gain access to the exciting and exotic Moroccan woman.

Selling Computers

The veiled Muslim woman has also found her way into a recent television commercial selling IBM computers and services. Also set in Morocco, this commercial focuses on two Moroccan men immersed in conversation about business problems. The conversation is conducted in a Moroccan dialect of Arabic with English captions. The background is out of focus and appears to show a crowded market. Arabic instrumental music can be heard in the background. Once the two men are finished with their conversation, the camera focuses slowly on a completely veiled (head and face covered) woman moving into the foreground. Her slow movements match the beat of the background music, which is getting louder as she comes into focus. Although her body and face are covered, she manages to create an atmosphere of sexual tension, attributable in part to her black promising eyes and in part to the loudening sound and climaxing beat of the background music.

The market for IBM products and services consists largely of educated, middle-class businessmen and entrepreneurs. Recent IBM commercials, relying on similar configurations, send the message that IBM products are so easy to use that even people who are not known for their technological adeptness can use them: a group of nuns discusses computer applications; a shepherd shows snapshots of his vacation on an IBM laptop; and two fashion models discuss IBM. The Moroccan commercial sends the message that IBM products and services are so easy to use and so indispensable that they have become a *sine qua non* for Moroccan men in a traditional Moroccan village. This advertisement, however, amplifies its message by suggesting that IBM products and services facilitate communication with the most inaccessible of women, the veiled woman. The creators of this ad exploit the stereotype that Western men want to conquer the "exotic" Muslim woman, whose "otherness" projects her as the ultimate object of conquest. This stereotype is assumed to be held by the targeted segment of the population, namely, middle-class, sexually active American men.

The commercial's focus on the eyes of the Moroccan woman reveals yet another advertising strategy when selling images of women. Only parts of a woman's body are shown. Often, these parts sell the product by selling sex but are unrelated to the advertised product.[8] Many Western travelers, especially males, have commented on the eyes of Muslim women. For example, John Foster Fraser comments in *The Land of Veiled Women* (1911, 75–76):

> They [veiled women] stood in groups apart from the men, and their *gandouras* showed harmoniously against the dark background of the night. It was all romantic. Some of them removed the veil in the shelter of the dusk and revealed their charms. But as I wandered by, their veils were dropped. A side-glance, and each woman peeping over the veil seemed to be looking at me with great liquid eyes, fixing upon me the bold glance of one conscious she could see without being seen. Often I felt there was something uncanny about those great eyes of the solemn women, always bright and always black. Big, unblinking, dreamy, sensuous eyes which filled one with a nervous curiosity as to what their owners were thinking about.[9]

It is this stereotype of the eyes of a Muslim woman promising a thousand and one pleasures that the commercial exploits. Since the eyes are the only part of the Moroccan woman that the veil does not cover, they become the object of attraction in the commercial. Also interesting is that the woman does not look at her two male costars but straight at the camera, out at the male gaze. Her eyes promise pleasure to any man who purchases the product.

Both the Jeep Cherokee commercial and the IBM commercial target a middle-class male audience. Both send the message that if the consumer buys the product, he will discover the mysterious woman behind the veil either by gaining her admiration or by being able to communicate with her. However, the veiled woman also appears in advertisements that target the female consumer in the United States. As we shall see, the creators of these ads rely on different stereotypes of Muslim women in order to sell their products.

Selling Cigarettes

The tobacco industry spent $6.02 billion in 1993 advertising and promoting products—almost $200 a second. In 1926, tobacco companies began to target women in their advertisements; between 1967 and 1970 four new brands of cigarettes were developed just for women. Ironically, since the 1980 Surgeon General's report on women and smoking, the tobacco industry has stepped up the introduction of cigarette brands that target women. Although tobacco advertising romances women with many different images, three distinct images are discernible: in 1928, when the first cigarette ad came out showing women smoking, smoking became a symbol of women's liberation. Now, the liberated woman was the one who smoked. When introducing the Lucky Strike brand in 1928, the cigarette industry relied on a strategy of associating smoking with a slender figure. Although slightly more subtle, today's tobacco ads convey the same message by using ultrathin models to hawk ultrathin cigarettes. The very name of some brands is indicative of this advertising strategy—Virginia Slims, for example. Another ploy of the cigarette industry is to sell smoking as glamorous. By focusing on style and chicness, the cigarette industry has made a successful entrance into women's magazine advertising. While at their inception these strategies targeted middle- and upper-class white women, they no longer do so. Surveys conducted in cities throughout the United States indicate that low-income Afro-American communities have many more tobacco billboards than neighboring affluent communities.[10]

Since the first ad appeared in 1928, tobacco companies have tried to sell the "perfect" identity. In order to be liberated, glamorous, chic, or slim, the consumer must buy the cigarette. Women in a low-income household may be most vulnerable to these ads. It may be difficult to feel liberated when depending on welfare. It may be challenging to appear glamorous and chic when surviving on food stamps. It is also more difficult to stay slim, considering that cheap food often has more calories than nutritional value.

Considered neither glamorous nor liberated by the Western media, the veiled Muslim woman has been utilized nonetheless by the advertisers of Virginia Slims. In a printed ad (FIG. 1.1), three women are shown wearing saris. They surround a man who is dressed in Western formal wear, including a bow tie, and a turban. Below the ad are two captions: one is framed and placed below the man. It reads, "The Sultan of Bundi Had Nothing Against Women. He Thought Everyone Should Own Two or Three." The other, located below two of the women, states, "You've Come a Long Way Baby." Before analyzing the message this ad tries to convey to the consumer, let us first address the cultural misidentification in this ad: the turban identifies the man as a member of the Sikh religion in Bundi, India. A Sikh is a member of a Hindu religious sect founded in the Punjab in about 1500.[11] This sect does not practice polygyny. Furthermore, the title of "Sultan" is usually reserved for a Muslim ruler. The ad exploits crude stereotypes by picturing a turbaned sultan and his harem. It claims that Muslim women—and we must assume that these are the ones the creators of the ad intended to portray—are treated like chattel or objects. They have no identity of their own. The ad insinuates that all women were men's chattel at one time but that some were able to leave these circumstances behind. These fortunate ones have come a long way. The message implies that smoking Virginia Slims will set the consumer apart from the submissive creatures in the ad. The consumer is a woman in her own right now. She does not have to be one among many women catering to the same master.

This ad demonstrates the differences in advertising strategies with regard not only to gender but to class. While the Jeep Cherokee and IBM advertisers, targeting the American middle class, show an authentic setting (Morocco) and rely on some regional familiarity on the part of the consumer, the Virginia Slims advertisers depict, intentionally or unintentionally, a delusory setting and crudely spell out the stereotype that in some sultanate veiled women continue to be man's chattel. This blatant misrepresentation of the status of the Muslim woman violated advertising guide-

FIG. I.I. Advertisement for Virginia Slims. The American-Arab Anti-Discrimination Committee (ADC), 1989 Activity Report.

lines established by the American-Arab Anti-Discrimination Committee (ADC). The ADC reported in a 1989 issue of its Activity Report: *"Virginia Slims Slams Muslims:* An offensive ad run by the Philip Morris tobacco company in major women's magazines such as *Cosmopolitan*, prompted a round of letters to the company's president Hamish Maxwell. ADC objected to the ad because it reinforced negative stereotypes of Muslim women, portraying them as submissive chattel. In response, a Virginia Slims representative told ADC that the company would not run the ad in the future."[12]

The veiled women in the Jeep Cherokee and IBM commercials convey the message that if the consumer buys the product, he will have access to a thousand and one pleasures. The veiled women in the Virginia Slims advertisement convey the message that if the consumer buys the product, she will be treated not as one among many women but as an individual. Smoking a Virginia Slims cigarette will help her stay liberated and a long way away from the times when she also was shackled and subservient to man's discretion and use. The veiled women in this ad were used to portray an image of woman that was expected to be abhorrent to the American consumer. The advertising strategy behind this ad is to reassure the consumer that she is nothing like the women in the ad and that by purchasing Virginia Slims she will never be like them. In order to determine if this strategy of portraying a contrast between Western and Middle Eastern women presents a paradigm, we need to look at the ads for other "image" products that target the female consumer.

Selling Perfume

One of the best-selling "image" products is perfume. In 1997, the perfume industry reached the $6 billion mark. The market consists, for the most part, of women of all social classes. Like advertisements for cigarettes, ads for fragrances sell an identity, an "image." They are packaged and marketed around a concept or theme that is supposed to capture the imagination of women and make a powerful emotional appeal. Perfume advertisements suggest that the product will turn fantasy into reality. They promise that a few dabs of a certain perfume will make the consumer beautiful, irresistible, successful, independent, and whatever else she would like to be. The ADC reports that in the April 1992 issue of *Vogue* and in other American fashion magazines, an ad for Bijan perfume appeared that portrayed a veiled, presumably Muslim, woman on one side offset by a woman with a baseball cap and bat on the other (FIG. 1.2). The caption beside the veiled woman reads "women should be obedient, grateful, modest, respectful, submissive, and very, very, serious."[13] An American flag is shown next to the woman in the baseball cap, and the caption reads "women should be bright, wild, flirty, fun, eccentric, tough, bold, and very, very, Bijan."[14] ADC explained in a letter to Bijan's management that "being Muslim and American are not a contradiction and therefore should not be portrayed as such by placing an American flag on the positive image and deleting it from the other." ADC reported that they received a written apology from Bijan.

Maintaining a high profile worldwide through some seventy monthly advertisements in more than eighty countries, the Beverly Hills designer Bijan, who hails from Iran, is acclaimed for his provocative and controversial image advertising and has featured several exotic models in his advertising campaigns. The function of the "exotic" woman in this ad is to show the contrast between the woman who wears Bijan and the one who does not. This ad claims that the woman who does not wear Bijan is obedient, grateful, modest, respectful, submissive, and very, very, serious. By contrasting this woman, identified as Muslim by her veil, with the woman with

FIG. 1.2. Advertisement for Bijan. *Vogue,* April 1992.

the baseball cap, it also implies that Muslim women are not bright, wild, flirty, fun, eccentric, tough, bold, and very, very, Bijan. Were it not for the veil, the woman in this ad would not recognize her "flirtatious," "seductive," and "exotic" sister in the Jeep Cherokee or IBM commercial. Advertising agencies use stereotypes of Muslim women that are tailored to the targeted market. When an advertisement targets the middle-class male consumer, stereotypes of veiled seductresses are exploited. When an advertisement targets the female consumer, images of submissive chattel are depicted.[15]

Selling Soup

When a product has a market that is difficult to categorize along lines of gender and class, advertisers still use images of veiled women to hawk their products but rely on a different marketing strategy. For example, the veiled woman has found her way onto the label of the President's Choice Instant Vegetable Couscous Soup (a packaged dried soup) (FIG. 1.3). Although Canadian-made, this soup is sold in some supermarkets in the United States. The blue veil and the mannerism of wrapping the veil around the face, concealing it except for the eyes, point to Tuareg origin. Among the

FIG. I.3. Photograph of label on box of soup. President's Choice Instant Vegetable Couscous Soup. Photograph taken by author.

Tuareg, however, it is not customary for women to veil; Tuareg men would wear the veil in the manner shown on the soup label.[16] The model's dark eyes are made up with black kohl; her slanted eyebrows are darkened and emphasized. The caption on the label reads in English and French "Under 500 mg Sodium, Under 250 Calories" "Too Good To Be True!" "Instant Vegetable Couscous Soup." Although President's Choice sells other soups, such as "French Onion," only the couscous soup features the face of a woman. The strategy of putting a veiled woman, albeit with the wrong color and type of veil, on the label establishes authenticity. The veil is supposed to convey to consumers that if they buy this soup, they buy authentic Middle Eastern food. By presenting the veil as emblem of Middle Eastern culture, the designers of the label target consumers of Middle Eastern origin.

Although veiled women sell a great variety of products in the United States, we can discern three major advertising strategies exploiting three different stereotypes about the Muslim woman: the mysterious woman hiding behind her veil, waiting to be conquered by an American man; the submissive woman, forced to hide behind the veil; and the generic veiled woman, representing all peoples and cultures of the Middle East.

Relying on different stereotypes about the veil, Western advertisers sell their products on the American market. In order to successfully sell Western products on the Middle Eastern market, advertisers have to abandon these Western misconceptions about the Muslim woman and focus on attitudes toward and (mis)conceptions about women that are ingrained in the Muslim mind. For example, Saudi advertisers of Western products have to appeal to mental structures that have determined the socioreligious significance of the veil to Muslims. An analysis of the function of the veil in ads for Western products that appear in the Saudi magazine *Sayidaty* reveals examples of these mental structures. While the Saudi market creates a demand for a certain Western product, Saudi culture and politics determine the nature of the ad for the product that successfully meets the demand of the market.

The Veil Sells Western Products in Saudi Arabia

The Market

The Arabian Peninsula is the birthplace of Islam and the site of some of the world's oldest civilizations. The area's early history was one of small trading centers surrounded by vast tracts of territory roamed by nomadic tribes. In the early part of the twentieth century, Ibn Saud, gaining the upper hand in tribal struggles, established the Kingdom of Saudi Arabia, and his descendants still rule today. The concept of separation of religion and state is foreign to Saudi society and governance. The constitution is the holy Qur'an and the *shari'a*.

Massive oil revenues have transformed Saudi Arabia's centuries-old pastoral, agricultural, and commercial economy. This transformation has been marked by rapid urbanization, large-scale development of economic and social infrastructure, the emergence of a welfare state and technocratic middle class, and the importation of millions of foreign workers—mainly from India, Pakistan, the Philippines, and Africa—for skilled and menial labor. It has also been marked by widespread expenditures of public funds in ways that improved the quality of life for most Saudis. In the early 1980s, Saudi Arabia had become a cash-rich, product-starved economy, and huge capital expenditures for infrastructure development and consumer demand produced sales opportunities for practically anything at enormously inflated prices. The market for U.S. exports to Saudi Arabia, however, has become more competitive in the 1990s. There are significant barriers to U.S. exports in several areas, as well as protective tariffs, which can run as high as 20 percent in the case of infant industries. In addition, Saudi Arabia also participates in the Arab boycott of Israel and bans products and investment from companies that are judged to contribute to Israel's economic or defense capacities.[17] Furthermore, government procurement regulations strongly favor Saudi citizens and the citizens of neighboring Gulf Cooperation Council (GCC) states. The government has also taken steps to reserve certain services for government-owned companies.

Saudi Arabia has been a relatively small market by world standards despite its high per capita income. Its indigenous population, however, has been increasing rapidly. By the year 2000, the Saudi national population should reach 10 million. Over the past two decades, one striking outgrowth of Saudi development—one that directly influences the nature of advertisements—has been the rapid migration of the population to the cities. In the early 1970s, an estimated 26 percent of the population lived in urban centers. In 1990, that figure had risen to 73 percent. With regard to spending decisions in the household, the husband alone makes one-third of food purchase decisions, the wife one-third, with the final one-third being made jointly. However, for consumer durable goods, the husband alone makes the purchase decision in almost 50 percent of cases, and less than one in seven wives accompanies her husband to the shop to undertake purchases.[18] Over 95 percent of Saudi households own a television set, and/or refrigerator, and/or washing machine. Between 60 percent and 70 percent own a hi-fi and/or video system; approximately 35 percent own a freezer, and only one in ten currently has a dishwasher.[19] Well-known American, Japanese, and European brands of consumer durable goods are available and, in many cases, are less expensive than elsewhere because there is no tax on them.

Advertising in Saudi Arabia

Barter is the traditional means by which nomads and farmers obtain each other's products, and weekly markets are held in villages and small towns. However, the Saudi economy is being progressively monetized and is now completely so in the towns and cities. Printed advertisements, including newspapers, magazines, and billboards, are now the principal means of advertising. Government radio does not carry advertising, but radio broadcasts from neighboring states that do so are received in Saudi Arabia. Television now accepts advertising but is under strict guidelines to exclude offensive commercials, violations of the Islamic code, and "hard sell" techniques. There are at least seven daily Arabic newspapers carrying advertising, and the monthly magazines published by various chambers of commerce also accept advertising.

Several multinational companies have launched major advertising campaigns in the Gulf States since the 1980s. They have to overcome many hurdles in order to sell their products on the Saudi market. In addition to securing native sponsors and avoiding the pen of the government censor, they have to decide if and how advertisements need to be tailored to appeal to local consumers. Companies that market their products worldwide are faced with the decision of whether to standardize their messages across countries or to individualize their messages with regard to the culture of the targeted country. Proponents of the universal approach, such as marketing experts Theodore Levitt and Richard Barnet, focus on the similarities that are shared among the people (basic human needs and instincts) all over the world.[20] Opponents of the universal approach believe that the universal standardization of advertising is not possible because significant differences, including language, culture, nationality, and consumer behavior, exist between nations.[21] They claim that the success of an international advertising venture lies within the awareness of these cultural and linguistic differences. When General Motors introduced the Chevy Nova in South America, it found out firsthand that there are limits to the universal approach to advertising. General Motors was apparently unaware that "no va" means "it won't go." After the company figured out why it wasn't selling any cars, it renamed the car Caribe in its Spanish markets. Many native speakers of Arabic are reluctant to purchase Nike shoes, since the word "nike" is pronounced similar to the Arabic "niki," the imperative form of "to have sexual intercourse." Not surprisingly, Adidas and other brands outsell Nike in Arabic-speaking countries. Many advertisers of Western products, however, do show an awareness of the culture and language of the targeted country or region. The advertisements of Western products that I found in Saudi publications suggest that these ads are tailored to Middle Eastern culture.

Selling Sanitary Napkins

A comparison between Kotex ads targeting the Western market and Kotex ads targeting the Saudi market reveals how advertisers deal with cultural differences in perceptions of the female body. In Western publications, Kotex ads exemplify that there is an evolution taking place in the Western perception of the female body and its functions. After army nurses found that Kimberly-Clark creped wadding, which was used as bandages during World War I, was also suitable for feminine care, Kotex was introduced in 1920 as the first readily available disposable product for menstrual hygiene.[22] At this time, however, the subject of menstruation was still shrouded in superstition and myth.[23] The menstruating woman was thought to be unclean—a belief that can be traced to a time when the Christian church prescribed rites of purification for the female after menses and childbirth. In the Old Testament, Leviticus 15:19–24, we are informed that God defines a menstruating woman as unclean for a period of seven days. Isidore of Seville (d. 636 CE) expresses most descriptively the superstitious attitude of the Christian church toward menstruation: "After touching [menstrual blood] fruits do not sprout, blossoms fade, grasses wither . . . iron rusts, brass turns black, dogs that taste it get rabies."[24] To avoid picturing a flesh-and-blood "impure" woman, Kimberly-Clark showed in its first Kotex advertising campaign in 1921 not photographs but illustrations of sophisticated women and sold its Kotex pads in a plainly wrapped, unidentified box. In 1928, when Kimberly-Clark put the photo of a real woman in its menstrual hygiene ad, the American public, including the model, was horrified. At that time, no decent woman would have associated herself publicly with menstruation. By the 1930s, however, women were shown in close-fitting gowns to demonstrate that there were no revealing outlines with the new "Phantom Kotex." For the first time, the ads discussed the Kotex belt to be worn with the pad. During the 1940s, Kotex ads supported the war effort. These ads encouraged young women to join the U.S. Cadet Nurse Corps and "keep going" in comfort by choosing Kotex products. Recognizing the large teenage segment of the population, Kotex ads of the 1950s clearly targeted young girls by claiming that Kotex educates young girls about menstruation. In the 1960s, in an effort to include the untapped market of Afro-American women, a Kotex ad featured a glamorous Afro-American woman in an evening gown wearing expensive jewelry.

The caption told the consumer to be mystical, magnetic, magnificent, and sure. By the 1970s, ads depicted a young girl wearing a T-shirt that read "Dear Mother Nature: Drop Dead." The implication was that Kotex gave consumers a product that allowed them to overcome nature, to conquer it. Interestingly, Pope Gregory the Great (d. 604 CE) stated that "the menstrual period is no sin, it is a purely natural event. But the fact that nature is so perverse, that it appears stained even without man's will, that comes from a sin."[25] Thus, by the 1970s, Kotex had made it possible for women to overcome this perversity of nature. The ads from the 1980s and 1990s show women in everyday situations; in a 1990s ad a woman plays with children on a bed. The captions claim that "Kotex Understands." It understands the special needs of women, during work or at home, day or night. In most of the ads, women are shown in whole-body poses in order to illustrate that women who wear Kotex pads have nothing to hide. They are self-confident, playing with their children or taking part in sports, protected from female nature.

Before analyzing ads for Kotex sanitary napkins in the Saudi magazine *Sayidaty,* we have to look at the religious context of menstruation as well as the cultural perception of the female body in the Middle East. In Islam, menstrual blood is surrounded by many taboos and restrictions. The Muslim scholar Ghassan Ascha explains in his work *Du statut inférieur de la femme en Islam* that "[l]e Coran décrit le sang menstruel comme un mal dont il faut se purifier" (the Koran decrees that the menstrual blood is an evil from which one must be purified).[26] Abdelwahab Bouhdiba supports Ascha's extrapolations about the stigma attached to menstrual blood in Islam in his work *Sexuality in Islam* when he quotes the point of view of Islamic jurisprudence (*fiqh*) on the subject of female impurity: "Janâba [ritual impurity] also derives from the menstrua, lochia and pseudo-menstrual emissions. . . . The fiqh merely passes on here an almost universal, in any case very widespread, attitude among ordinary people. Menstrual blood arouses considerable revulsion. More or less everybody in the world popular tradition accuses it of aborting serious projects, of turning milk sour and food rotten."[27]

Thus, just like the Kotex advertisers in the West, the Kotex advertisers in the Middle East need to eradicate the stigma of impurity attached to menstruation in order to successfully market their product. As we saw, Kotex accomplished this by showing first illustrations and then photographs of the whole body of a female model. This whole-body pose allows the female consumer to see for herself that the product is invisible when worn. Indeed, this invisibility makes menstruation per se invisible and irrelevant. Kotex makes the wearer pure and clean.

This advertising strategy of showing the whole body of the model to convey purity does not work in the Middle Eastern context. In Middle Eastern culture, female impurity is not limited to menstruation but is extended to the whole body of a woman. Ascha, citing many Muslim scholars, concludes that "[l]a femme, en Islam, est un être auquel il est préférable de ne pas se frotter sans prétexte (occasion) légal. Il a été rapporté que le prophète n'a jamais touche aucune femme qui ne lui appartînt" (In Islam, the woman is a being with whom one should avoid contact unless one has legal circumstances. It has been transmitted that the Prophet never touched a woman who did not belong to him).[28] The Prophet is also reported as having said: "Woman is something shameful and impure ('awra)."[29] Fedwa Malti-Douglas explains that, in literary Arabic, 'awra "signifies at the same time something shameful, defective, and imperfect; the genitals; and something that must be covered."[30] Thus, if the entire female body is considered impure, something that needs to be covered, the Western strategy of showing the entire body of a female model in order to demonstrate purity would constitute an affront to Middle Eastern mentality were it to elude the pens of the censors of the Saudi government.

How then does Kimberly-Clark advertise its sanitary napkins in Saudi Arabia? The text of the ads is almost identical to the text of the ads in recent Western publications: one ad (FIG. 1.4) reads "Kotex understands my needs. It understands that I need protection. It also understands that I like to feel at ease." Another ad (FIG. 1.5) reads "Kotex understands what it means to be a woman." Both ads also include information about the texture and quality of the napkin and show photographs of the faces of young women. What is striking, however, is the color of the models' veils and the whiteness of their teeth: in one ad (FIG. 1.4), the model wears a light yellow veil; in the other (FIG. 1.5), the model in the center of the photograph wears a white veil and a white blouse. Interestingly, the colors white and, to a degree, yellow are the most intolerant of blood. When investigating honor and poetry in a Bedouin society, Lila Abu-Lughod found that while the color black expresses shame, particularly sexual shame, its opposite, white, is the color of religion and purity.[31] By wrapping the models' heads in white

FIG. 1.4. Advertisement for
Kotex sanitary napkins.
Sayidaty, October 1996.

FIG. 1.5. Advertisement for
Kotex sanitary napkins.
Sayidaty, February 1994.

and light yellow veils and by showing their gleaming white teeth, the advertisers have successfully conveyed to the consumer an image of purity. They have successfully concealed the functions of a woman's body behind a clean white curtain. They target the readership of the magazine by claiming that Kotex understands woman's need to be pure. Kotex knows what it means to be an "impure" woman and has found a solution to overcome her polluting nature. Although Kotex ads in Saudi Arabia differ dramatically in appearance from Kotex ads in Western publications, they employ the same strategy: both claim to be able to make female nature invisible and irrelevant.

Selling Toothpaste

Toothpaste ads in Western fashion magazines often depict a close-up shot of the lips and teeth of a woman. A recent ad for Rembrandt toothpaste, titled "Dazzling White," provides information about the product and shows, along with a photograph of the tube, photographs of teeth before and after the use of Rembrandt. The "after" shot depicts gleaming white teeth framed by lips wearing bright red lipstick.[32] The advertisers employ a strategy of fragmentation of woman's body, a strategy of fetishizing a woman's mouth, in order to portray sex appeal. The message embedded in this image is that if the female consumer uses the advertised brand of toothpaste, her teeth will be so bright and clean, her mouth will be so sexy, that she will be irresistible to the opposite sex. The ad suggests that if the consumer uses the product, she will exude eroticism, no matter how plain the rest of her may be.

Toothpaste ads in *Sayidaty* try to convey a quite different image of woman. Before analyzing this image, we need to look at the Middle Eastern perception of female sexuality. There are substantial cultural differences between East and West in conceptions not only of woman's body and its functions but also of woman's sexuality. Western culture allows the media to bombard the audience with sexual imagery of the female body or parts of it in order to hawk products. For centuries, women have been objects of male desires, male fears, and male theorizing, and many women have internalized their status as objects, especially as sex objects. It is only on this premise that the Rembrandt ad can work. The ad promises the consumer that by using the Rembrandt toothpaste she will transform herself into a sex object.[33]

In Middle Eastern socioreligious ideology, the Muslim woman is not considered a sex object. The concept of *fitna* plays a major role in this ideology. Fatima Mernissi defines fitna as chaos provoked by women's sexuality: "The Muslim woman is endowed with a fatal attraction which erodes the male's will to resist her and reduces him to a passive acquiescent role. He has no choice; he can only give in to her attraction, whence her identification with fitna, chaos, and with the anti-divine and anti-social forces of the universe."[34] The concept of fitna makes woman not the object but the agent. Malti-Douglas gives a semantic analysis of woman's role as aggressor: "The Arabic word for seduction is very telling. *Futina bi,* to be seduced by, is in the passive. The woman is the source of the action, the man its object. More important, this verb is also the grammatical root that gives us *fitna.*"[35] The idea that a woman has the power to cause fitna is deeply ingrained in the Muslim mind. When a man and a woman are together, fitna may occur. The *hadith* "when a man and a woman are isolated in the presence of each other, Satan is bound to be their third companion"[36] expresses this fear of fitna. According to Mernissi, "the entire Muslim social structure can be seen as an attack on, and a defence against, the disruptive power of female sexuality."[37] Polygyny, repudiation, veiling, and sex segregation have been seen by many scholars, religious and feminist, as attempts to channel, control, legalize, and tame woman's sexuality.

The premise that women should not associate with unrelated men has been the basis for all Saudi restrictions on the behavior of women, including regulations regarding the separation of boys and girls in the educational system and laws stipulating that women have a male chaperon when traveling, not study abroad without a male chaperon, not check into a hotel alone, and not drive a car in the kingdom. Sex segregation has made it difficult for Saudi women to join the workforce, especially in professions in which contact with the opposite sex is difficult to avoid. Many Saudi women, willingly or unwillingly, fulfill what conservative Muslim thinkers consider woman's main purposes, namely, to be a good wife and a good mother. It is in the role of mother that woman will find paradise at her feet, as a well-known proverb declares. That Saudi women take this proverb to heart is demonstrated by the fact that the average number of children born to the Saudi woman is 6.5 (estimated for 1995), as compared to 1.8 for the American woman.[38]

The ad for Signal toothpaste (FIG. 1.6) in *Sayidaty* should be understood in this context. Just like the text of the Kotex ads, the text of the Signal ad does not reflect cultural differences between East and West. It describes the effectiveness of the product in exaggerated terms: "Now, a toothpaste whose effect lasts and lasts and lasts long after you have stopped cleaning." Like the photograph in the Kotex ad, the one in the Signal ad reveals cultural differences. The photo shows a happy family. Parents wearing traditional clothes stand behind a boy who wears Western clothes and squeezes toothpaste from a tube of Signal onto his toothbrush. Both mother and father hold out their brushes for the boy to squeeze toothpaste onto them. The father looks down, while the mother smiles into the camera, showing shiny white teeth. Her smile is not a smile of sexual allure but of motherly pride and happiness. The photo captures the solipsism of a happy family, self-content, wholesome, and far from chaos. This ad tells the consumer that in order to be a wife and mother who wants the best for her family, she needs to buy the Unilever product Signal. The ad appeals to the consumer's desire to be a good wife and a good mother. The family becomes united in the use of Signal.

This advertising strategy of suggesting to the consumer that she is a good wife and mother if she buys a certain product or uses a certain service is also employed in ads for food items such as certain brands of milk, butter, and yogurt, which the Saudi woman may actually purchase by herself. But this strategy is also exploited in ads for products and services that she most likely would not purchase by herself, for example, tickets for British Airways, or the services of a certain air conditioning company. This strategy is, of course, also used on Western consumers, although I have not found one ad featuring mother and child in a recent issue (May 1998) of *Elle*.

Selling Watches

The ads in *Sayidaty* do not rely on sexual imagery to sell products. That is not to say, however, that the ads in *Sayidaty* do not exploit woman's desire for romance and love. In a series of contextualized ads, the Swiss watchmaker Concord relies on romantic illustrations complemented by poetry and enlarged photographs of Concord watches to sell an illusion of romance. This illusion can be realized with the purchase of an expensive gold-and-diamond watch, which in the ads becomes identical with a desirable beautiful woman. While the Concord advertisers sell an image in the *Sayidaty* ads, they sell facts and information about the watches in their ads

FIG. 1.6. Advertisement for
Signal toothpaste. *Sayidaty,*
June 1991.

in the fashion magazines published in the West. The ads in Western magazines show an enlarged photograph of the watch with some information
about it, including the price ($3,990 for the Concord Saratoga SL, $8,500
for the Concord Veneto, and $8,900 for the Concord La Scala).

The first ad for this brand of watch (FIG. 1.7) appeared in the October
1993 issue of *Sayidaty.* Interestingly, that year Saudi Arabia and the United
Arab Emirates set the world record for the purchase of gold jewelry. The
sales volume in these two countries reached $11.3 billion a year. We may
assume that the Concord watchmaker has garnered a substantial share of
that market.

In the 1993 ad, we find in the foreground a woman who wears a black
transparent face veil (*niqab*), exposing only her heavily accentuated eyes.
Her black cloak (*abaya*) has a trim of gold embroidery, and the part of the
veil across her forehead is decorated with a chain of gold coins, identifying
her as Bedouin.[39] The background depicts a crescent moon, blue sky, sparkling stars, and an intricately latticed arch. Underneath the illustration are

FIG. 1.7. Advertisement for Concord watches. *Sayidaty,* October 1993.

centered four lines of calligraphy, interspersed with dots reflecting the stars in the sky. The lines read:

As charming and as soft as the moon, like the first early nights of
   the moon
As swift, and accurate as the strokes of the artist's brush
Chosen by the elite for special occasions.
It is the Swiss watch Delirium, from Concord.

Below the photographed watch in small print we read, "Concord Delirium ladies watch, 18 karat gold, leather band, enameled in white color, set in four diamonds, also available for men."

   The shape of the crescent moon in this illustration is reflected in the arch of the woman's brows and in the shape of her heavily made-up eyes. While the light of the crescent moon is clearly visible in the illustration, the outline of the full moon is hinted at; it is painted a shade lighter against the nightly blue of the sky and superimposed on the band of stars. In the lunar calendar, the moon is full on the fourteenth day. In Middle Eastern culture, fourteen is also the age when a girl is most beautiful and desirable. It is the age to get married. A woman with a face as soft and round as the full moon is considered the most beautiful in Middle Eastern aesthetics. Many proverbs attest to this beauty ideal. For example, a proverb from Bahrain states "I saw a beautiful woman in a tent who appeared like the full moon in the sky." A Kuwaiti proverb translates as "God commanded me to love you, o you moon-faced woman." The beauty of the moon-faced woman is also the subject of many *qasidas*. For example, al-Mutanabbi, considered by many as the greatest poet in the Arabic language, rhymes "pale moon reflects her day of face, that she and I may double see as one."[40] What the crescent moon in the illustration thus implies is that the beautiful woman is waiting for the full moon, when she will be the most desirable and ready to get married.

The next ad in this series (1994) (FIG. 1.8) shows the same illustration but without the woman. Since readers are still able to visualize the beautiful face from the 1993 ad, its absence in the 1994 ad creates suspense. The reader waits for the moon to become full and for the beautiful woman to return. The poem, again in calligraphy interspersed with dots and centered underneath the illustration, uses moon as metonym for woman in "dreaming of embracing the moon" and thus underscores the atmosphere of suspense created by the illustration:

Shining like a star
Dreaming of embracing the moon
Charming colors
Like musical notes played on string
It is the Swiss Concord Delirium
It is the four season watch from Concord
Chosen by the elite for special occasions

The attributes described in this poem are those of the watch as well as of the beautiful woman featured in the 1993 ad: "Shining like a star" refers to the sparkling diamonds on the watch, and "charming colors" refers to the various colors of the different leather bands in which the watch is available.

The next ad in this series (FIG. 1.9), from the November 1994 issue, builds even more suspense. It shows an illustration of a Bedouin wearing

FIG. 1.8. Advertisement for Concord watches. *Sayidaty,* October 1994.

the traditional white *kafiya* and *agal* and galloping on a black horse. The urgency of his desire to unite with the beautiful woman who is waiting for him in the first ad is made perceptible by his speed, which is expressed by the galloping stride of his horse and by his kafiya, torn back in swift artist's strokes. The background is the typical scenery of a desert. The moon and stars are now absent. Again the text is in calligraphy but is no longer interspersed with stars. It reads:

> The Swiss watch Saratoga for which hearts long, because of its
>   beauty, perfection, and fineness
> A faithful companion, whose outstanding performance increases
>   over the years
> Chosen by the elites because of its deep-rootedness [*'araqa*] and
>   steadfastness [*al asala*].

The double entendre created by the use of the Arabic feminine possessive pronoun in this poem is arresting; the pronoun refers to the woman as well as to the watch, which has a feminine gender in Arabic (*al sa'a*). Beauty, perfection, fineness, deep-rootedness (*al 'araqa* also means ancient ancestral line), and steadfastness (*al asala* also means noble descent) are desired characteristics in a watch as well as in a woman. The woman and the watch are interchangeable; they have become identical. This fusion between woman and watch is illustrated in the next ad in this series. In the Concord Papillon ad (February 1995), the beautiful face of the woman becomes the beautiful face of the watch.

Starting with an ad in the May 1995 issue (FIG. 1.10), both the beautiful woman and her Bedouin suitor are portrayed, with the woman in the foreground and the Bedouin at a distance in the background. Interestingly, this ad is titled *al-khay(y)al,* which can mean, without diacritical marks, "imagination" as well as "the horseman." The ad suggests that the woman is imagining the horseman whom we met in the previous ad. Looking out the window of a car, she imagines him at a distance, letting his falcon fly toward her.

FIG. 1.9. Advertisement for Concord watches. *Sayidaty,* November 1994.

FIG 1.10. Advertisement for Concord watches. *Sayidaty,* May 1995.

Finally, in a Concord ad in the October 1996 issue (FIG 1.11), titled *al-raghba* (desire), we see the woman in the foreground and the Bedouin suitor riding through the desert sand toward her. Since we met him first in November 1994, he has changed horses and clothes. The veil of the woman has also changed: the embroidered trim of her abaya is noticeably wider and attached to the chain across her forehead are no longer coins but gold nuggets in the shape of desert roses. The text of this ad reads:

> The pieces of diamonds are swimming in a golden sea of eternal
> harmony
> Saratoga SL—a watch to mesmerize
> It fulfills the ultimate desire to buy beauty

This ad implies that the purchase of the watch will fulfill the consumer's desire for romance, love, and harmony. The watch will fulfill her dreams. The man of her dreams will come looking for her and they will be united in "eternal harmony." This series of ads invites what Judith Williamson in *Decoding Advertisements* calls an "irrational mental leap" from what things mean to us to the meaning we give to products.[41] In other words, the Concord ads entice the consumer to project her desire for romance, love, beauty, and harmony, which is fulfilled by the Bedouin horseman in the ads, on to the features of a Concord watch.

These ads are tailored to appeal to Saudi women, and women from other Gulf states, who can claim noble ancestry. For these women, having a noble ancestry is often synonymous with having access to wealth and thus being able to purchase the Concord watch. The prices of the watches are not mentioned in the ads in *Sayidaty;* they are sold over the Internet with price tags ranging as high as $13,900 for the Concord Delirium and $57,000 for the 18-karat-gold Concord Saratoga. Furthermore, the consumer is likely to live in a town, as 73 percent of the Saudi population does, and returning to the desert may have become a nostalgic dream for her. She most likely understands the metaphors and metonyms in the ads, which were used for centuries by the Bedouins. All these prerequisites enable her to give her dreams a concrete shape in the form of a Concord watch.

The ads in *Sayidaty* for products as diverse as sanitary napkins, tooth-paste, and watches are tailored to meet the cultural specificities of the Saudi

FIG. I.II. Advertisement for Concord watches. *Sayidaty,* October 1996.

market. Reflecting the cultural values of Saudi Arabia, these ads are quite different from ads for the same product but targeting the Western consumer. They demonstrate the advertisers' awareness of the cultural differences between East and West and their willingness to exploit these differences.

Conclusion

The veil has as many meanings as it has colors and shapes. This semantic versatility has made the veil a lucrative tool for advertisers in the East and the West. Advertisers, using the principle of homeopathic or sympathetic magic, rely on its "exoticism" and "eroticism" to seduce Western men into buying Jeep Cherokees and IBM computers. Cigarette and perfume advertisers stress the "backwardness" of the veil in order to hawk their products to Western women. The veil becomes an emblem of authenticity when ethnic foods are sold to Middle Eastern consumers in the United States and Canada. When selling sanitary napkins to Saudi women, the white veil sells purity, helping consumers overcome the perversity of nature. In ads for products and services as diverse as Signal toothpaste and British Airways, the veil identifies the traditional woman in her role as good wife and good mother. In ads selling Concord watches, the embroidered veil decorated with chains of gold coins and desert roses is part of the Saudi consumer's dreams of romance in the desert sand that have become identical with the Concord watch.

Images and photos of veiled women have become a powerful weapon in the advertisers' arsenals, in the United States as well as in Saudi Arabia. It is noteworthy, however, that the advertisers in Saudi Arabia use mostly Lebanese and other non-Saudi models in order to elude the eager pen of the government official and in an effort to keep the image of Saudi women "pure" and "honorable," without the stigma of being an object.[42]

2 Veiled Images in American Erotica

The Target Market of *Penthouse, Playboy,* and *Hustler*

Advertisers of products as diverse as Jeep Cherokees and sanitary napkins rely on the semantic versatility of the veil in order to sell their goods to target markets. For example, as we saw in chapter 1, when trying to sell Jeep Cherokees, advertisers exploit the Western stereotype of the exoticism and sensuality of the veiled woman in order to sell jeeps to American middle-class men. *Penthouse, Playboy,* and *Hustler* also exploit this semantic flexibility of the veil in order to sell sex and politics primarily to male consumers.[1]

However, these three magazines do not all appeal to the same segment of the American male population. Mediamark Research Inc. estimates that in 1998 the readers of *Playboy: Entertainment for Men* had a median age of thirty-two years and a median household income of about $39,000. For the same year, the readers of *Penthouse: The Magazine of Sex, Politics, and Protest* had a median age of thirty-three years and a median household income of about $40,000.[2] The subscribers to *Penthouse*'s online version have a median age of twenty-nine years and a household income of more than $53,000. Since these median household incomes reflect the income of mostly single males, it may stand to reason that the average reader of *Penthouse* as well as *Playboy* is a young, sexually active, middle-class male. Mediamark Research does not include data about the readership of *Hustler: For the Rest of the World*. Most magazines conduct demographic surveys of subscribers in order to sell advertising space to advertisers of products that may appeal to the surveyed subscribers. The nature of the advertisements in *Hustler*, however, may not necessitate such market research: The only advertisements in *Hustler* are pages upon pages of ads for phone sex and some ads for sexual aids—ads that will most certainly appeal to sexually active readers of pornographic magazines. The few quasi-investigative articles in *Hustler* aim to incite readers with sensationalist and testosterone-laden journalism. We may conclude that the average reader of this magazine is young and relatively unsophisticated and delights in viewing the intimate details of the female anatomy.

Do these three magazines contribute to the imprinting and perpetuation of sweeping generalizations and stereotypes about the veil? Since their first publications in 1953, 1969, and 1976, *Playboy, Penthouse,* and *Hustler* have offered more than 250 images of the Middle East[3] to their American consumers.[4] The vast majority of these images feature women wearing the veil. How many Americans saw these images? According to Standard Rates and Data Services (SRDS), *Playboy* had about 3.24 million subscribers in 1991 and about 3.25 million in 1993. *Penthouse* had about 1.3 million subscribers in 1991 and more than 1.5 million in 1993.[5] For spring 1999, Mediamark Research estimates 4.5 readers per copy for *Penthouse* and 2.8 for *Playboy*.[6] If we assume that *Playboy* and *Penthouse* had the same number of readers per copy in 1991 and 1993, we may conclude that more than 9 million Americans read *Playboy* in 1991 and 1993. We may also conclude that 6 million Americans read *Penthouse* in 1991 and almost 7 million in 1993. Taking into account the small number of adult female readers of *Penthouse* (about 12 percent) and estimating the adult male population at about 90 million in the early 1990s, we may estimate that approximately one in seventeen American adult men saw the images of the veil in the May 1991 issue and that one in fourteen saw them in the September 1993 issue; these issues of *Penthouse* are discussed below.

Mediamark Research estimates that in spring 1999 *Playboy* had a total readership of close to 9 million, while *Penthouse* had only about 4 million readers, a decrease of 3 million readers as compared to 1993. This decrease in subscriptions to *Penthouse* is partly because of the popularity of *Penthouse*'s subscription online site, which allows consumers to avoid the embarrassment of subscribing to or purchasing the printed version.[7] SRDS has not received circulation numbers for *Hustler* since 1988. *Hustler* is also not included in the list of magazines for which Mediamark Research estimated circulation numbers for 1999; however, its publisher Larry Flynt claims that *Hustler*'s readership grew by 500 percent in 1997 mostly due to the publicity caused by the movie *The People vs. Larry Flynt* (1996). We may deduce from these numbers of readers that for the last several decades *Playboy*, *Penthouse*, and *Hustler* have made a significant contribution to the typecasting of the veiled woman in popular culture. Furthermore, the circulation numbers above do not include minors. In testimony given to the Attorney General's Commission on Pornography Hearings, in Houston, Texas, in 1985, the following data were made public: 100 percent of all high school age males surveyed reported having read or looked at *Playboy* or similar "men's entertainment" magazines; the average age when viewing the first issue was eleven years old; 16.1 issues was the average number seen by male high schoolers; 92 percent of males in junior high reported exposure to *Playboy* or similar magazines.[8] These children experienced Middle Eastern culture and sexuality by looking at images of veiled women in erotic magazines without having the knowledge and resources to critically assess these images. The role of these magazines in the imprinting of stereotypes about the Middle East in general and the veil in particular may, therefore, not be a minor one.

Playboy, *Penthouse*, and *Hustler* sell sex as well as politics. Thus, on one hand, stereotypes about the veil are visually presented in order to sexually stimulate the reader; on the other hand, these stereotypes are presented in cartoons to mock and ridicule certain aspects of the social and sexual behavior of Middle Easterners. Any exploration of the semantic versatility of the veil in these magazines, therefore, has to have a dual trajectory: one that investigates the sexual significance of the veil in photographs and one that explores the political import of the veil in cartoons. It is the photographs of nude women in erotic and pornographic poses that sell the magazines.[9] The cartoons in these magazines are not intended to sexually stimulate the reader. They are drawings that caricature or symbolize, often satirically, some event, situation, or person of topical interest. In *Playboy, Penthouse,* and *Hustler,* cartoons often make political statements by mocking certain aspects of a person's or people's sexuality. Thus, one may expect that the use and relevance of the veil in the photographs are different from that in the cartoons.

The Veil Sells Sex

The Pleasures of the Orient

When selling products to the Western male consumer, the veil is most often ascribed an erotic meaning. In order to sell sex, *Playboy, Penthouse,* and *Hustler* exploit this erotic image of the veil. What is the underlying assumption prevalent in the West that facilitates the equation of sex and veil? Centuries of Western misinterpretations of Middle Eastern sexuality and culture have led to an image of the Middle East as a world of virgin pleasures and unbridled passions. Many Westerners acquire their information and prejudices about the Middle East from the tales of *The Thousand and One Nights.*[10] Indeed, these tales convey a tantalizing image of sexuality in the Middle East. This medieval narrative constitutes a veritable encyclopedia of sexology. The subjects covered include bestiality, frigidity, homosexuality, impotence, orgy, polygyny, sodomy, voyeurism, and all other sexual behavior known to mankind.[11] The tales of *The Thousand and One Nights* create an image of the Middle East as a world revolving around debauchery, perversion, and sexual illicitness. According to *Playboy, Penthouse,* and *Hustler,* it is the world of the seraglio inhabited by cruel sultans, voluptuous odalisques, and loyal eunuchs—a world of sexual megalomania where not only carpets fly and lamps are magical, but sex is close to supernatural.[12]

Furthermore, the abundant existence of manuals of Muslim erotology intensified the Western image of Oriental libertinism.[13] To mention a well-researched manual, *The Perfumed Garden of the Shaykh Nefzawi* describes twenty-five coital positions for a heterosexual couple of analogous build. Shaykh al-Nefzawi further elaborates on coital positions for the humpbacked, tall, small, obese, and pregnant.[14] Alan Hull Walton, in his introduction to Sir Richard Burton's translation of *The Perfumed Garden,* explains that "the peoples of the Orient are much less sexually inhibited than we" (the people of the West).[15] Thus, to protect Western modesty, the translators of *The Thousand and One Nights* as well as *The Perfumed Garden* have omitted chapters of the Arabic originals.[16] In its January 1965 issue, *Playboy* published a story from *The Perfumed Garden*. This tale, titled "The Trial of a True Friend," describes the adulterous exploit of a beautiful young woman married to an impotent old man, and the sexual adventure of her sister. The tale is illustrated by a drawing of two women in reclining poses wearing transparent harem pants, bras, and face veils.[17]

Another important source of information on the sexual mores of the Muslim world is provided by Western interpretations of the Qur'an and Islam in general. The Christian West has traditionally seen Islam through Dante's eyes as "The Inferno." According to Dante, Islam is not a religion, but a life of licentiousness. Western medieval writers and clergymen portrayed the Prophet Muhammad as an impostor and the Qur'an as his pretentious fabrication. They described Islam as a licentious way of life, both here and in the next world. Echoing medieval interpretations of a "licentious" Islam, Mohammed Pickthall, a modern commentator on the Qur'an, explains the difference between the Christian and the Muslim approach to sexuality in marriage: "For Christendom the strictest religious ideal has been celibacy, monogamy is already a concession to human nature. For Muslims, monogamy is the ideal, polygamy the concession to human nature."[18] Some modern Western authors have attempted to show that Islam is a "sensuous faith," permitting its followers a number of sexual practices that led to a "false" religion.[19]

Western fantasies about the Orient and misinterpretations of Islam created an image of the Middle East as a world in which every sexual behavior known to humankind is allowed and enjoyed. It is a world in which men are permitted as many women as they can satisfy and veiled women revel in submission to their master. The West transformed the sexual reality of the Middle East by manipulating the meanings of objects such as the veil and concepts such as the harem, and by presenting these objects and concepts in such a way that they became alienated and often severed from their original meaning. In this manner, entirely new images were created and new meanings were assigned to them. Orientalism—photographic and literary—has, over several centuries, led to the creation of fixed images of the Middle East.[20] For example, by the end of the nineteenth century, Europeans had created their own image of life in the harem. The photographs of life in the harem taken in a studio were so different from the actual subject they claimed to portray that the real images seemed no longer "authentic." The "created" and "imaginary" idea of the harem was now the only acceptable one.[21] The veil, no matter in what form, shape, color, or size, had now come to signify not "real" Middle Eastern women, about whom little was known, but the heroines of *The Thousand and One Nights*. The veil had become the trademark of the wanton woman who finds pleasure in her subjugation to an often sadistic master.

The Veil Promises a Thousand and One Pleasures

Genuine travelogues, tales of imaginary voyages in novels set in exotic places, and "Oriental" erotica provided European writers with a poetic backdrop of "Oriental" authenticity. For example, in 1869, Gustave Flaubert wrote of a particular brothel owned by a woman known to her clients as "La Turque," the Turkish woman.[22] La Turque, according to his writings, added to the poetic character of the "Madame's" establishment. Flaubert authenticated his novel by naming the madam La Turque. This strategy of authentication is also employed by the photographers of *Penthouse* and *Playboy*. By veiling their models, they strive to create an atmosphere of an "authentic" Middle East, saturated with sexual possibilities and the wantonness depicted in *The Thousand and One Nights*.

The veil in the photo-stories in *Penthouse* (May 1991; September 1993) is intended to prove that the depicted sexual poses are indeed those of the Middle East. The veiled heroines and the turbaned heroes in these photo-stories authenticate a Middle Eastern setting and thereby serve to evoke Western fantasies of Oriental sexual abandon. Interestingly though, in the photo-story of May 1991, the title of the story, "Jeannie and Lawrence," as well as the captions, indicates that the photo-story visualizes the sexual dream of an American college student named Jeannie involving her professor, Lawrence, who plays her sheik. One caption reads: "'Welcome to my seraglio,' the sheik would beckon to his newfound mistress. 'You will be my Scheherazade and delight me with erotic tales of a thousand and one Arabian nights.'" The professor is identified in the caption of the last photo as Lawrence of Arabia. The veil and the turban visually identify the sexual behavior of the protagonists as that described in *The Thousand and One Nights*. This photo-story employs Western images of Oriental libidinousness that are, except for the presence of the veil and the turban, detached from Middle Eastern reality. The veil and the turban function as visual nexus between Western fantasies about the Orient and Middle Eastern reality.

The veil and the turban are also prominent in a photo-story in the September 1993 issue of *Penthouse* that depicts a couple in different sexual poses. This series of photos takes us on an odyssey of misrepresentations of the Middle East. On the first page, the heroine wears an embroidered, transparent, hood-shaped veil over her blond locks. She is nude under her veil except for tassels on her nipples. The hero wears a colorful turban, and his face, shown in profile, has more the Mongolian features of Genghis Khan than those of an Arabian knight, as the title of the photo-story claims. The caption of the first photo in this series reads: "Diane had always felt pulled toward the Middle East. In college she had earned her doctorate in the history of the region, then she moved there to learn all she could about the culture of these desert lands. When she met Ghassan, she knew she'd stay forever." The caption of the third photo tells us that Diana and Ghassan are in the Sahara, where the desert wind fuels their lust. In the next photograph, Ghassan wears a scimitar, embroidered ankle warmers made of fur, and Turkish slippers. The caption of the last picture in this series explains that "this Arab prince and his Western princess became forever one under the starlit desert sky." Neither the actors nor their clothes with their diverse accessories belong to the Sahara, but they may well constitute echoes of *Arabian Nights,* to which the title of the photo-story "Arabian Knight" alludes. The veil and the turban, although adjusted to conform to the dictates of an erotic magazine, anchor the story visually in a Middle Eastern context.

The veil is worn by women identified as Western in the captions in order to rouse images of Oriental wantonness in the Western male viewer. A veiled centerfold in the December 1973 issue of *Penthouse* is identified as Helga Schiller from Bremen, Germany. This series of photographs is titled "Helga of the Dunes," pointing to the dunes of the Sahara as the setting for this series. The architecture and Arabic as well as French writings that appear on a sign depicted in the photographs suggest a village or an oasis in North Africa. The caption reads: "For Helga is a drifter . . . a Siddhartha of the seventies . . . a blond Venus on the sunburned perimeter of Islam." The veil and the mention of Islam in this caption signify that Helga is a true "Oriental" woman and, as such, eager to provide the pleasures of the Orient. Interestingly, in these three photo-stories, the veil is not worn by Middle Eastern women but by Western women who, by doing so, hope to trigger Western male fantasies of *The Thousand and One Nights* in the first two series and of the "sensuousness" of Islam in the third series. In all three series, the veil symbolizes woman's willingness to partake in male fantasies.

The Veil as Western Fetish

In the photographs discussed above, the veil is exploited to galvanize fantasies of Oriental licentiousness in the reader. The object of desire is the woman under the veil. In some photographs, however, the veil itself functions as object of desire. It becomes a fetish. The definitions of sexual fetish are numerous. Wilhelm Stekel, a sexologist writing in the early twentieth century, explains that "there is not an organ of the human body, not a single article of clothing or of daily use which may not become an object of fetishism."[23] For fetishists, the shoe may be sexier than the foot it adorns, the veil more enticing than the anatomy it screens. Fetishism is a translocation of desire. The sexual impulse is directed away from genitalia and toward an object such as the shoe or the veil. So varied are the types of fetishism that have been studied in the last century that a plethora of subcategories exists. One that may be of interest to us is called *hyphephilia*. This term is applied to arousal by human hair, animal fur, leather, and fabrics, especially upon erogenous zones. The veil of diaphanous chiffon and the sheer material of harem pants are fetishes that the late designer Gianni Versace translated into high fashion.[24]

The Canadian playmate in the May 1989 issue of *Playboy* wears a veil made of embroidered diaphanous white lace. She is screened by her veil, except for one eye and some blond hair, but at the same time she is exposed to the gaze of the viewer. Although the transparency of the veil does not leave much to the imagination, the veil creates a transparent barrier between the model and the viewer. The ethnographer Kelly Dennis maintains that veiling nude models creates an "erotic aura of not being too close."[25] He argues that "it [the veil] distinguishes erotica from obscenity, art from mass culture, for both art and erotica depend upon effacement of the female sex which is enacted by veiling."[26] However, in addition to screening part of the model's face and her breasts, the white veil in this photograph has another function: the whiteness of the veil serves to purify the playmate's nudity. The white transparent veil creates the illusion of the virginal whore. As substantiation of this paradox, the veil becomes the object of the viewer's desire, a fetish.

An illustration in the September 1994 issue of *Penthouse* also depicts the veil as fetish. Here, the Japanese artist Hajime Sorayama uses a super-realism illustration technique that makes his artwork almost indistinguishable from a photograph.[27] His illustration shows a dark-skinned model wearing a lavender-colored head scarf and a white transparent face veil. Her breasts and vagina are screened by veils made of several strands of small-linked chains that are hooked to crescent moons. The lower veil is, in addition, decorated with coins resembling the jewelry usually worn by belly dancers around the hips. The model also wears a snake arm bracelet of gold and wrist bracelets. High-heeled, black thigh-high leather boots with buckles complete her outfit. She holds one breast in her hand in a pose of self-stimulation. Her fingers have long purple-painted nails. She aims to please consumers who fetishize chains, diaphanous fabrics, long sharp fingernails, and kinky boots. The transparent face veil, the purple head veil, and the veils made of chains attached to crescent moons serve not only to identify the model as Middle Eastern but to convey Oriental submissiveness. High-heeled, thigh-high boots and long sharp fingernails gouging into muscular flesh are well-established fetishes of dominance in the West. For many years, high boots have been the trademark of prostitutes specializing in sadomasochism.[28] Thus, the model embodies Oriental submission and Western dominance at the same time. She substantiates a paradox. In sadomasochistic terminology, she embodies the slave as well as the master. Interestingly, Sorayama exploits the veil as antipode to Western fetishes of dominance.

To conclude, in the photographs in *Penthouse* and *Playboy* and in Sorayama's artwork in *Penthouse,* the function of the veil is to rouse in the consumer fantasies of an Orient where voluptuous women eagerly submit to the sexual demands of a master. In the photo-stories, this delusion of a thousand and one pleasures is created by employing the veil as signifier of Oriental sexuality. When the veil functions as fetish, it symbolizes the virginal whore and the submissive dominatrix; both are a paradox. *Hustler* does not feature photographs of veiled women. Dennis's assertion that the veil distinguishes erotica from obscenity may explain why there are no photographs of veiled women in a magazine that relies on graphic depictions of human nudity and sexual acts.

The Veil Sells Politics

U.S. Relations with the Middle East

Cartoons in erotic magazines are not intended to sexually arouse the consumer, but to entertain by satirizing and caricaturing a person's or a people's social and sexual behavior. Thus, it is not surprising that there is a direct correlation between the frequency and content of cartoons in *Playboy, Penthouse,* and *Hustler* set in the Middle East and the nature of American relations with the countries of the Middle East. A brief outline of these relations may shed light on the semantic exploitation of the veil in these cartoons and thereby facilitate a categorization of the different meanings of the veil.

Despite an oil embargo in 1967, U.S.–Middle East relations were relatively stable until the oil embargo of 1973–74. In 1973, Arab oil-producing nations moved to prohibit shipments to the United States, Western Europe, and Japan in retaliation for their support of Israel. This cutoff precipitated an energy crisis in the industrialized world. In 1974, when worldwide inflation caused dramatic increases in the cost of fuel, food, and materials, the oil-producing nations boosted prices, heightening inflation. At this time, the economic growth slowed to near zero in most industrialized nations. After 1974, relations between the United States and Middle Eastern nations improved and were again stable in 1978, when U.S. president Jimmy Carter arranged peace talks between Israeli premier Menachem Begin and Egyptian president Anwar Sadat at Camp David. In that same year, however, Mohammed Reza Shah Pahlavi, who had the support of the United States, imposed martial law to put an end to violent antigovernment demonstrations in Iran. In response, the self-exiled Ayatollah Khomeini called on his compatriots to topple the Shah. In 1979, Ayatollah Khomeini realized his vision of a theocratic government, and the Islamic Republic of Iran was born. Iran's political leaders were now weary and suspicious of Western influence in the region, a situation that culminated in the hostage taking at the U.S. embassy in Tehran. In 1980, the United States cut ties with Iran and, when Iraq invaded Iran, sided with Iraq. In the following years, U.S.–Middle East relations were marred by reciprocal violence: in 1983, a pro-Iranian Lebanese bombed the U.S. Marine installation in Beirut in a suicide mission; in 1986, U.S. planes under the order of President Ronald Reagan bombed the cities of Tripoli and Benghazi in

Libya in retaliation for Libya's involvement in international terrorism, especially the bombing of a Berlin discotheque in April 1986; in 1988, a bomb exploded on Pan Am Flight 103 over Lockerbie, Scotland, allegedly stowed there by a Libyan terrorist. In 1990, talks between Kuwait and Iraq over issues of oil prices and territory failed, and Iraq under Saddam Hussein's leadership annexed Kuwait, assuming that its longtime ally, the United States, would not intervene. Concern over oil supplies and massive public relations campaigns, largely financed by Kuwait, mobilized U.S. opinion against Hussein and drove a U.S.-led coalition to bomb Iraq in January 1991 in Operation Desert Storm.[29] Defeated, Iraq was forced to leave Kuwait and submit to a U.N.-monitored program of disarmament. Despite intense efforts by the leading Western powers, Israel, and Saudi Arabia to have Hussein assassinated, or his regime overthrown by a coup, he survived.[30] His military and intelligence apparatus remained effective. In the United States, in the meantime, four Muslims were convicted in the 1994 bombing of the World Trade Center and more Muslims were tried for a wide-ranging plot of terrorist attacks.

The following analysis of the semantics of the veil as portrayed in cartoons warrants a caveat. While the cartoons considered were published in *Playboy, Penthouse,* and *Hustler* during the period just outlined, their content will not always be specifically reflective of the events occurring at the time they appeared. For example, we may find that the veil's meaning changed with the Iranian Revolution but did not change from cartoons intended to mock the social and sexual behavior of the Ayatollah Khomeini to those aimed at ridiculing Muammar al-Qaddafi or Saddam Hussein. Categories of veiled women are, therefore, arranged thematically and, if feasible, these categories or the most telling examples thereof are related to and contextualized with political events.

The Harem Unveiled

The December 1962 issue of *Playboy* contained the first in a series of cartoons set in the Middle East. A turbaned man, presumably a sultan, and two women watch as two servants, presumably eunuchs, wrap a nude woman in gauze, starting at her pelvic area. One servant says to the other: "He's never satisfied! Now he wants her gift wrapped!" The translucent veil being wrapped around her represents the gift wrap. She is wrapped in order to be unwrapped by the sultan, to whom she will be presented as a gift. Since this is a December issue of *Playboy,* we may assume that she will be his Christmas present. Interestingly, in this cartoon, a Christian holiday is superimposed on a harem setting. The sultan, celebrating Christmas, is no longer satisfied when presented with just a nude woman. He has been presented with plenty of those before. Only the anticipation he feels when unveiling the wrapped woman will rouse his interest now. The veil in this cartoon adds extra pleasure for the sultan, whose wives and concubines are usually presented to him in the nude, according to the cartoons in *Playboy.*

A turbaned, usually obese, hero and several women, either completely nude or wearing translucent harem pants, are sufficient to create a harem setting in *Playboy.* In these settings, the veil is superfluous to the depiction of Oriental sexuality. In the cartoon described above, as well as in a cartoon in the December 1966 issue of *Playboy,* this Oriental sexuality merges with icons of Christianity. In the 1966 cartoon, we see four voluptuous women lounging, either half-naked or fully naked, wedged between a Christmas tree and some wrapped presents. In the center, we find an obese sultan, sitting on the ground barely able to cross his legs in the typical fashion. He wears shiny harem pants, a pair of gold hoop earrings, and a feathered turban. In his right hand, he holds a *hukkah* (water pipe), while his left hand rests on his knee. His facial expression is rendered in a comical manner, with a goatee, upward-slanting mustache, raised eyebrows, and eyes open wide in obvious surprise. One of the four women, completely naked, is stretched out on her stomach and engaged in conversation with him. Two of the women are talking to each other. The caption reads: "He's easy to please. He wants the same thing every Christmas." These two cartoons are significant insofar as they offer a Westernization of the harem. Although they present the stereotype of the insatiable sultan and odalisques who are ever-willing to please him, they make Oriental sexuality less alien to the Western consumer by having the sultan celebrate Christmas. Islam has not yet become an issue for *Playboy* cartoonists and *Playboy* readers.

Another technique used to "Westernize" the harem scene was to endow women with a beauty that complied with Western ideals. The odalisques were portrayed as paragons of Western beauty and as such they were unveiled. In the cartoons of 1966, harem women look like *Playboy* versions of Jeannie in the then-popular TV sitcom *I Dream of Jeannie,* starring Barbara Eden. Sidney Sheldon's creation, which aired first in September 1965, brought a Westernized version of Oriental sexuality to American living rooms. The name of the protagonist, "Jeannie," is a phonetic cognate of "genie" or "jinni." In Arabic mythology and in the tales of *The Thousand and One Nights*, a jinni is a supernatural spirit, capable of assuming human form and said to dwell in all conceivable inanimate objects. Jinn delight in punishing humans for any harm done them; however, those human beings who know the proper magical procedures can exploit the jinn to their advantage. The American Jeannie takes the form of a beautiful woman who, after having been rescued by Captain Anthony Nelson from the confines of a bottle, vows to accept him as her master and serve him devotedly. The harem women in the *Playboy* cartoons of 1966 are modeled after this Jeannie in their appearance and willingness to please their master. In *Playboy* fashion, however, they are completely nude or wear translucent harem pants.

In the December 1966 cartoon discussed above, the four women have hairdos almost identical to that of Jeannie: long hair is swept up into a bun on top of the head and then flows down the back. A cartoon in the January 1966 issue (FIG. 2.1) shows an obese mustachioed sultan surrounded by women who also wear their hair in typical Jeannie fashion. Some of the

FIG. 2.1. Cartoon, *Playboy,* January 1966. Reproduced by special permission of *Playboy* magazine. Copyright 1966 by *Playboy.*

women even have Jeannie's blond hair color. Here, the sultan, looking cozy in their midst, explains: "My other wives don't understand me." A cartoon in the July 1966 issue displays a servant carrying a topless Jeannie look-alike to an obese pasha reclining on a litter. The caption reads: "How about one more for the road, Pasha?"

This technique of populating the harem with Western paragons of beauty was employed to entertain the *Playboy* consumer with images that were familiar to him. Cartoons are only effective in mocking and ridiculing a person or a people if they relay images whose implications the reader is able to grasp. In the 1960s, average Americans had a very limited understanding of the reality of Middle Eastern women and Middle Eastern culture in general. The images of the women in *The Thousand and One Nights* were still thought to represent real Middle Eastern women; these images were reinforced by popular shows such as *I Dream of Jeannie.* Another image of the Middle East that originated at this time was that of the fabulously rich OPEC oil sheik living in the desert and drowning in oil reserves. In the 1960s, oil-rich countries in the Middle East had impressive revenues from the export of oil, but their economic and political power did not yet frighten the industrialized nations.[31] The cartoons of 1966 make it clear that the West did not yet feel threatened by the Middle East. They mock sultans for their sexual prowess and single-mindedness but seem to begrudge the sexual opportunities allotted to these men, as well as the obvious willingness of their women to please them.

The harem setting is still a popular subject in the *Playboy* cartoons. The women in this setting are usually nude and unveiled and, for the most part, they are examples of Western ideals of beauty. The cartoons continue to be drawings of voluptuous long-haired brunet or blond playmates. The master is usually portrayed wearing a turban and Turkish slippers; only in a cartoon in the March 1989 issue and one in the September 1992 issue does the master wear a *kafiya* and *agal* (headdress and the tie around it), identifying him clearly as an Arab. The messages of the cartoons vary, however, depending on the nature of U.S. relations with the Middle East. When relations were troubled in 1983, an illustration of Oriental sexuality took a decidedly cruel turn. A cartoon in the July 1983 issue (FIG. 2.2) shows an evil-looking sultan clasping a whip and shepherding a flock of handcuffed nude, mostly blond, women wearing iron collars. A man in the background explains to another: "He's stocking up a new oasis." In this car-

FIG. 2.2. Cartoon, *Playboy,* July 1983. Reproduced by special permission of *Playboy* magazine. Copyright 1983 by *Playboy.*

toon, women are portrayed as chained chattel forced into sexual slavery by a cruel sultan. The focus in this cartoon is no longer on the sexual prowess of the sultan, but on his cruelty toward women. This cartoon does not attack the institutions of the harem and polygyny per se, but the brutal way in which the sultan uses these institutions.

Veiled Women Fly on Carpets

In the cartoons showing scenes from the harem, women are not veiled and are often identified as Westerners. In cartoons featuring flying carpets,[32] women again wear the veil in order to help authenticate the *Arabian Nights* setting. A cartoon in the March 1977 issue of *Playboy* (FIG. 2.3) shows a copulating couple on a carpet flying over a forest of minarets. They are watched by a big-eyed, sharp-nosed man wearing a fez, clinging to a rope suspended from the sky. This cartoon may have been intended as an exercise in taking voyeurism to new heights, but to Muslim sensibilities a cartoon showing a couple engaged in intercourse directly above minarets is an exercise in blasphemy.

FIG. 2.3. Cartoon, *Playboy,* March 1977. Reproduced by special permission of *Playboy* magazine. Copyright 1977 by *Playboy.*

A cartoon in the September 1981 issue of *Playboy* is clearly intended to offend Muslims. A nude woman wearing a transparent face veil and an obese, hook-nosed man wearing a large feathered turban and Turkish slippers sit on a carpet flying over the roofs of mosques and minarets. Right behind them, the carpet has a staircase going down. Over the stairs is an arrow pointing downward, with the words "Rest Rooms" written above. By featuring rest rooms over mosques this cartoon is blasphemous. It depicts Middle Easterners soiling their own religion. This cartoon was published at a time when the United States had started to conceive Islam, embodied by Ayatollah Khomeini, more and more as a threat to American interests in the region. In January 1981, the U.S. Embassy hostages were freed, after 444 days in Iranian captivity and after a failed U.S. rescue attempt in 1980. What is striking about this cartoon, then, is not so much the cartoonist's attempt to blaspheme Islam, but the cartoonist's reliance on the imagery of *The Thousand and One Nights* in order to deliver the message. We may assume that the cartoonist used these timeworn images because the American media and the American public knew little about Iranian reality.[33]

The Veil as Muslim Fetish

The veil, like the flying carpet and the turban, is exploited in the cartoons to "authenticate" an Oriental setting. It is also used in some cartoons as the most immediately perceptible characteristic of Muslim society. When employed as such, the veil becomes a fetish of the Muslim, an irrational devotion or translocation of desire. When the veil is depicted as a fetish signifying Oriental submissiveness in the photographs discussed above, its purpose is to sexually arouse the consumers of *Penthouse* and *Playboy*. As fetish of the Muslim, however, the veil is ridiculed in many cartoons in *Playboy, Penthouse,* and *Hustler.* The Muslim institution of veiling becomes conflated with a Muslim fetishization of the veil.

In the November 1967 issue of *Playboy* (FIG. 2.4), a cartoon set in a physician's office shows a woman, nude except for a white face veil, stand-

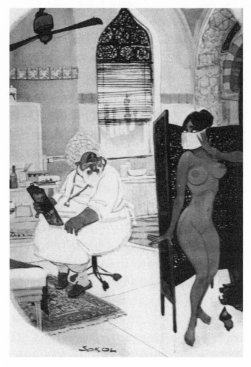

FIG. 2.4. Cartoon, *Playboy,* November 1967. Reproduced by special permission of *Playboy* magazine. Copyright 1967 by *Playboy.*

ing behind a screen. She looks anxiously in the direction of an obese turbaned man in a white coat with a stethoscope around his neck who asks
her: "Everything off?" The woman's reluctance to take off her veil is portrayed as irrational. To the male gaze focusing on her nude body, her fear of
taking off the veil seems ludicrous. By devoting herself seemingly irratio-
nally to her veil, she makes a fetish of the veil. A cartoon in the January 1986
issue of *Penthouse* also depicts the veil as woman's fetish. This cartoon portrays a woman who is nude except for a white face veil dancing in front of
a group of men wearing either turbans or fezzes. One of these men tells her
to "Take it off!" The motivation of the stripper to keep her face veil may be
simply her desire to protect her anonymity. But the nature of cartoons per
se as well as the political context of this one calls for an interpretation that
ascribes to the stripper an irrational devotion to her veil. This cartoon thus
reflects Western incomprehension of the institution of veiling in particular,
and of Islamic culture in general.

In a cartoon in the October 1986 issue of *Penthouse,* this irrational devotion of Muslims to the veil carries overtones of bestiality. This cartoon
shows, against a backdrop of tents and sand, a camel wearing a face veil.
One in a group of three Arabs, wearing *galabiyas* and kafiyas, says: "I'm
beginning to worry about Abdulla." Abdulla has started to veil his presumably female camel. In addition to portraying Abdulla as a zealous advocate
of the veil, this cartoon implies that Abdulla is involved in bestiality. The
goal of the cartoon is to insult the Arab Abdulla. This cartoon appeared in
October 1986, about six months after U.S. planes under the order of President Reagan had bombed the cities of Tripoli and Benghazi in Libya in
retaliation for Libyan advocacy of and involvement in international terrorism (in particular, the bombing of a Berlin discotheque in April 1986). We
may, therefore, assume that the depicted Abdulla is most likely Muammar
al-Qaddafi.

Qaddafi, however, was not the only Muslim who provoked the wrath of
American erotica in 1986. Not only his sexuality became a subject of satire
for cartoonists but also that of Ayatollah Khomeini. In the April 1986 issue
of *Playboy* (FIG. 2.5), an ayatollah stares excitedly at a three-page poster of a
figure who wears a shapeless full-body veil. Only the eyes and two bare feet
show. A bangle adorning one ankle identifies the figure as a woman. The
three-page poster of a woman in a magazine reminds the *Playboy* reader of
the playmate of the month. While the *Playboy* reader is supposed to be

FIG. 2.5. Cartoon, *Playboy,* April 1986. Reproduced by special permission of *Playboy* magazine. Copyright 1986 by *Playboy.*

aroused by the nudity of the playmate, the ayatollah is depicted as getting excited over a shapeless figure wearing a bangle. In this cartoon, the veil embodies a translocation of desire: The ayatollah is aroused not by the nude body of a woman but by the veil itself. This cartoon ridicules the sexuality of an ayatollah, most likely that of the Ayatollah Khomeini, by attributing a veil fetish to him. It also echoes Western criticism and incomprehension of the institution of veiling that is enforced by the Islamic Republic of Iran.

Sex under the Veil

Another category of cartoons that ridicules the institution of veiling consists of ones that depict the veil in the shape of a tent. In the January 1989 issue of *Playboy,* a cartoon shows two women wearing heavy full-body veils. They are portrayed as two walking tents with openings for the eyes. One woman says to the other: "Anything interesting creep into your tent lately?" In this cartoon, the place "under the veil" becomes the locale of illicit activities. This theme is also picked up in a 1991 issue of *Hustler.* Here, a cartoon shows an American GI looking perplexedly at a bulky veiled figure: facing each other, two feet in slippers and two naked feet stick out from beneath this tent of black fabric. The veil seems to hide a couple in *flagrante delicto.*

In these two cartoons, the veil creates opportunities for licentious behavior. Muslim advocates of the veil claim, of course, that the institution of veiling is supposed to prevent exactly this kind of behavior, which could lead to *fitna*. These cartoons are examples of the semantic versatility of the veil—a versatility that includes diametrically opposed meanings. They show that the relationship between the veil (the signifier) and sexual behavior (the signified) is determined by the interpreter.

The Veil in Blatantly Racist Politics

Many of the cartoons in *Hustler* exploit the veil in a blatantly racist political manner. In the December 1986 issue, a cartoon depicts an Arab wearing a kafiya and fatigues and holding an Uzi in his hand. He is accompanied by an obviously pregnant woman wearing a face veil and a head scarf. She also wears a T-shirt saying "Future Suicide Bomber" with an arrow pointing to her pregnant belly. The veil in this cartoon is worn by a woman who will be the mother of a future suicide bomber. This cartoon may refer to the suicide bombing in 1983 of the U.S. Marine installation in Beirut by a pro-Iranian Lebanese Muslim.

A cartoon in the September 1988 issue also portrays a Muslim man as a terrorist and a Muslim woman as a supporter of terrorism. This cartoon shows an Arab wearing a kafiya and fatigues reading a sign that says: "Arab High School, Class Registrations." The courses offered are "Plane Hi-Jacking, Hostage Murder, Rock Throwing, Embassy Bombing, Flag Burning, Utilizing Media." Behind the Arab, we see a completely veiled woman, possibly a fellow student. These two cartoons imply that the veil is worn by mothers and supporters of terrorists and as such becomes a symbol of terrorism.

Hustler's cartoonists were most prolific in 1991, the year of Operation Desert Storm. Two cartoons criticize incisively a victimization of the Muslim woman in Muslim society. One cartoon shows three women with a man wearing a galabiya and kafiya. The women wear black veils with pieces of the fabric cut out in different places: one woman's veil is cut to display her pubic area, another's is cut to show her breasts, and the other's is cut to reveal her eyes. This cartoon implies that the Arab needs three women in order to have all the parts he desires in a woman. The veil reduces each woman to only a part of her body. By fragmenting her body, the veil becomes a symbol of her victimization.

An illustration in the June 1991 issue also exploits the veil in order to portray the Muslim woman as victim. This illustration shows a woman with closed eyes. She wears a face veil and a full-body veil opened to display her nude body. Her clearly visible vagina is stitched up. She seems to hide her pain behind closed eyes and a face veil. An Arab wearing a kafiya and a sneering grin stands in the background. Looming behind the mutilated woman is the shadow of a satanic beast displaying long sharp teeth, an arm with three claws, and an erection. The illustration alludes to the *hadith* "when a man and a woman are isolated in the presence of each other, Satan is bound to be their third companion."[34] This illustration conveys the message that in order to avoid fornication, Muslim society subjects women to the barbaric practice of infibulation. Her screams of pain are stifled by a face veil. The blatant racism underlying this cartoon manifests itself in the fact that infibulation, as well as female circumcision, is not practiced in Iraq, the setting of this cartoon. Infibulation and female circumcision are not practiced in 80 percent of the Muslim world, including Saudi Arabia, Jordan, Iran, Iraq, and Turkey, while it is practiced in non-Islamic parts of Africa, including areas from Mauritania to Cameroon, across central Africa to Chad, and in Mali and Somalia.[35]

These four illustrations portray Muslim men as terrorists and barbarians. Muslim women are portrayed as supporters as well as victims of these terrorists. The veil figures prominently in all four illustrations: it is the badge of the supporters of terrorism, and it functions as a weapon used against women, by reducing them to body parts and by stifling their screams. The veil symbolizes the "otherness" of Islamic society. These veiled images belong to a society that is cast as a hostile amorphous "other" with which Americans have little in common and to which the best response is war, according to *Hustler*. The same stance of "us against them" served to boost the resolve of American troops to rally against Saddam Hussein. We may assume that *Hustler*, which is widely read among American troops, did its share to widen the chasm between non-Muslim Americans and Muslim Middle Easterners.

From Symbol of Wantonness to Symbol of Victimization

In her exquisite analysis of Western representations of the Muslim woman, Mohja Kahf focuses on literary texts from the eighth century to the eighteenth century.[36] She shows that over this period of a thousand years, the Muslim woman metamorphosed from termagant to odalisque. Interestingly, as Kahf demonstrates, the termagant—the exuberant and overbearing Muslim woman—disappeared as soon as Europe gained dominance over the East. In the eighth century, Europeans seem to have expressed their fear of the all-powerful East in their representations of the Muslim woman. As Kahf explains, the Bramimonde of *La Chanson de Roland* was aggressive and loud. She was anything but the submissive creature that, centuries later, describes the Muslim woman. Once Europe had subjugated the Middle East, however, it "feminized" it. Now Europe expressed its feminization of the East by degrading the Muslim woman to a prisoner of the seraglio. The odalisque was born. The European texts that Kahf investigates as well as the cartoons discussed above show that Western representations of the Muslim woman are intrinsically linked to political relations between East and West. Alas, the termagant may never rise again. In American erotica, Muslim women and Western women in Oriental settings are portrayed as odalisques endowed with a wide range of characteristics, from wanton slave to mutilated victim.

Recalling woman's wantonness and man's sexual megalomania in the tales of *The Thousand and One Nights,* photographs of veiled women serve to arouse the viewer. This same licentiousness of the tales, however, is also used in cartoons to ridicule the sexuality of the Middle Easterner. When the veil is utilized to symbolize sensuousness and licentiousness, the female wearing the veil is identified most often as Western woman. In the photostories, we met Jeannie the American college student, Diane who holds a doctorate in Middle Eastern history, and Helga from Bremen. The cartoons introduced us to Jeannie look-alikes and other paragons of Western beauty—veiled and unveiled. For the photographers and cartoonists of *Playboy, Penthouse,* and *Hustler,* the veil symbolizes wantonness only when it is worn by a Western woman.

The veil is shown as fetish in the photographs to titillate the Western consumer. The models in these photographs represent a virginal whore and a submissive dominatrix. Both belong to the realm of male fantasy. In the cartoons, the veil is shown as fetish of the Muslim either as irrational devotion or as translocation of desire. Both of these meanings of fetish are exploited in the cartoons to illustrate the irrationality of Muslims, their "otherness." The blatantly racist politics of *Hustler* transform this "otherness" into an amorphous evil.

Although depictions of the veil in *Playboy, Penthouse,* and *Hustler* cartoons confound a chronological categorization, a general transformation in meaning is noticeable: The veil as symbol of Oriental licentiousness changed into a symbol of woman's victimization whenever the United States had an enemy in the Middle East whose dark shadow had reached American shores. Did American erotica, with *Hustler* in the lead, try to encourage their readers, especially GIs, to go and rescue veiled women from the evil and barbarian Muslims? Was the veil as symbol of woman's victimization exploited as justification for racism and, in 1991, as rallying cry for war against Saddam Hussein? A semantic transformation of the veil that is effected by politics is, however, not unique to American erotica. As we shall see in chapter 4, Iranian politics also exploit the semantic versatility of the veil to meet political agendas.

3 The Cinematics of the Veil

Cinematic Functions of the Veil

Visual media, in the West and in the East, often eroticize the veil. American erotica such as *Playboy* and *Penthouse* use the veil to titillate the reader. Western advertisers exploit the veil of the Muslim woman to coax Western consumers into thinking that by buying the advertised product they will also buy the favors of the mysterious and exotic woman behind the veil. Saudi advertisers of Swiss watches sell watches by relying on the romantic image of the veiled Bedouin woman. Filmmakers, in the East and the West, use the veil to tantalize and arouse the spectator. They entice the gaze of the audience in order to make their movies commercially successful.

The ideologists of the Islamic Republic of Iran have been on what is now a twenty-year quest to eradicate improperly dressed women, whom they consider prostitutes, from the screen. They want to deny the spectator's gaze, which they associate with sexual pleasure. The Islamic government has implemented strict laws that govern the cinema: Iranian filmmakers have to get approval for the script; they have to get a production permit; they have to submit a copy of the film to the film review board; and, finally, they have to get a screening permit. Many Iranian filmmakers have found these laws intolerable and have chosen exile and isolation. Other filmmakers continue to make movies in Iran and have come up with ingenious ways to comply with these laws.

In turning from a consideration of Iranian movie making to Indian popular cinema, we enter another world of cinematic aesthetics and expression. Indian filmmakers, who also have to submit to government censorship with regard to explicit sexual scenes and violence, rely on the eroticism associated with the veil in order to create sexual tension. They use the veil to draw the spectator's gaze. Sneaking a peek under the veil of a beautiful woman becomes a tantalizing game not only for the male protagonist but also for the spectator. The huge success of the Indian film—the Indian movie industry is the largest in the world—inside India as well as outside, especially in the Middle East, shows that the Indian filmmakers' use of the veil appeals to large audiences.

The famous Italian director Bernardo Bertolucci relies on the erotic appeal of the veil in his film *The Sheltering Sky* (1991). In this film, the heroine adopts the veil in order to disguise herself as a Tuareg man. Although the veil is supposed to be a disguise, the heroine's acts of veiling and unveiling are undertaken in such a way as to taunt and titillate the spectator.

Denying the Gaze

Censoring Cinematic Expression

The Iranian cinema first drew international attention in the early 1970s with European-influenced artistic films such as Dariush Mehrjui's *The Cow*. The Iranian Revolution in 1979 brought filmmaking only to a temporary halt. Since the mid-1980s, government centers, headed by the Farabi Cinema Foundation, have encouraged serious artistic works capable of competing on the international level. The international acclaim of Iranian films today proves that the Farabi Cinema Foundation has established a respectable position for the Iranian film at the global level.[1]

Iranian directors have always been tightly constrained by censorship. They had to submit to harsh political censorship under the late Shah of

Iran. For example, Mehrjui's *The Cow* (1969) so infuriated the government that it first kept it out of distribution and then forced the filmmakers to put a disclaimer at the beginning of the film, explaining that it depicts events that happened prior to the Shah's rule. The film shows the abject poverty of a village and how the villagers are affected by the loss of the village's single cow. This portrayal of abysmal poverty clashed dramatically with the Shah's vision of a "great civilization."[2]

Since the 1979 Islamic Revolution, Iranian filmmakers have been required to submit to the censorship of the Ministry of Culture and Islamic Orientation. In the years immediately following the revolution, film production dropped dramatically to an annual average of eleven feature films during the period from 1979 to 1985, compared to sixty feature films annually in the six years preceding the revolution. Today, Iran's film production matches prerevolution numbers, and Iranian films receive international recognition. This international acclaim has put the censors in the Ministry of Culture and Islamic Orientation in a precarious position: censors with a more liberal attitude admit that Iranian filmmakers have dramatically helped change the unfavorable image of Iran in the West, but politically intransigent censors claim that filmmakers adhere to Western criteria and values. This chasm in attitudes may well explain the arbitrariness of the laws of censorship. In the summer of 1996, the Ministry of Culture published rules for the Iranian cinema, with a detailed code of what is legal and what is not. Forbidden are tight feminine clothing; the showing of any part of a woman's body except the face and hands; physical contact; tender words or jokes between men and women; jokes about the army, police, or family; negative characters with beards (which may allow the spectator to associate them with religious figures); foreign or coarse words; foreign music or any type of music that brings joy; favorable depiction of a character who prefers solitude to collective life; and policemen and soldiers who are badly dressed or have an argument. The rules also stipulate that films should always include a prayer scene, exalt religion and heroism during war, and denounce Western cultural invasion.[3] An article in the Iranian daily *Abrar* (July 19, 1997) claims that for some Iranians these regulations, especially those concerning the *hijab,* are not comprehensive enough. A revolutionary guard from Tehran who chose to remain anonymous complains that the film industry complies only with the laws of hijab but does not actively promote the form of hijab (chador) that Ayatollah Khomeini recommended as the best form of coverage for the female body.

The fact that Iranian filmmakers are so productive and successful on the international level, despite the restrictions, makes their accomplishments even more admirable. The kind and extent of censorship enforced in Iran has made many filmmakers skillful, resourceful, and determined. They have learned to choose their subjects carefully and to practice indirect, allegorical storytelling. Filmmakers use subjects that appeal to the audience and elude the censor's pen. In *Gabbeh*, Mohsen Makhmalbaf tells the tale of star-crossed lovers who belong to a nomadic tribe that weaves elaborate carpets, called "gabbehs." Circumstances prevent the beautiful heroine, who is also called Gabbeh, from marrying a persistent suitor who follows her through the changing seasons. Gabbeh wears a colorful head scarf made of gauze, and the upper part of her turquoise-colored tribal costume fits tightly. Tribal women have not been compelled by the Islamic government to obey the strict codes of hijab; they continue to wear their colorful tribal clothes. By using a nomadic tribe as backdrop for his film, Makhmalbaf is able to circumvent the laws that prescribe the proper hijab for female protagonists. Moreover, by emphasizing the aesthetics of colors such as turquoise blue, turmeric yellow, and henna red, Makhmalbaf gives an illusion of cinematic possibilities that the stark reality of censorship denies. Striving to focus the spectator's attention on aesthetics instead of character development, the filmmaker Bahram Bayzaei relies on a similar strategy. In films such as *Perhaps Another Time* (*Shayad Vaqte Digar*) and *Travellers* (*Mosaferan*), the camera focuses repeatedly on the strikingly beautiful face of the female protagonist.

A genre of film that has been popular with Iranian filmmakers before as well as after the revolution is the children's film. This kind of film allows filmmakers to deliver an oblique social commentary and depict intimate situations. Abbas Kiarostami's *Where Is the Friend's Home?* (late 1980s) may be considered the prototype for the Iranian "kid quest" films. The story line is deceptively simple: a little boy is trying to exchange notebooks with a schoolmate. The subtext of this film, however, echoes with the resonance of allegory. The protagonist in *The White Balloon* is Razieh (Aida Mohammadkhani), a determined seven-year-old girl who wants nothing more than a certain beautiful goldfish to decorate her family's house for the New

Year.[4] Although this film is about children, it is not really a children's movie. During most of the movie, the atmosphere is one of threat and doom. *Children of Heaven* portrays human hope and beauty against a harsh economic and political landscape.[5] The film also shows the close relationship between a brother and sister. The events in this film are seen through the children's ingenuous eyes, a view that is helpful in circumventing government censors. But even when filmmakers focus on children, they have not always been able to escape censorship. During the Seventeenth Fajr International Film Festival (February 1–10, 1999), which also coincided with the twentieth anniversary of the Islamic Revolution, an episode by Rakshan Bani-'Etemad in the six-episode *Kish Island* was blocked by state censors, because the protagonist, a thirteen-year-old girl, showed too much hair peeping from under her scarf.

The rules that have undisputedly transformed Iranian filmmaking since the Islamic Revolution revolve around the dress and behavior of the female protagonists. These rules were first put into effect in 1982 and have remained virtually unchanged since then: women are required to cover their hair and wear loose-fitting garments when in public. Although a woman may be "at home" in the context of the film, the censors consider her to be "in public" when her image appears on the screen. Hamid Naficy explains that "these general and ambiguous guidelines have had profound effects on the use and portrayal of women in cinema."[6] These rules have also distorted the image of normal family life. Women are shown veiled in the privacy of their home, in the presence of father, son, husband, brother, or uncle. The heroine is even shown wearing a head scarf while she is sleeping. Since the censors require the female protagonists to be veiled in what seem to be "private" situations, the movie makers must find situations that are "private" and at the same time "public." For example, when the script calls for a scene between wife and husband in the bedroom, the camera swings repeatedly to the bedroom window that opens to a crowded street. Since passersby are able to see the woman in the bedroom, she has to wear her veil. Other filmmakers show female protagonists sharing quarters with guests or other renters, a circumstance that would justify the wearing of the veil at all times. *Children of Heaven* shows a family sharing quarters with other families, a situation in which the women have to veil, because they are in and out of their rooms and share the courtyard with others.

Since the Islamic Revolution, almost all Western movies have been banned because of the severe restrictions governing the ways in which women can be portrayed. The images of unveiled women were cut from existing Iranian films. Naficy explains that "when cutting caused unacceptable narrative confusion, the offending parts were blacked out directly in the frames with markers. In local productions, women were excised from the screens through self-censorship by a frightened industry unsure of official attitudes and regulations regarding cinema."[7] In the mid-1980s, women were shown in domestic roles, blending into the background. Women's roles also did not require a lot of body movements so as to prevent emphasizing the contours of the body.

Furthermore, according to Islamic law, a woman may be "intimate" only with members of her own family. Intimacy includes activities such as touching and hugging, which cannot be portrayed on screen unless the actors are related. Of course, these restrictions make it difficult for filmmakers to portray husband and wife characters if the actors are not married in real life. Naficy claims that because of these restrictions, "both women and men were desexualized and cinematic texts became androgynous. Love and the physical expression of love (even between intimates) were absent."[8] When Ayatollah Khomeini declared that "we are not against cinema; we are against prostitution," he meant that he was against any woman whose form was revealed too clearly on screen, or whose behavior could be in any way construed as sexual.

Censoring the Spectator's Gaze

Why do the censors of the Islamic Republic go to such lengths to regulate women's appearance on the screen? What is offensive about the woman who is veiled but not properly so? Had the rules and regulations governing women's attire not been so detailed and comprehensive and had the censors been less intransigent, this censorship could have been considered a backlash against the nudity and sexual explicitness common in films made during the reign of the late Shah. But for the censors in the Islamic Republic, nudity and sex scenes are not the issue, since these are so unthinkable that they are not even mentioned in the rules and regulations. Ayatollah Mosavi Khoei in his *Tozih al Masa'il* even rules that a man should not look at the photo of any *namahram* (non-related) woman.[9] An identical ruling was issued by Ayatollah Hajj Sayyad Ali Behbahani.[10]

What is the ideological basis for censorship that aims at hiding all traces of sexuality? What is the harm to the spectator who sees a wayward strand of hair peaking from under the veil or who witnesses a clandestine touch between husband and wife? A brief discussion of the relationship between the act of looking and the sexual pleasure it can provide may supply some answers. Sigmund Freud postulated that people find pleasure when looking at other people's bodies as (particularly, erotic) objects; he referred to this pleasure as scopophilia. In the darkness of the cinema, the spectator may look without being seen either by those on screen or by other members of the audience. The spectator therefore becomes a voyeur. Discussing conventional narrative films in the "classical" Hollywood tradition that focus on a male protagonist and assume a male spectator, Laura Mulvey argues that the cinema facilitates for the spectator both the voyeuristic process of objectification of female characters and the narcissistic process of identification with an "ideal ego" seen on the screen: "As the spectator identifies with the main male protagonist, he projects his look onto that of his like, his screen surrogate, so that the power of the male protagonist as he controls events coincides with the active power of the erotic look, both giving a satisfying sense of omnipotence."[11]

In his discussion of the Iranian cinema, Naficy mentions a third type of look, a masochistic one, that, according to him, corresponds with the Islamic understanding of the gaze. He explains that this look is necessitated by Islamic principles of modesty because "masochistic identification seems to account for ascribing 'excessive' power to women over men by pointing to the aberrant pleasure the men draw from being subjected to this female power."[12] According to Naficy, the male spectator finds pleasure in being humiliated by the female protagonist. As for the female spectator, Naficy explains that she also finds masochistic pleasure "from being 'controlled' by looks from men, and from watching women being looked at, controlled, and possessed by men."[13] Although film theorists disagree about the kind of pleasures spectators obtain by watching a movie—voyeuristic, narcissistic, or masochistic—they agree that spectators find pleasure in the gaze.

According to some Muslim scholars, the eyes are an erogenous zone. For example, Ayatollah Ali Meshkini claims that "looking is rape by means of the eyes . . . whether the vulva admits or rejects it, that is, whether actual sexual intercourse takes place or not."[14] Fatima Mernissi concludes that the eye is "an erogenous zone in the Muslim structure of reality, as able to give pleasure as the penis."[15] Clearly then, according to Islamic thinking, the male spectator receives sexual pleasure by looking at the female body on the screen. It is not the eroticization of the eye, however, that leads to a censorship of the gaze, but the Muslim conception of sexual pleasure. Sexual pleasure for the sake of pleasure alone is discouraged by Muslim scholars. Al-Ghazali (1050–1111) in *The Revivification of Religious Sciences* claims that if the desire of the flesh dominates the individual and is not controlled by the fear of God, it leads men to commit destructive acts.[16] According to al-Ghazali, sexual pleasure can lead to social chaos (*fitna*). He also explains that "sexual desire was created solely as a means to entice men to deliver the seed and to put the woman in a situation where she can cultivate it, bringing the two together softly in order to obtain progeny."[17]

The Qur'an advises Muslims to lower their gaze:

Say to the believing men that they should lower their gaze and guard their modesty: that will make for greater purity for them: And God is well acquainted with all that they do.

And say to the believing women that they should lower their gaze and guard their modesty; that they should not display their beauty and ornaments except what (must ordinarily) appear.[18]

The gender disparity displayed in these verses is most revealing with regard to the gaze. The male believer is told that unless he lowers his gaze and guards his modesty, his purity will be diminished. This verse explains to the male believer that by looking at a woman, he will obtain sexual pleasure and thus his purity will be in jeopardy. The female believer is not specifically told that her purity will be greater if she lowers her gaze and guards her modesty. The believing woman is not explicitly told that by gazing at a man she will feel sexual pleasure. Instead, she is told not to display her beauty and ornaments. In other words, she is told not to attract the male gaze. These verses seem to presuppose a gender dynamic in which man is the agent of the gaze and woman is the object of his gaze. This gender disparity with regard to the gaze is reflected in the rules and regulations governing the Iranian cinema. By focusing on the proper hijab for female protagonists, the government censors reveal their concern for the purity of the

male spectator. The purity of the female protagonist is only important insofar as it denies the male gaze and thereby male sexual pleasure in a context
that is outside procreative purposes.

Beyond the Male Gaze

The "purification" process in the Iranian cinema not only has effected substantial changes with regard to themes, subjects, and techniques but has
led to an emergence of women behind as well as in front of the camera.
Naficy explains that the emergence of female directors "was made possible
partly by the incorporation of a complex system of modesty (*hejab in its
widest sense*) at all levels of the motion picture industry and in the cinematic
texts."[19] The cinema has now become an acceptable place of employment
for the Muslim woman. Before the revolution, only two women, Forugh
Farrokhzad and Shahla Riahi, had directed films.[20] Today, there are at least
seven women directors active.[21] Abiding by the rules and regulations governing the Iranian cinema, female directors often portray women as victims
of Iranian laws. For example, the films of Rakhshan Bani-E'temad, the
leading film director, tackle topics such as divorce and polygyny. The film
Divorce Iranian Style (1998), directed by Kim Longinotto and Ziba Mir-
Hosseini, demonstrates that Iranian law gives the right of divorce to men
and automatically awards custody to the father. This film also gives hope to
the Iranian woman by illustrating how daily social change chips away at the
monolithic authority of the law. Tahmineh Milani's films focus on the
problem of woman's self-determination in the Islamic Republic of Iran. In
her *Legend of the Sigh* (1991), she portrays two women intellectuals. In *Two
Women* (1999), she juxtaposes the life of a modern woman from Tehran
who makes her own decisions and the life of a traditional woman whose
father and husband make decisions for her. The theme of male power over
women is also portrayed by Samira Makhmalbaf, the eighteen-year-old
daughter of Mohsen Makhmalbaf, who has burst onto the cinematic scene
with a film called *Apple*. This film is based on a true story about an Iranian
man who confines his twin daughters to a small house for twelve years.
Interestingly, Samira Makhmalbaf's movie establishes that the father is not
a monster who abuses his daughters but is himself a victim of the doomsday
ideology disseminated by the Iranian clergy. Most of the films by female
directors focus on the social reality of women's lives and assume a female
spectator. They often try to assure the viewer that change is possible and

that there is space in which she can reconcile personal happiness with her faith. The implications of the male gaze seem to have little or no significance for female filmmakers.

Romancing the Veil

The Indian Popular Cinema

The cinematics of Iranian films revolve around rules and regulations whose purpose is to deny the spectator's gaze by purging the film of sexual stimuli. In contrast, Indian filmmakers, who also have to submit to censorship of sexually explicit scenes, seek to draw the gaze by titillating the audience with the veil. Indian filmmakers may be rivaled in this intense focus on the veil only by Iranian poets, especially those of the constitutional period, as we shall see in chapter 6. The purdah, chador, hijab, *niqab, burqah,* and *ghuunghat* are mentioned in hundreds of films, with protagonists from many different ethnic and religious backgrounds.[22] The films discussed below have been selected based on two criteria: they have enjoyed great popularity in India as well as in the Middle East; and they rely on the veil to create sexual tension.

India boasts the biggest film industry in the world, producing between 800 and 900 films a year. In 1993, films in Hindi numbered only 182 out of more than 800, but they cater to the all-Indian market and are understood by the majority of the Indian population.[23] Indian films are seen not only in South Asia and Southeast Asia but also in East Africa, Mauritius, the Caribbean, the Middle East, Britain, Canada, Australia, the United States, and the countries of the former Soviet Union. For example, in 1988, the Arabian Gulf imported 179 Indian films; the United Kingdom and Ireland, 67; Malaysia, 33; Sudan, 31; and Kenya, 22.[24] In *Veils and Videos,* Minou Fuglesang explains that watching Indian movies has become a social event for Muslim as well as non-Muslim women in Lamu, a town on the northern coast of Kenya. These women whose native tongue is Swahili are, according to Fuglesang, especially fond of Indian romantic melodramas, which are usually shown without subtitles.[25]

The Indian cinema produces two major genres of film: "art" films and commercial "popular" films. The artistic films, which constitute only about 10 percent of the total output, seek to capture a segment of Indian reality.

These are the films that compete with Iranian films at international film festivals. Popular films are seen by the vast mass of Indian moviegoers. They are largely melodramatic, often musicals, conveying simple moral messages; they represent a distinctively Indian approach to cinema as a form of mass entertainment. There are clear differences in terms of theme, style, and technique between the two kinds of Indian films.

The Indian popular cinema has been greatly influenced by Hollywood and is often referred to as "Bollywood"—that is, they are Hollywood-type films produced in Mumbai (formerly called Bombay). The development of the story line distinguishes the Indian film from its Western counterparts. Instead of the linear and direct narratives of Hollywood films, popular Indian films are assemblages of moving tableaux. These films are aptly called *masala* films (*masala* in Hindi means a mixture of various spices) because the story line is interspersed with elements of action, tragedy, comedy, eroticism, plots within plots, and musical passages of song and dance. Most films contain five or six song-and-dance scenes, often based on a title song that reflects the story and communicates its meaning in a vivid manner. The films often have a predominance of nonverbal elements. This may explain the popularity of Indian films outside India in countries such as Kenya where people do not understand the language spoken in the films. Although many films do not have subtitles, the spectator can often follow the story line because the symbolism of the films is clear and characters' actions, gestures, facial expressions, and speech are often exaggerated.

The Indian popular cinema has several common themes and subjects: romantic love, male friendship, motherhood, fate, respect for tradition, and social injustice. Indian films are basically morality plays, where the forces of good and evil vie for supremacy, and where the social order, disrupted by the actions of immoral and villainous people, is restored by the power of goodness. We may speak of a binary, black-and-white dramaturgy. The antagonism between good and evil, the clash between moral and immoral, is the main ingredient of the melodrama. Melodramas, by definition, deal with characters who are easily recognizable, often stereotypical, and who incarnate the forces of good and evil. For example, the "good" heroine is beautiful, innocent, and modest. She is sexually pure and obeys traditional rules. She is allowed to engage in romance. The "bad" woman is portrayed as a sexual, sensual being who has immoral intentions and lures the hero into falling in love with her. The "romantic" hero is good-looking, thoughtful, vulnerable, intelligent, but also rebellious. He is ultimately rewarded with the hand of the heroine and often with her wealth. The villain often drives an American car and wears black clothes and sunglasses, in contrast to the hero, who often wears white.

Indian films reflect India's religious diversity. Secular India is home to Hinduism, Islam, Christianity, Buddhism, Jainism, Sikhism, and many other religious traditions. Today, there are about 100 million Muslims living in India.[26] Hinduism is practiced by 80 percent of Indians. After Hindus, Muslims are the most prominent religious group and are an integral part of Indian society. In fact, India has the second largest population of Muslims in the world after Indonesia. The films discussed below feature Muslim as well as Hindu protagonists and show that veiling is customary among traditional Muslim women as well as among Hindu women. Whereas Muslims use the veil and seclusion to safeguard women from men outside the family, Hindus use the same devices to enforce women's subordination to their in-laws, to order the domain of family and kinship.[27] However, Muslim and Hindu ideologies with regard to women are subsumed in a larger "Indian" ideology. This dominance of "Indian" ideology manifests itself in the sari, the traditional garment of the Indian woman. Although Muslim women, especially in northern India, wear sari blouses that cover the midriff, back, and arms, the often bright color and the shape of the sari infringe upon the laws of hijab implemented by the Iranian clergy. The Indian Muslim woman, just like the Indian Hindu woman, has to submit to the rules and regulations of Indian society that severely circumscribe her life.

Indian films praise traditional Indian society, where women's roles are essentially those of daughter, wife, and mother. The films idealize the woman who is subject in childhood to her father, in youth to her husband, and, when her husband is dead, to her children. The Indian popular cinema rewards the heroine who is unwaveringly obedient to her husband. She is, of course, allowed to indulge in romantic love; indeed, many movies rely on romance in order to appeal to the audience. This romantic love is depicted as all-consuming, absolutely pure, and eternal. The heroine who seeks this kind of romantic love and lives by traditional norms is allowed to find happiness. The "bad" woman who transgresses traditional norms is punished and victimized. Most Indian films convey sexuality by showing disguised acts of sexual excitement. The Indian cinema operates on the assumption that the female form is more exciting veiled than nude.

Romancing the Veil in Song

The Indian movie is a combination of three elements: instrumental music and dance, a pictorial aspect, and dialogues and lyrics. Song lyrics, instrumental music, and dance are significant in conveying the meaning of the story and in generating the desired emotions. Songs generate emotion, underline moral messages, convey eroticism and sexuality whose overt expression is not allowed on screen, and create the mood for audience participation. It is understood that a popular song (excluding the classical ragas and classical compositions) in India cannot make it just on the merit of its lyrics, its singer, or its composer. In order for any popular song to sell in India, which has a very competitive music market, it must originate in a successful movie. In many cases, a movie becomes a hit at the box office simply because of its great songs. Many moviegoers can instantly remember a movie and its stars just by recalling or hearing the music and lyrics of a song.

The song lyrics of popular films abound in references to the veil.[28] The romancing of the veil in song serves as cinematic stimuli in the Hindi film *Mere Huzoor* (1969).[29] Covering Muslim culture, its manners and mores, this musical melodrama deals with the complex and tragic relationship between two close friends who love the same woman. In the song "Rukh se zaraa naqaab uThaa do, mere huzoor," in which both *niqab* and *purdah* are used, one of the friends addresses the beloved woman:

Rukh se zaraa naqaab uThaa do, mere huzoor (Please remove the veil from your face, my lady)[30]
[Please] Let me take a look at your beautiful face.
[Please] Let me commit a beautiful sin [with all those looks at your beauty].
[Oh, please] Love of my life, remove this veil from your beautiful face.
Let my heart repent [for all its foolish desires] today.
Oh, you queen of my heart, please unveil your beauty to me just once.
Having you is like having a companion for lifetime.
It's like finding the moon on a dark scary night.

Tell me, my queen of heart, where did you wake up [on this path
   of love]?
Unveil yourself to me just for a moment.
After seeing your beauty and youth in the mirror, I have lost my
   senses upon seeing such a display of [your] beauty.
If it's possible, oh you my queen, please bring me back to my
   senses.
Unveil yourself to me just for a moment.
I love your soft hands and your scented body.
So many feelings [gardens] of love have crossed my heart.
Oh, you queen of my heart, please help this love in my heart
   bloom now.
Oh, you queen of my heart, please unveil yourself to me just for a
   moment.[31]

The cinematic success of this song relies on the pleasure the spectator receives by being privy to an intimate situation between the veiled woman
and the hero who is beseeching her to unveil. This scene awakens the
viewer's drive to become a voyeur by looking in on a "private" world.[32]
Stephen Neale explains that this drive is dependent upon the maintenance
of a distance between subject (spectator) and object (veiled woman).[33] The
contrast between the dark movie theater and the brilliance of the shifting
patterns of light and darkness on the screen helps promote the illusion of
voyeuristic separation. The veil removes the heroine's face even further
from the spectator's reach and thus intensifies the illusion of intruding into
a private world.

   The spectator's distance from the screen and the additional distance
created by the veil produce a fantasy that sustains the spectator's desire to
get a glimpse of the heroine's beauty. This song aims more at staging a
desire than at fulfilling it. In other words, the filmmakers expect the spectator to be more excited when fantasizing about the heroine's beauty than
when actually seeing it. This fantasy is nurtured by the cliché that the veil
always hides beauty. When the hero reassures the audience that indeed he
has glimpsed her beauty in the mirror, he confirms this cliché. His pain and
suffering at not being able to look at her serve to convince the spectator of
her beauty. The hero foments voyeuristic anticipation through his repeated
pleas to the heroine to unveil for just a moment. The mention of the
heroine's soft hands and scented body further increases the spectator's ex-

citement. In this scene, the filmmakers expect the veil to tantalize and titil-late the spectator. This cinematic appeal to voyeuristic pleasures also shows that the filmmakers assume a male spectator—an assumption generally made by the makers of masala films.

A song from the movie *Amar Akbar Anthony* (1977) also entices the spectator to fantasize about the beauty behind the veil.[34] This movie, a tale of religious syncretism, is about three brothers who are separated at birth and raised as a Hindu (Amar), a Muslim (Akbar), and a Christian (Anthony). Akbar sings to one of the three heroines:

Pardaa hai, pardaa hai, pardaa hai pardaa

(There is a veil, there is a veil, there is a veil)[35]
I will pour a little bit of wine [of love] on [her] blossoming youth.
I will throw/send this [beautiful] rose to a real beauty.
[The beauty is hiding] behind a veil.
[The beauty is hiding] behind a veil, behind a veil.
The beauty is hiding behind a veil, behind a veil, and behind the
    veil is the beauty!
I will remove the veil of all those beauties behind the veils.
[And, if I don't unveil them] my name is not Akabar.[36]
[The beauty is hiding] behind a veil, behind a veil.
I like the people to look wherever my eyesight goes.
They better watch where my eyesight goes and where it stops.
Oh, you love of my dreams, here I am, Akabar Ilaahabaadi.
Oh, you love of my dreams, here I am, Akabar Ilaahabaadi.
I say poetry for all the beauties and love those beauties with shiny
    foreheads.
[Oh, you my love] I will never leave you.
I will break down all the blinds [chilmans] [behind which you are
    hiding].
Oh, you cruel one, don't be afraid of this world [or our community
    folks], or expected manners or excuses [to show love].
Oh, please show me your beautiful face, beautify my scenarios for
    me.
[If you don't do as I say] I may call your name [in this gathering]
    and blame you for something.

And if I don't bring ill repute to you in this gathering, then [I warn
   you that] my name is not Akabar.
[The beauty is hiding] behind a veil, behind a veil.
Thank God, your face is now a bit visible.
All those shades of shyness and blushes are spread all across your
   eyes [and face].
[Just imagine how strange it is that] someone is dying [after your
   unveiled beauty],
and someone is [just sitting down and] blushing.
Just imagine, someone is shedding tears, and someone is just care-
   lessly smiling.
The world teases us this way and those who rule our hearts seem to
   enjoy it very much.
These are their traditions, their cruelties [to their lover] are famous
   [all over].
And if you get angry and hide your face again [behind the veil],
   then remember, oh, you owner of such [cruel] beauty.
If your beautiful youth is like a fire, then my love is like cold water.
And if I don't cool down by your anger, then my name is not
   Akabar.
[The beauty is hiding] behind a veil, behind a veil.[37]

This song goes beyond the confines of romance where the lover beseeches
his beloved to fulfill his desires, and the beloved complies, and they live
happily ever after. It touches on the realm of sadomasochism: the cruel
heroine smiles carelessly while Akbar is suffering and shedding tears. When
Akbar claims that he is dying of his desire to see her unveiled, she simply
blushes but does not comply with his demands to unveil. Ultimately, sexual
tension is created through the power struggle between the hero and the
heroine. She is angry and refuses to show him her beauty. He becomes
angry at her for denying him visual pleasure and retaliates by threatening to
bring her into disrepute. In their struggle, the heroine uses her veil as a
weapon against Akbar, a weapon that she will most probably relinquish,
since her good repute is her most valued asset. This song shows that the
"cruel beloved" syndrome belongs to the repertoire of patriarchal fiction.
In a traditional society, in which man's word is superior to woman's, the
hero could, with one single statement, check his beloved's cruelty. The

heroine's submission to the hero's desires is thus guaranteed from the beginning.

This scene appeals less to voyeuristic than to sadomasochistic pleasures. The male spectator who is expected to identify with Akbar obtains masochistic pleasures by being humiliated by the cruel beloved and subjected to female powers. Moreover, when Akbar blackmails his cruel beloved into submitting to his wishes, the male spectator is awarded sadistic pleasures. By identifying with the cruel heroine, the female spectator may also enjoy sadomasochistic pleasures, albeit in reverse sequence.

In the last two songs, in which the hero courts the heroine, the veil is again used to create sexual tension. Do songs in which the heroine romances the hero also aim at tantalizing and titillating the male spectator? A song in the Hindi movie *Mother India* (1957) may provide an answer.[38] This film, set in Rajasthan, is considered a national epic that addresses topics associated with motherhood, patrimony, and revenge. *Mother India* centers on the life of Radha, an old woman, as she recounts her past: her happy married life with three sons in a rural Indian village. Eventually her husband leaves her, so she must raise the children alone while fending off financial as well as sexual pressures from the landlord. One son dies in a flood; another son, Birju, gets in trouble with the landlord's daughter and runs away to join a gang of robbers. The third son, Ramu, remains dutiful. This film was a spectacular commercial success, and its plot and characters became the models for many subsequent Indian films. Naushad's music is a special highlight of this film, with songs including "Duniya mein hum aaye hain," "Nagri-nagri dware-dware," and "Ghuunghat nah kholungi saiyan tere agge." In the latter song, the landlord's daughter sings to Birju, with whom she has fallen in love and who is trying to seduce her:

Ghuunghat nah kholungi saiyan tere agge

(I will not open the veil in front of you)
I will not open my ghuunghat in front of you [my love].
I feel shy because of emerging emotions.
The ghuunghat is over my face, but you, my sweet heart, are in my
    eyes.
In my heart [inside myself] I am smiling.
Try to understand what my heart is saying,
Because I don't know how to say it [I am too shy to explain my
    feelings to you].

[From the depth of my emotions] My heart and my body both are
trembling.
I will not open my ghuunghat in front of you [my love].[39]

The Hindu heroine explains to Birju why she will not discard her veil in his
presence. Her confession of shyness and her plea for his understanding may
imply that she uses the veil as a shield behind which she can hide. However,
her veil is transparent, and she allows Birju, as well as the spectator, fre-
quent glimpses at her beautiful face. Thus, the heroine employs the veil as
a toy in a coy and coquettish game of hide-and-seek. This is not the only
way, however, in which the heroine creates sexual tension. Her confession
that her body trembles in anticipation and her description of her emotions
and reactions aim at titillating the spectator. The viewer may receive pleasure not only by looking behind the veil but by being told about the sexual
arousal of the heroine. When the heroine confesses that she is looking at
the hero, that he is in her eyes, she shows her vantage point.[40] The spectator, especially the spectator who identifies with the hero, may feel vulnerable to her gaze and may be pleasurably stimulated by being the object of
the heroine's voyeuristic regard.

To conclude, the cinematic function of the veil in songs is the creation
of sexual tension. By focusing on the hero's reaction to the heroine's
beauty, softness, and scent, "Rukh se zaraa naqaab uThaa do, mere huzoor" creates an atmosphere saturated with sexual possibilities. The song
"Pardaa hai, pardaa hai, paraa hai pardaa" produces sexual tension by
staging a power game between the cruel and beautiful beloved and the
smitten and ruthless hero. The scene of the third song, "Ghuunghat nah
kholungi saiyan tere agge," in which the heroine romances the hero, gen-
erates sexual tension by giving the spectator glimpses of the heroine's face.
This tension is further amplified by the heroine's description of her arousal
in the hero's presence. Interestingly, the function and effect of the veil in
these musical interludes is independent of cultural ideologies with regard
to the veil. In Muslim as well as Hindu settings, the veil is used to titillate
the audience.

Sneaking a Peek

The movie *Chowdhveen ka chaand* (Moon of the fourteenth night),[41] released in 1965 and very popular also in Pakistan, has all the themes of the
Indian melodrama, and its story line revolves around the veil. The protago-

nists of this movie are three young men ready to sacrifice their lives for one another and a beautiful young woman aptly called Jameelah, which means beautiful. The movie is set in the city of Lucknow, a Muslim-dominated city in the state of Uttar Pradesh, which is well known for its religious piety, cultural elegance, and refinement. The introductory scene of this movie shows young women, veiled and accompanied by female chaperones, shopping in the bazaar in the evening. Young men stroll in the congested bazaar, passing time and looking for opportunities to sneak a peek behind the veil of a potentially beautiful woman. Young women unveil themselves with seeming innocence by pretending to inspect advertised merchandise, to the consternation of the chaperones who are doing their best to keep the young women behind veils. The camera then focuses on Jameelah, who is shopping with her mother, and on the three young men, Piyaaray Mian (or Nawaab Sahib), Aslam, and Musarrat, all from respected families, who are roaming the bazaar ogling veiled women. Piyaaray Mian gets a glimpse at Jameelah's face, is overwhelmed by her "innocent" beauty, and decides to marry her. His quest to find out her name takes up the rest of the film. A plot within a plot has Aslam marry Jameelah, unbeknownst to Piyaaray Mian. Aslam also does not know that his wife is the woman whom his best friend Piyaaray Mian wants to marry. On his wedding night, Aslam sings the theme song "Chowdhveen ka chaand" in praise of the beauty of his bride Jameelah:

Chowdhveen ka chaand

(The moon of the fourteenth night)
[I can't decide whether] You are as beautiful as the Moon of the
    fourteenth night, or as beautiful as a golden sun! Whatever it is,
    by God, there is no one as beautiful as you are!
Your beautiful long hair is like clouds bowing to your shoulders.
[holding your moon-like beautiful face]! Your eyes are like beauti-
    ful cups full of a desired wine! You, yourself are like a wine,
    which is playfully intoxicating by desires of love!
Your face is like a smiling lotus in a wild lake! Or you are like a love
    poem, which is being sung accompanied by the instrument [mu-
    sic] of life!
Oh, my spring-full soul [love], you are like a poet's dream [who
    may be the only one capable of fully describing your beauty in
    all Completeness].

Your lips are playful with the naughty smiles of lightening! Even
   the Milky Way [acknowledges your beauty and] bows along the
   paths you walk!
You are [my dear!] the climax of all that beauty and love in this
   World![42]

Upon hearing this song, Jameelah falls in love with Aslam. Piyaaray Mian
continues his search for his beloved mystery woman. After a switching of
veils between Jameelah and her cousin Nasima, Piyaaray Mian thinks
Nasima is his beloved and asks her family for her hand. When Aslam finally
realizes that Piyaaray Mian's mystery woman is his own wife, he experiences great emotional distress: he loves his wife, but he feels obligated to
give up Jameelah in order to fulfill the wish of his good friend. Eventually
he decides to give Jameelah to Piyaaray Mian, but Jameelah refuses to leave
him. So Aslam decides to commit suicide on Piyaaray Mian's wedding day.
Meanwhile, Piyaaray Mian still has no idea that he is about to marry
Nasima and not Jameelah. Eventually he realizes that Aslam's wife is his
mystery woman and that Aslam is willing to give her up for his sake. Upon
this realization, he cancels his wedding, locks himself in his room, and
commits suicide by swallowing the diamond on his engagement ring.
Aslam is too late to save him. The movie ends with Aslam admonishing
Jameelah to veil her face at all times so that no other man will die because
of her beauty. He is convinced that Jameelah caused the death of his friend
by allowing him to look at her beautiful face.

Chowdhveen ka chaand has many of the themes of the masala film: male
friendship, veiled beauty, romantic love, arranged marriages, obedience of
the wife, and suicide. The film also has all the ingredients of the Indian
melodrama: comedy, songs, drama, tragedy, and convoluted plots. This
three-hour movie is carried by the veil. The veil provides comedy: the scene
in which Jameelah swaps veils at a birthday party and thereby frustrates
Piyaaray Mian's quest makes for good comic relief. The veil provides tragedy: when Jameelah exchanges veils with her cousin Nasima, tragedy en-
sues. The tragic flaw seems to lie not in the *dramatis personae* but in the veil
itself. The veil submerges the audience in an atmosphere of impending
doom. When Jameelah swaps veils with Nasima, the audience knows in-
stinctively that this swap will have tragic consequences. Even the moral of
this movie hinges on the veil. The audience is told by Aslam that Jameelah's careless and flirtatious unveiling led to the death of his best friend.
Aslam's accusation echoes Islamic sentiments with regard to woman's

body being the cause of chaos and male ruin. The Iranian laws of hijab, which also apply to the Iranian cinema, aim at preventing the chaos caused by woman's body and man's loss of control at the sight of it. Interestingly, while this film tells the male spectator about the destructive effects of female beauty, it elicits the male gaze. The male moviegoer is expected to gaze at Jameelah's devastating beauty, an act that causes the demise of Piyaaray Mian.

In this film, the veil is used not only to stage different moods but to appeal to different senses. The audience is treated to voyeuristic pleasures: tantalized by first glimpses of Jameelah's face at the beginning of the movie, the spectator finds his voyeuristic anticipation satisfied when the bride reveals her face on the wedding night. The melody and lyrics of "Chowdhveen ka chaand" allow the audience to experience the wedding night. Piyaaray Mian's mention of the feminine scent of Jameelah's *dupatta* entices the spectator to recall a feminine scent, thereby intensifying the spectator's excitement.[43]

Veiled Cross-Dressers

Both the Iranian and the Indian film are geared toward the gaze, although one attempts to deny the gaze by veiling the female protagonists while the other draws the gaze by allowing the spectator tantalizing and titillating peeks under the veil. The cinematics of the veil, however, go beyond the focus on scopophilia. Because of its screening property, the veil can also be used as disguise. Cinematic cross-dressing has many implications and takes many forms. In the 1980 BBC documentary *Death of a Princess,* a young Saudi man who is in love with a Saudi princess adopts the veil in order to leave Saudi Arabia undetected and join his princess in London. Unfortunately, his disguise is discovered because he wears his own shoes. His oversight leads to his and the princess's public execution. In the Iranian movie *Snowman,* directed and written by Davoud Mirbaqeri, the hero, played by Akbar Abdi, dreams of living in America. He applies for a visa at the American Embassy on three different occasions and is rejected each time. Desperate to get to America, he adopts the hijab and thereby dresses like an Iranian woman. For $6,000 he is to marry an American man who will take his new "wife" home to the United States for a green card. Along the way, however, he falls in love with a virtuous head-scarf-wearing Iranian woman in Turkey. They marry and return happily to Iran. The Shi'i passion play (*Ta'zieh*), popular in Iran, also resorts to cross-dressing: women are not allowed to appear in these productions, and thus female roles have to be played by male actors who wear the veil.[44] To be sure, in none of these productions in which men adopt the veil does the act of cross-dressing take on sexual overtones.

But it is not just men who cross-dress in movies or on stage. Cross-dressing was employed most successfully in the 1999 Academy Award–winning *Shakespeare in Love*.[45] In this merry farce, Lady Viola finds herself stagestruck in the Elizabethan era, when women are forbidden to appear on the boards. She decides to dress as a man to win the Romeo role, and a young man dresses as a woman to play Juliet. Lady Viola's cross-dressing, in addition to carrying the romantic plot, has powerful sexual connotations. The movie that many Western moviegoers associate with carnal pleasures and woman's cross-dressing by veiling may well be Bertolucci's spectacle *The Sheltering Sky* (1991).[46]

The Sheltering Sky, based on Paul Bowles's 1949 novel, focuses on Kit Moresby and, to a lesser extent, on her husband, Port. They are idle rich Americans who consider themselves intellectuals, stressing that they are "travelers," not tourists. They embark on a voyage of self-discovery in Tangiers, in the company of their socialite friend, Tunner, who is in love with Kit and who gives Port interested glances. Tunner, however, abandons them, as their trip becomes more of a trial. Kit and Port explore North Africa in an attempt to understand the exotic and the forbidden, while becoming more self-indulgent along the way. Dazed by the brightness of the desert sun, seduced by the darkness of the labyrinth of the kasbah, confronted by a society that does not shy from expressing its sensuality, Kit and Port lose their moorings and become restless and dissatisfied. Finally, the city grows too restrictive to the Moresbys, and they embark on a journey deep into the Sahara. Port gets sick and dies of typhoid fever. In shock over the loss of her husband, Kit wanders aimlessly in the Sahara until she notices a long caravan of veiled men mounted on camels approaching her. She stops the caravan and motions to one of the veiled men to give her a ride on his camel. She rides for days with the Tuareg traders, sharing a camel with a young Tuareg named Belqassim.[47] They fall in love and, before the caravan reaches Belqassim's town, we witness a scene in which Belqassim buries Kit's clothes and shoes in the desert sand. When the caravan reaches town, Kit wears the blue veil and clothes of the Tuareg men, and Belqassim shows her how to act like a Tuareg man. He takes her to a room on the roof of his house and locks her in. They start a passionate love affair. Eventually, the women of the house become suspicious of the activities on the roof. Thus, one day, when Belqassim is not at home, the women and children of the household gather in front of Kit's room, clap and chant, and beat their drums. Kit gets nervous and quickly slips into her male disguise. A young Tuareg woman opens the door and lets Kit know that she must leave the house immediately. Kit walks through the door, with her head held high, looking at the crowd. Slowly she unwraps her turban and confirms the crowd's suspicion that indeed she is a woman. The next shot shows Kit, wrapped again in her turban, in the marketplace begging for food. The market crowd turns on her and forcefully unwraps her turban. The next scene shows Kit in the hospital recovering from her ordeal. The film ends with Kit looking at the window of the restaurant that she had visited with her husband and their friend when she first came to Tangiers.[48]

The cinematographer, Vittorio Storaro, brings the desert alive, right down to the flies on the skin of the actors. Debra Winger and John Malkovich give convincing performances as jaded, tired American intellectuals immersing themselves in the North African culture and climate. But this movie leaves many questions unanswered. Roger Ebert in his review of this movie comments that "Bertolucci has done almost everything right in this movie except to communicate the theme."[49] Bertolucci's failure to communicate becomes especially obvious in the last part of the movie, in Kit's encounter with the Tuareg. This part would have been easier to understand had Bertolucci provided subtitles for the dialogues conducted in Tamershak, the Tuareg language. To be sure, even with subtitles, many questions would have been left unanswered. For example, why does Kit run away from the dead body of her husband to join a Tuareg caravan? Why does Belqassim dress her as a Tuareg man? Why do the Tuareg women and children drum Kit out of Belqassim's house?

Although this movie is based on Paul Bowles's book, it leaves out, glosses over, and even censors several events described in the novel that are crucial to our understanding of the narrative and the motivations of the protagonists. While the movie portrays Kit's affair with Belqassim as self-indulgent adventure, the book describes Kit's life after her husband's death as an attempt at self-destruction. The movie does not show that, while traveling with the caravan, Belqassim allows another member of the caravan to rape Kit. The movie also does not show that after Kit has fled from Belqassim's house, she submits her body to Amar, who is described in the book as "tall, thin and very black,"[50] and who steals all her money. The movie also does not clarify why the women in Belqassim's house want Kit to leave. The novel explains that Belqassim already had four wives, the number of wives allowed by the Qur'an. Furthermore, Belqassim was not neglecting his wives while he carried on his affair with Kit and "even if that had been the case, and they had believed a boy to be the cause of it, it never would have occurred to them to be jealous of him."[51] The author explains that it was out of pure curiosity that Belqassim's wives sent Othman, a Negro urchin, to spy on the young stranger.[52] In the movie, Kit is urged by women and children to leave Belqassim's house; in the novel, Kit flees the house after bribing Belqassim's wives with the jewelry Belqassim had taken away from them and given to her. Kit has to leave not only because Belqassim's interest in her is waning but because Belqassim's wives are poisoning her.

Bertolucci is unable to communicate the movie's theme mostly because he has purged the movie of all events that cast the Tuareg in a bad light. This cinematic whitewashing of Bowles's portrayal of the Tuareg muddles Kit's as well as Belqassim's motivations and character. In the book, Kit feels that the only way to continue living after her husband's death is by totally submitting her body and mind to any man who is willing to dominate her. Belqassim is willing to make her his sexual slave. After he has shared the pleasures of her body with another member of the caravan, he eventually claims complete ownership of her body. He marks this occasion by burying her clothes and by dressing her like a Tuareg man. Her cross-dressing as depicted in the book is nothing but a device that makes it possible for Belqassim to keep his property. The movie, however, transforms sexual slavery into romance. The master-slave relationship of the novel is cinematically whitewashed by the camera's repeated focus on the aesthetics of the gaze. The camera focuses repeatedly on Belqassim's veiled face, where only his beautiful sparkling dark eyes are exposed. His eyes seem to be speaking to Kit with desire, and she returns the gaze with lust and passion. The movie makes us believe that the two have fallen in love. When Belqassim buries Kit's clothes and shoes and gives her the Tuareg veil, we are made to hope for a happy ending to this unlikely romance. When Belqassim locks Kit in the room on the roof, Kit is shown to enjoy her imprisonment, indulging herself in decorating the room with pages torn from her journal and eagerly waiting for Belqassim to unveil her. When Kit leaves the room, she unveils to the beating of drums, revealing her beautiful face to the women and children.

In many scenes, Bertolucci uses the veil to tantalize and titillate the spectator. Kit's cross-dressing is not so much a disguise as it is a pretense for sensual unveiling. The spectator is treated to scenes in which Belqassim passionately unveils Kit. In some scenes, Kit wraps her face in a coquettish way. For both protagonists, the veil has become part of an erotic game of hide-and-seek. The cinematic focus on the veil glosses over the darker aspects of their sexual games. Kit's seemingly joyous game with the veil diverts the viewer's attention from her status as Belqassim's prisoner, locked in a room on top of the house in which his family lives. Belqassim's passionate but gentle unveiling of her camouflages the fact that she is his property and that he can dispose of her as he sees fit. It may not be too reckless a thought that by focusing on the veil as titillating device, Bertolucci is able to hide events that would alienate and offend moviegoers. Bertolucci may not have gone far enough in his censorship of Bowles's novel. The film critic Chris Hicks speculates that some moviegoers will 'no doubt be offended by the film's graphic sex scenes, not to mention a peculiar close-up shot of Malkovich's genitals at one point."[53]

Gazing at the Veil

Religious and cultural values with regard to the gaze determine the cinematic use of the veil. The Islamic Republic of Iran strives to forbid the male spectator sexual pleasure that is not strictly in the context of procreation. The Iranian censors thus deny the gaze that may bring sexual pleasure to the male moviegoer. Female protagonists are required to hide any part of their bodies that may elicit a sexual reaction in the audience. Moreover, the restrictions and rules that aim at deterring the gaze have transformed the Iranian cinema. Filmmakers have been forced to focus on themes and subjects that do not necessitate the portrayal of sexual dynamics, not even in the form of romance.

In contrast, the Indian popular cinema is based on the romantic melo-drama. Since sexual explicitness is subject to censorship, Indian filmmakers romance the veil in order to convey their sexual messages. They use the veil to tantalize and titillate the audience. The hide-and-seek game behind the veil is the subject of many Hindi songs. These songs not only make for relaxing musical interludes but often convey the message of the whole film. The function of the veil in the Hindi films is to create an atmosphere taut with eroticism.

Bertolucci's *The Sheltering Sky* relies on the Tuareg veil to create sexual tension. This film focuses on the eroticism of the veil, worn by the male as well as the female protagonist, to divert the audience's attention from the darker aspects of sexuality such as sexual slavery and rape. By using the veil to draw the gaze, Bertolucci is able to elide those events in the novel that would have offended many moviegoers. We may conclude, then, that Ber-tolucci censors the literary truth by using the veil to distract the spectator's gaze.

4 Iranian Politics and the Hijab

Unveiling, Reveiling, and Properly Veiling

The veil has proven to be a lucrative advertising tool for selling Western-made products to Western as well as Saudi consumers. Advertisers of products as diverse as Jeep Cherokees and sanitary napkins have relied on the semantic flexibility of the veil to market their products. Not only advertisers exploit the veil to fit their needs. Iranian politics have defined, redefined, and properly defined the meaning of the veil. In the early twentieth century, Reza Shah's modernization politics called for women to unveil. In 1979, Ayatollah Khomeini's realization of a theocratic government called on women to comply with the religiously sanctioned dress code for Muslim women. The Iraqi invasion of the budding Islamic Republic in 1980 forced Ayatollah Khomeini to consolidate his power and mobilize his troops to defend Iran's territory and religion. During the Iran-Iraq war (1980–88), the dress of the Iranian woman was under intense scrutiny. Posters, banners, and even postage stamps taught her the correct way of veiling. Also during this period, we find a noticeable semantic fusion of *hijab* and *jihad* (holy war) in the context of martyrdom. In the 1990s, the graffiti in metropolitan towns, sanctioned and perhaps written by members of the Hizbollah, proves that the veil was still employed to promote the political agenda of the Iranian clergy.

Removing the Veil by Force

In 1990, agencies of the Islamic Republic of Iran published two documents, which had been classified as secret until then. These documents contain correspondences of Reza Shah between 1924 and 1933 and prove most revealing with regard to the process of unveiling under the regime of Reza Shah.[1] When Reza Shah returned from a visit to Turkey, where Kemal Atatürk had started to implement secular reforms including unveiling, he called his cabinet members and told them: "We must change our image and tradition to that of the West. The first step is to change [men's traditional] hats to chapeaus. Then, the unveiling process must take place. Obviously this is a difficult task for ordinary people to undertake all at once. Thus, it is your duty, ministers of government offices, to take your wives [unveiled] to the 'Iran Club' once a week." Reza Shah then ordered Hekmet, his minister of education, to see to it that female teachers and students in girls' schools remove their hijabs and that access to the schools be denied to them if they resist his order.[2]

These orders clearly state Reza Shah's reason for abolishing the veil. After he had ousted the Qajar dynasty and established himself as dictator, Reza Shah embarked on his quest to modernize the state by imitating the Western model of men's and women's dress. His reign marked the beginning of a period of socioeconomic reforms and the secularization of Muslim culture—a process that continued during the reign of his son, Mohammed Reza Shah Pahlavi. Although Reza Shah introduced modern civil and penal codes in 1928, the provisions of the civil code were taken mostly from Islamic law, the *shari'a*. Thus, these codes did not challenge men's prerogative over women or change the patriarchal structure of the Iranian family. Clearly, Reza Shah's order to his cabinet to effect the removal of the veil was not rooted in his desire to reform the status of his female subjects but in his belief that, in order to be modern, Iran must only look Western. Perhaps his three unveiled wives were the best examples of his stress on image rather than substance.

Reza Shah's orders to his cabinet also indicate the manner in which the abolition of the veil was to be implemented. While Atatürk encouraged Turkish women to abandon their veils, Reza Shah ordered Iranian women to unveil. Many, including the clergy, resented this order and tried to prevent its execution. We read in one of the "secret" documents:

> Department of Gendarmerie of Sabzevar to Governor's Office of Sabzevar, 42 Farvadin 1317 [1928 AD]
> Ministry of War, Department of Gendarmerie, Regiment No. 12 of Khorasan,
> one page attachment No. 521, on 24/01/1317
> Confidential
> Sabzevar Governor's office. Copy of report No. 47 dated 23/01/1317 of Davzan Guard Station is attached. As I have observed myself at that location, the order of unveiling has by no means been carried out there. The questioning of numerous people showed that a person by the name of Mirza Mahmud Khan, who is one of the local landlords and an influential person, along with a cleric and the local deputy are preventing it. As has been heard in the investigations, some time ago, the unveiled wife of the director of the cotton factory was insulted by Mirza Mahmud and the above-mentioned cleric, who used obscene words in addressing her and, although the director of the factory has made a complaint, no one has investigated the matter. Since the harm of the failure to implement the above-mentioned order will befall your Excellency, please take the appropriate steps to implement this order and stop the power of such influential people.
>
> Inspector of the Department of Gendarmerie, Lieutenant Colonel . . .[3]

Reza Shah took these appropriate steps to implement his order when he launched the anti-veil offensive in 1936. At that time, police were instructed to use force to remove women's veils in the streets. They were ordered to rid the streets of the most conspicuous sign of backwardness, and that was, according to Reza Shah, the chador. Many women from traditional families, afraid of being attacked by Reza Shah's police, refused to leave their homes. After five years of forced unveiling, Reza Shah was ousted by the Allied Forces (1941), and clerics cried for the return of the veil. Women who had been forced to unveil were now forced by social and religious pressures and by a clerically organized mob to veil again; many older women in the cities resumed the veil.

Like his father Reza Shah, Mohammed Reza Shah, who came to power in 1941, walked a tightrope, trying to modernize and appease his Western advisors while keeping a powerful clergy at bay. After briefly losing power, in 1953 Mohammed Reza Shah, in a CIA-backed coup d'état, toppled the popular government of Mossadegh and began an era of terror, targeting all political parties and oppositional groups including the clergy and women's organizations.[4] In 1963, strongly encouraged by his American advisors, the Shah agreed to reforms. These reforms, the White Revolution, included women's enfranchisement and other reforms favoring women. The Family Protection Act, passed by the Majlis in 1967, did not represent a radical change from the *shari'a*. It did modify the civil code in favor of women with regard to divorce and child custody; it restricted polygyny without outlawing it; and it was altogether silent about temporary marriage for pleasure (*mut'a*).[5] Considering that this act was passed in an atmosphere of political repression denying democratic rights to all subjects, it could hardly be seen as a radical break with tradition. It did, however, face strong opposition from the clergy. Ayatollah Khomeini, for example, condemned the government for not upholding the explicit words of God and the sacred Islamic texts. When he came to power in 1979, the suspension of the reformed Family Protection Act was one of the first items on his "revolutionary" agenda.

Reza Shah's abolition of the veil and Mohammed Reza Shah's reforms did not lead to fundamental changes in the status of Iranian women. The modernization efforts of the Pahlavis led, however, to a visible schism among Iran's women: unveiled educated women living in towns tended to belong to "Westernized" upper and middle classes; veiled women living in towns were educated at home, often by tutors, in religiously sanctioned subjects; and veiled women living in rural areas were mostly illiterate, having been taught only the rudiments of Islam. It was the unveiled "Westernized" Iranian woman who became a scapegoat for the demagogues of the Islamic Republic of Iran.

The Veil and the Revolution

Women's status in Iranian society was changed little by the modernization efforts of the Pahlavis. In 1979, women were still considered men's subjects, and they were eager to change that even if it meant supporting the clerics who had a history of opposing legislation that would have given women more rights. The Islamic Republic of Iran, however, quickly squashed women's hopes and ambitions for improving their lives. It introduced many new rules and regulations concerning all aspects of women's lives. Now there were rules as to the nature of the jobs women could hold and the subjects they could study. Now a woman had to ask for her husband's permission if she wanted to work. Women were aggressively encouraged to have large families; female sexual abstinence was declared a sufficient reason for divorce.[6] And women were now persuaded, often by force, to veil. Women who appeared unveiled in public were assumed to be opposed to the tenets of the Islamic Revolution and were thus not only religiously but also politically suspect. In the eyes of the revolutionaries, unveiled women represented Western values, which the Islamic regime wished to eradicate from Iranian society.

Two men were instrumental in defining the ideology of the hijab in the new regime: the Ayatollah Motahari and the intellectual Ali Shariati. Both rejected Iran's domination by the West by rejecting the "modern" Iranian woman. Both considered "modern" women as embodiments of Western decadence, as "greedy painted under- or overdressed Western dolls." In his book *Mas'aleh-ye Hejab* (The question of hijab), Motahari discusses the history of the hijab and speculates on the logic and reasons for its existence.[7] In his *Weltanschauung*, women's sexuality can lead to *fitna* (social chaos), unless it is properly controlled. According to Motahari, the hijab provides a barrier between the sexes and thus serves to uphold the social order. He insists that through unveiling, "half the population has been transformed into idle creatures preoccupied with clothes, cosmetics, and attracting men."[8] In her work *Populism and Feminism in Iran,* Haideh Moghissi argues that it was for a larger reason that Motahari presented gender equality as a Western plot and renounced women who advocated secular reforms as agents of the West. She concludes that by criticizing the most powerless segment in Iranian society, namely, women, Motahari effectively used a code to criticize the Shah's despotic rule and his socioeconomic dependence on the West without invoking a harsh response from Reza Shah's police.[9]

Ali Shariati, who had studied at the Sorbonne and enjoyed a reformist Muslim upbringing, frames his criticism of Mohammed Reza Shah's politics by juxtaposing "the painted Western doll" with the modest independently thinking Muslim woman. He writes: "A woman who has attained the level of belief chooses her own life, her way of thinking, her very being and even her own form of adornment. She actualizes herself. She does not give herself over to television and passive consumption. She does not do whatever consumerism tells her to do. She is not afraid to choose the colors of dress because it may not be in style this year! She has returned and returned vigorously! To what? To the modest dress of Islam. As what? As a believer and committed human being."[10] According to Shariati, the Iranian woman "actualizes" herself as a believer who negates Western values. The revival of Islam will lead her to independence, and she will no longer be a plaything in the hands of foreigners. For Shariati, the hijab becomes a symbol of independence from the West, of progress in general. Again, we see the semantic versatility of the hijab, from a symbol of backwardness under Reza Shah to a symbol of progress within the ideology of the Islamic Revolution. Moreover, the hijab had become a rallying point of the revolution. However, the constitution of the Islamic Republic of Iran, based on Islamic principles and approved in a referendum held throughout Iran in 1979, does not address the topic of the hijab.[11] The law of hijab was originally not a law but a recommendation made by Khomeini in the spring of 1980.

Mobilizing the Hijab for War with Iraq

In 1983, an amendment was added to the constitution that states that women who harm public chastity by appearing in public without the religiously sanctioned veil are subject to receiving up to 74 lashes.[12] In 1986, another amendment was added that states that those in public view whose dress and makeup are in violation of religious law and those who cause the spread of corruption or violate public chastity will be arrested, given priority when tried in the proper court, and accordingly sentenced to one of the punishments listed in the addendum.[13]

The law of hijab is enforced by *komitehs* (from the French *comité*). The komiteh patrols are also known as "guardians of the Islamic Revolution." The duty of the komitehs, which are composed of both male and female believers, is to safeguard people's moral conduct in public by looking for women who show a "bad hijab."[14] "Bad hijab" refers to any garment, adornment, or appearance that, intentionally or unintentionally, might have the potential to draw the male gaze. It can include letting the hair show from under the veil, wearing clothes that cling to the body or are otherwise ostentatious, and using makeup, lipstick, nail polish, or perfume.[15] Punishments for bad hijab were up to the discretion of the komiteh members and ranged from scolding and name-calling to jail sentences and fines. Rumors circulated that some zealous komiteh members had used handkerchiefs in which razor blades were hidden in order to wipe off lipstick.

Interestingly, the criminalization of offending public chastity by not veiling properly coincided with Iran's mobilization in 1980 for war against Iraq. The harshness and vigilance of the komitehs were felt much more strongly during the Iran-Iraq war (1980–88). One possible explanation for this may be that policing the hijab diverted attention from the horror of the fronts; it drew the nation's attention to a situation that, unlike the war, was more controllable and thus gave the nation a unifying boost. However, the war with Iraq, which had turned more and more bloody and costly, could not be won by merely drawing the nation's attention inward, toward improperly veiled women. The hijab had to take on another semantic dimension, one that separated Iran from the enemy Iraq on an ideological level. It could no longer be a mere symbol of progress in the context of Islamic revivalism; it had to become a symbol of Shi'i Iran. It had to embody not so much Islamic but Shi'i ontology. While up until 1980 the veil was exploited to distinguish the Muslim woman from the "Western" doll, during the war with Iraq the veil was used to distinguish the Shi'i from the Sunni Muslim.

The *casus belli* was multifaceted, ranging from centuries-old Sunni-versus-Shi'i and Arab-versus-Persian religious and ethnic disputes to a personal animosity between Saddam Hussein and Ayatollah Khomeini.[16] Hussein had viewed the revolution in Iran as both an opportunity for Iraq to gain territory and a threat to Iraqi political stability. He invaded Iran in 1980, thinking that an army led by mullahs[17] would not deny him control of the Shatt al-Arab waterway[18] and control of the Gulf. Furthermore, Hussein feared that the success of Iran's Islamic Revolution would inspire the Shi'is in Iraq to revolt against the Iraqi government. There was some basis for his fear. Although the Shi'is constitute more than 50 percent of the Iraqi population, they have been politically impotent and economically depressed. Saddam Hussein himself, the top officers in the security services, and most of the army's corps commanders are Sunnis. The majority of the Shi'is live in southern Iraq, the most depressed region of the country. It is also true that Ayatollah Khomeini and the Iranian revolutionaries had mounted intense propaganda barrages challenging Iraqi Shi'is to join the Islamic Revolution and drive the Sunnis from power. It is noteworthy that the Iraqi Shi'is are Arabs, not Persians, and that they have been the traditional enemies of the Persians for centuries. The Iraqi government exploited this animosity by promoting the war as part of an ancient struggle between the Arab and Persian empires. The fact that Iraqi Shi'is have continued to defend the Iraqi regime may be seen as evidence for the success of Baghdad's anti-Persia propaganda.

In the attempt of Iran's religious leaders to rally Iran's and half of Iraq's population around Shi'i ideology, a new semantic dimension of the hijab became tangible. Posters, billboards, and even stamps promoted the war by heralding the "ideal" woman. On the occasion of "Woman's Day" (April 25, 1981), Ayatollah Khomeini described the duties of ideal women: "You, respected ladies, are charged with bringing up pious children. Your job is to rear pious children and deliver them to society. . . . You should bring up children who will safeguard the Prophet's wishes and aspirations. The assistance of the women is many times more valuable than that of men. May God protect you in bringing up human beings, the job of the Prophets."[19] According to Ayatollah Khomeini and the Iranian clergy, the ideal woman is the mother who raises pious children for the Prophet's kingdom. The image of this ideal woman was plastered all over Iran to promote the war with Iraq. Although the preamble of the Iranian constitution forbids the use of woman's image in commercials for services and goods in the private sector, woman's image was freely used to promote the ideological cause of the Islamic Republic of Iran. Her veiled image was everywhere: throughout the cities, on public walls, inside each and every business (both private and government), outside and inside public transportation facilities, and in every learning institution. She called the men to war on banners erected in public squares, inside every Iranian airport, in public resorts, parks, and swimming pools, on hiking trails and ski slopes, and even inside holy shrines.[20]

Posters, banners, billboards, even postage stamps depicted women as strong supporters of the war.[21] Covered by her hijab, the Iranian woman represents the chaste pious daughter, sister, wife, and mother of the soldier. These posters are always accompanied by slogans about the goodness of the hijab. We find quotes by various Shi'i imams including Ayatollah Khomeini praising Fatima Zahra, the daughter of the Prophet Muhammad. In Shi'i hierology, the ideal pious woman is Fatima Zahra, who is revered as the most excellent of women.[22] Her direct lineage to the house of the Prophet and her marriage to 'Ali ibn Abi Talib, the first Shi'i imam, as well as her being the mother of two grandsons of the Prophet, Imam Hassan and Imam Hussein, clearly establish her religious importance for the Shi'a. Early biographical dictionaries and *hadith* collections have captured her world primarily as one defined by her marital and maternal functions. And it is as wife of 'Ali and mother of Hassan and Hussein that Fatima promotes the war against Sunni Iraq. Shi'i support of the claims of 'Ali and his line of descendants to presumptive rights to the caliphate and leadership of the Muslim community had led to the first great schism of Islam, that between Shi'is and Sunnis. The Shi'i veneration of Fatima as ideal female image, as opposed to the Sunni veneration of 'A'isha, the Prophet's favorite wife and daughter of the first caliph Abu Bakr, reflects this religio-political split. The veiled woman on the posters, representing Fatima, served to remind the Iranian population of the differences between Iran and Iraq. But images of good wives and holy mothers were not enough to keep the Iranian population fighting an enemy who was equipped with the latest Soviet weaponry and had the clandestine backing of the United States.[23]

The Iranian clergy did find ideological ammunition that helped check Saddam Hussein's territorial ambitions. It called upon Iranian soldiers to avenge the "Tragedy of Karbala." In 680 CE, Hussein, the grandson of the Prophet and the second son of Imam 'Ali, was on his way to Kufa to claim the caliphate from Yazid when he was attacked by Yazid's army in the desert of Karbala and lost his life. Although a minor skirmish in military terms, this battle gave the Shi'i cause an aura of tragedy and martyrdom, which came to emanate again in the war against Iraq.[24] The "Tragedy of Karbala" was exploited by the clergy to legitimize the "imposed" war and justify the deaths of thousands of young Iranian men.[25] They were considered martyrs, soldiers of Hussein, whose deaths were not to be mourned but celebrated.

Martyrdom is an integral part of Shi'a Islam and Iranian history. During the Iranian Revolution, many of those who died fighting the forces of the Shah were considered martyrs. Justifying the war with Iraq, Ayatollah Khomeini spoke of martyrs and martyrdom: "Think about the fact that the best people at His own time, His Holiness the Lord of the martyrs [Imam Hossein], Peace be upon Him, and the best youths of Bani-Hashim [the tribe of the Prophet Muhammad and Imam Hossein], and his best followers were martyred, leaving this world through martyrdom. Yet, when the family of Imam Hossein was taken to the evil presence of Yazid, Her Holiness Zeynab, Peace be upon Her, said: 'what we experienced was nothing but beautiful.'"[26]

Zeynab's "beautiful experience" refers to the belief that martyrs ascend straight to heaven, where they are rewarded for the love of their religion. Knowing about martyrs' rewards in the afterlife, believers celebrate their death. For Zeynab, the death of her brother Hossein was thus an occasion for celebration. Ayatollah Khomeini explains: "The departure of a perfect person, the martyrdom of a perfect person is beautiful in the eyes of the saints of God—not because they have fought and have been killed, but because their war has been for the sake of God, because their uprising has been for the sake of God. Regarding martyrdom as a great blessing is not because they are killed. People on the other side also get killed. Their blessing is due to the fact that their motivation is Islam."[27]

Thus, in order to mobilize the hijab for the war with Sunni Iraq, it had to change its semantics yet again. No longer could it just symbolize the perfect mother, wife, sister, or daughter; now it had to be worn by the mother, wife, daughter, or sister of a martyr. It became synonymous with the holy war against Iraq. Sending her son, father, brother, or husband to war was a woman's contribution to martyrdom and to the hoped-for glorious victory against Sunni Iraq.

Arresting is a postage stamp introduced in 1988 on the occasion of the "Eighth Anniversary of Sacred Defence" (FIG. 4.1). This stamp portrays a veiled woman who stands behind three men who appear to be her son, father, and husband. The military uniforms worn by these men indicate their readiness to go to war. Their red and green headbands read "Ya Hus-

FIG. 4.1. Iranian stamp, 1988.

sein" (Oh Hussein) and "La ilahu illa Allah" (There is no god but Allah). The headbands invoke Hussein's martyrdom in defense of Islam. The first part of the *shahada* (Muslim creed) on the headbands further testifies to the men's eagerness to fight and die in the jihad, the holy war.[28] Interestingly, shahada means creed as well as martyrdom. The word *shahid* (martyr) can be traced to the same morphological root. Green and red are the colors of Islam and blood and thus signify martyrdom in the name of Islam. The veiled woman behind the three men seems to agree with the men's enthusiasm to defend the holy cause. She gives her sisters the message that it is the duty of every Iranian woman to defend her country even if this means sending her son, father, husband, and brother to their deaths as martyrs.

A number of posters show the same constellation as the postage stamp. They picture a veiled young woman who stands behind three generations of men: an elderly man who could be her father, a young man who could be her husband, and a young boy who could be her son. The message of these posters is that the Iranian woman supports the war even if she loses all of the important men in her life. For her, this is a religious duty and obligation. She supports the jihad at any cost without showing sorrow or shedding a tear. She makes the ultimate sacrifice in her life on earth and will be rewarded for her sacrifice(s) in paradise, as daughter, wife, sister, and/or mother of a shahid. Her message to the soldier is that his duty is not toward his family but toward his religion and country. These posters tell the fighter that he is absolved from family obligations in the face of a much greater cause, the defense of God and country. Moreover, they serve to make the soldier feel like a sinner when he shows love for his mother, wife, or daughter and in moments of weakness doubts his holy mission. Moghissi explains that every day, Iranian newspapers published letters or "Martyrs' Wills," written by young Iranian men killed in the Iran-Iraq war during the early 1980s. "In these letters the predominantly teenage writers passionately asked their parents' forgiveness for their 'unpardonable sins.'"[29] These feelings of having committed "unpardonable sins" may have been partly invoked by these posters. The soldier whose mother sends him to war to become a martyr may perceive his fear of getting killed as failure in his duty toward her.

A poster titled *Negahbane Noor* (Guards of light) by graphic artist Kazem Chalipa, well known in Iran, shows the image of a family gathered under a portrait of Ayatollah Khomeini (FIG. 4.2).[30] The color scheme in this poster displays Iran's ideology. A black-veiled mother pushes her red-faced son, who wears a red shirt, assumedly toward his death as a martyr. The son represents one in a wave of youths who fed the front lines. The bandaged father is dressed in green, the color of Islam. Overshadowing them all is the glowing white beard of Ayatollah Khomeini, whose portrait hangs above them. The color of his beard symbolizes his purity. The colors red, green, and white are the colors of the flag of the Islamic Republic of Iran. By using the colors of the Iranian flag, this poster clearly signifies the active role of the son, father, and Khomeini in the holy war against Iraq and the future of Iran. The poster also reveals the role of the Iranian woman. The black of her veil is not on the flag. But, by pushing her son toward martyrdom, she is allotted a supportive role in Shi'a Islam and Iranian politics.

A stamp issued in 1986 to honor Fatima Zahra, which was also selected

FIG. 4.2. Poster by Kazem Chalipa titled *Negahbane Noor. A Decade with the Graphists of the Islamic Revolution, 1979–89.*

for Woman's Day, takes even further a mother's willingness to sacrifice her child for the holy cause (FIG. 4.3). It shows a young mother clad in a black chador with a small baby boy. The baby wears a red headband with the inscription "Ya Zahra," evoking Fatima Zahra. The green upper part of the stamp reads: "Allahu Akbar" (Allah is greatest). The lower half of the stamp portrays a number of women in red and black (black for mourning and red for martyrdom), some of whom are depicted with their hands clutched in fists. This postage stamp sends to the whole world the message that the willingness of the Iranian woman to sacrifice her baby boy for the holy cause will lead to a final victory over Iraq. Here, the hijab symbolizes martyrdom but also the ultimate victory of the true religion. The veil becomes synonymous with jihad.

This fusion of hijab and jihad is best illustrated on posters that show women wearing the traditional chador and holding a gun, with faces showing determination and sometimes anger (FIGS. 4.4 and 4.5). These women are portrayed as fighters for and defenders of the true faith, although they were not allowed to participate actively in the war and become martyrs in their own right.[31] These posters symbolize the resolve and determination of Iranian women to support the fighters.

A stamp with the title *hijab* inscribed on the lower left corner further

FIG. 4.3. Iranian stamp, 1986.

Left: FIG. 4.4. Poster. *A Decade with the Graphists of the Islamic Revolution, 1979–89.*

Below: FIG. 4.5. Poster. *A Decade with the Graphists of the Islamic Revolution, 1979–89.*

FIG. 4.6. Iranian stamp.

elaborates on this fusion of hijab and jihad (FIG. 4.6). This stamp was issued to honor the hijab and the women who fought against Iraq. It depicts an eye whose pupil is a woman clad in a conservative black veil with the barrel of her gun showing. As pupil of the eye, the veiled woman with her gun is crucial to the Iranian government. Moreover, as pupil of the eye she becomes the focal point of government strategies. She embodies both religion and war.

Guarding the Veil in Post-War Iran

Although the war with Iraq is over, little has changed with regard to the Islamic Republic's scrutiny of women's dress. The government, however, curbed excesses of violence against improperly veiled women. In 1992, it established the Law Enforcement Forces of the Islamic Republic of Iran, under whose auspices both the official armed forces and the komitehs have been grouped. In this way, the government is able to reward the komitehs for "guarding the revolution" in the years since 1979 by allowing them to continue in this role, while simultaneously establishing, for the first time, some sort of official control over them. Such control apparently was necessary in order to halt abuses by the more zealous komiteh members.

Images of veiled women still flood Iran, even though the war is over and

FIG. 4.7. Poster titled *Simaye Efaf.* Agency for the Fight against Social Corruption/ Agency for Public Education.

their mission is accomplished. Although they still promote the hijab for the cause of the revolution and Islam, their mission has taken on more didactic overtones. From billboards, posters, and stamps, women praise the hijab as the most ideal garb for the Iranian woman. The inscription on a promotional poster published by the Agency for the Fight against Social Corruption/Agency for Public Education reads "simaye efaf" (face of chastity) (FIG. 4.7). The poster shows two women with one superimposed on the other. The superimposed woman, shown in profile, wears a light-blue veil—an unusual color for the veil, which normally has a somber color. The lower part of her blue hijab is darker and shows the outlines of the seven continents. She incarnates a new generation of Iranian woman, chaste and cosmopolitan. She belongs to a new wave of youths who are ready to conquer the seven continents. She is a pious role model who may be able to convince the world to follow her way of life. The second young woman is depicted in a frontal pose and rendered on a smaller scale. She sits at a desk with microphones in front of her. She seems to be announcing to the world the arrival of the "new" Muslim woman.

Another poster published by this agency presents an excellent example of a textual and visual advertisement for the hijab (FIG. 4.8). This poster elaborates on the "accepted" and "preferred" styles of veiling in Iran:

Decree of Imam Khomeini on the subject of Islamic coverage. The body is the instrument of the soul, and the soul is divine air. This sacred instrument must not become a plaything of the desires, passions, and debauchery of anyone. Attention: Working sisters must observe the following: (a) At the place of work, they must appear in full cover in conformity with the presented models without any sort of adornments; (b) The color of the manteau [the outer gown] should, preferably, be black, dark blue, brown, or dark gray; (c) The use of flat [low-heeled] shoes in the workplace is mandatory; (d) The use of tight and fashionable clothing and any sort of makeup is prohibited. Committed brothers and sisters, we are ready to receive your constructive opinions and suggestions with regard to fighting social corruption.[32]

In addition to this statement, the poster features drawings of two women in conservative types of preferred or recommended hijabs. Above these

FIG. 4.8. Poster titled *Pattern of Islamic hijab.*

two figures is a one-line quotation from Khomeini: "Respected ladies of Iran proved that they are a strong fortress of chastity." Below the figures appears the inscription "Pattern of Islamic hijab." This poster tells the Iranian woman that by abiding by Imam Khomeini's dress code, she will be a fortress of chastity. Interestingly, while Reza Shah's order to unveil did not entail any major reforms for women, Khomeini's fixation on the proper hijab also did not improve the lot of the Iranian woman. A good hijab will not protect her from a civil law that allots her few rights.

In addition to printed material, metropolitan cities abound in graffiti declaring the virtues of the good hijab.[33] In the summers of 1995 and 1996, I found slogans such as the following:

Veiling represents your personality and dignity.

The best adornment for a woman is to preserve her veil.

My sister, your dignity and honor is in your observance of Islamic cover.

A woman's veil and chastity show her personality.

Your veil is your dignity.

Greetings to veiled women.

My sister, add veiling to the list of your virtues.

My sister, adorn your beauty with the glory of veiling.

Veiling is a divine duty.

Veiling is a sign of her Holiness Fatima Zahra.

The stronghold of the Muslim woman is her veil.

The worth of a woman is in her veil.

In these slogans, the veil symbolizes dignity, chastity, honor, duty, piety, and self-worth. Other slogans promise the woman who wears the proper veil safety and protection from the male gaze and from her own sexuality, as some clerics claim: "Veiling is safety, not restriction"; "Islamic cover and veiling is a woman's safety"; "Veiling protects the jewel of a woman's chastity and dignity"; "My sister, do not sacrifice the cover of your soul for the cover of your body"; "Veiling for woman is like a guard of flowers"; "A woman in her veil is like a pearl in its shell"; and "Your veiling prevents corruption." One slogan claims that "a woman's freedom is bound to her veil." Another slogan even promises that "veiling nurtures pious children."

I also found graffiti claiming that the improperly veiled woman offers herself and that she is a toy of Satan. The improperly veiled woman is also

FIG. 4.9. Photograph of graffiti in Tehran, 1997. "If unveiling is a sign of civilization, then animals must be the most civilized." Photograph taken by author.

accused of having an improper mind or a psychological disorder. Furthermore, she invites the glances of strangers. Still another slogan offends the men who are responsible for the improperly veiled woman: "A woman's improper veil shows her man's lack of honor." The slogans about the improperly veiled woman convey male fear of female sexuality. There are many different interpretations as to the reasons for man's fear of woman's sexuality. Some Muslim scholars believe that the veil and sex segregation in general protect woman from male aggression. Others argue that woman is not in control of her sexuality and, therefore, must be constrained by society.[34] However, all believe that, unconstrained, women's sexuality has the potential to cause fitna, civil war, and the destruction of Muslim society. The slogan "If unveiling is a sign of civilization, then animals must be the most civilized" implies that the veil is a *sine qua non* of civilized society and that any society that does not veil its women belongs to the animal kingdom (FIG. 4.9).

Interestingly, it is not just the unveiled woman but the improperly veiled woman who becomes the nation's enemy: "Death to the improperly veiled woman" and "The improperly veiled woman is a stain on the Islamic Republic of Iran and must be eliminated immediately." The clergy promotes the traditional form of the hijab, which consists of a black chador and a black *maghnaeh* (a tight-fitting head cover). Other forms of hijab are considered, especially by members of the Hizbollah, as imports from the West. This association of some forms of the hijab with Western corruption makes the improperly veiled Iranian woman the scapegoat of Iran's politics toward the West, especially toward the great Satan, the United States. The moral defense of the Islamic Republic of Iran seems to rest painfully on the shoulders of the properly veiled woman. She has become Iran's bulwark against the cultural assault of Western nations.

The Veil and Male Politics

The hijab and Iranian politics are closely intertwined. Political needs defined and continue to define the semantics of the veil. Indeed, the veil has become the trajectory of Iranian politics. That is not to say, however, that the status of the Iranian woman has followed this trajectory. Although allotted a few human rights in this century, she has not been able to escape the patriarchal yoke. The fact that gender equality is seen as a Western concept by the Iranian clergy also has not helped her cause. We may even contend that the politics of the veil do not involve the wearer of the veil but the guardian of the wearer. The Iranian woman is a pawn in men's power games. Addressing the masculine character of Iranian history, Reza Baraheni wrote in 1977 that in Iran, "man, the ruling sexual force, creates a social atmosphere which is totally male and which conditions women according to male peculiarities."[35] In this regard, the Islamic Republic represents a continuum of the masculine character of Iranian history. In the Iranian theocracy, religious law prevents women from becoming ayatollahs or mullahs and thereby prevents them from contributing to the character of Iranian history.[36] Women are segregated and therefore not part of the social "public" atmosphere. Furthermore, male peculiarities, justified on religious grounds in the Islamic Republic, condition women's lives. The Iranian woman was forced to unveil to fit Reza Shah's delusions of grandeur and forced to reveil to fit Ayatollah Khomeini's visions of true religion. She was told that by donning the veil, she would fend off the assault of Western culture. She was also told that by sending her son to martyrdom, she would help save the Islamic Republic of Iran and support the defense of Islam. Ten years after the war with Iraq, she was told that by not veiling according to the guidelines of the clergy, she would cause the downfall of the Islamic Republic. In Iranian politics, the veil has proved to be the most effective weapon of the rulers, secular and clerical.

5 Militarizing the Veil

Before the Battle

Does Islam allow women to participate in battle? The Qur'an does not provide a definite answer, *hadiths* differ about the permissibility of women's active participation in jihad, and historical precedent shows that at the time of the Prophet, women fought alongside men on the battlefields. Thus, there is leeway in answering this question, and Muslim societies have applied different rules at different times. The most famous woman who participated in battle is 'A'isha, the Prophet's favorite wife. Her participation in the Battle of the Camel, a major military conflict in the first civil war in Islamic history, caused much controversy, and her defeat has been used as a rallying cry against women's participation in battle.

Thirteen hundred years after the Battle of the Camel and the first Muslim *fitna* (civil war), the question of women's participation in battle is still debated. Threatened by Saddam Hussein's efforts at expanding Iraq's territory and resources, the United Arab Emirates, in order to increase the size of its armed forces, founded the first military school for women in 1990. Its female military force contributes to the Emirates' defense while, at the same time, complying with Islamic law in terms of sex segregation and dress code. In Saddam Hussein's Iraq, women receive training in the handling of guns and participate in combat. These Iraqi women volunteers are known as *fauj lil majida* (brigade belonging to the glorious one). The Islamic Republic of Iran has not allowed women to actively participate in the war against Iraq and become martyrs in their own right, but it does allow women to become *komiteh* members and police other women who are improperly veiled. Another group of Iranian women, however, actively participates in battle against the Islamic Republic of Iran. These women belong to the Mujahedin-e Khalq.

Most pertinent to the discussion of the meanings of the veil is the way in which these female soldiers have combined Islamic law concerning woman's seclusion—behind harem walls as well as behind the veil—with the dictates of soldiery. 'A'isha's participation in the Battle of the Camel could be interpreted as complying with the Qur'anic injunction prescribing the seclusion of the "Mothers of the Believers," since she went to battle sitting in a closed litter on her camel. She was thus segregated from and invisible to her troops. The female soldiers of the United Arab Emirates follow Islamic law; they adjust their uniform to the Islamic dress code for women. Most female volunteers in the Iraqi armed forces wear fatigues and head scarves. The komiteh members in the Islamic Republic of Iran are properly veiled when policing their improperly veiled sisters. The women of the Mujahedin-e Khalq wear fatigues and head scarves.

An investigation of the appearance of and the limitations imposed on female soldiers in the armed forces as well as in the militias of these countries promises to reveal ideologies associated with or expressed by means of the veil.

'A'isha's Participation in the Battle of the Camel

One of the best-known and most written-about women in Islamic history is 'A'isha bint Abi Bakr (d. 678 CE). The implications and ramifications of her participation in the Battle of the Camel still permeate any analysis of the roles that Muslim women play in today's armies and militias: first, because 'A'isha is still a role model for many Sunni Muslims; and second, because the socioreligious issues that her participation in this battle raised are still debated in contemporary Muslim societies.

'A'isha's marriage to the Prophet, when she was still a child, was supposed to strengthen the ties between the Prophet and 'A'isha's father, Abu Bakr, the Prophet's chief follower. When the marriage was consummated, she was about ten years old. Like all the wives of the Prophet, she received the honorable title "Mother of the Believers." At eighteen, 'A'isha became a childless widow and, like all the Prophet's wives, was forbidden by a Qur'anic injunction to remarry. She was and still is revered as the Prophet's favorite wife. The importance of 'A'isha's public and political life was rendered entirely by men almost 150 years after her death and in a social milieu much more misogynist than that of the original Arabian setting. The earliest written sources date from the 'Abbasid period (750–1258 CE), when women had been excluded from access to the public domain and banished from the battlefield. Thus, accounts of the Battle of the Camel may have distorted the qualities and motivations of 'A'isha.[1] The investigation of the role of women in battle does not necessitate an in-depth analysis of 'A'isha's qualities and motivations for going to battle, which would go beyond the scope of this chapter. It does, however, call for a brief description of the reason for 'A'isha's participation in this battle.

The Battle of the Camel was the major military conflict in the first fitna in Islamic history. The *casus belli* was the assassination of the third caliph, 'Uthman, who like his predecessors was linked to the Prophet by marriage. Calls to avenge his murder and disputes over succession culminated in a battle near Basra in which 'A'isha and Talha and al-Zubayr, two of the Prophet's companions, were defeated by 'Ali ibn Abi Talib, first cousin and son-in-law of the Prophet and the fourth caliph of Islam. The battle came to be known as the Battle of the Camel because the fiercest struggle took place around the camel bearing 'A'isha's closed litter:

> 'A'isha was present during the fighting on a camel, in a palanquin the cover of which had been reinforced by plates of iron and other materials (al-Mas'ûdî, *Murûdj*, iv, 315) and the camel was protected by a kind of armature (al-Dînawarî, 159); at the end of the battle, the palanquin had so many arrows stuck in it that it looked like a hedgehog.

'A'isha was not hit; all she received was a scratch on an arm. The fighting round the camel was particularly fierce; the defenders followed one after the other while declaiming verses; those who fell handed the bridle of 'A'isha's camel to other fighters and there were many dead.[2]

Talha and al-Zubayr lost their lives. 'A'isha was treated with respect by the victorious 'Ali and retired to private life after this defeat. Leila Ahmed concludes that 'A'isha's retreat from public life is representative of the future limited role of all women in the Islamic community.[3] 'A'isha's defeat in this battle was used by some historiographers to demonstrate the danger that female participation in public life can pose to the Islamic community. The term *fitna* denoting civil war in the seventh century came to mean "chaos caused by women's sexuality" in the ninth century.

In the twelfth century, the Shi'i author Ibn Shahrashub (d. 1192 CE) wrote that 'Ali had tried to persuade 'A'isha not to go to battle by advising her: "Fear Allah, O 'A'isha and return to your dwelling and cover yourself with your veil."[4] The basis of 'Ali's quote is the Qur'anic verse: "Wives of the Prophet, if you safeguard your dignity, you are not like any other women. . . . Stay in your homes and do not display your finery as women used to do in the days of ignorance."[5] However, when Ibn Shahrashub quotes 'Ali in the twelfth century, 'Ali's advice takes on a different semantic dimension. By this time, women had been effectively banished from public life; they were forced to return to their dwellings and cover themselves with their veils. While in the seventh century seclusion was the prerogative of the Prophet's wives, in the twelfth century seclusion in the harem and behind the veil had been imposed on all women with social standing. The veil, worn by the Prophet's wives to show their distinction and social status, was now used to segregate women and exclude them from public life. A sign of distinction had been transformed into a sign of exclusion.

Noteworthy and relevant to the investigation of women's roles in today's armies and militias is the fact that 'A'isha sat in a closed litter on her camel and was thus invisible to her troops as befitted her elevated status as "Mother of the Believers." At the time when Ibn Shahrashub quoted 'Ali, women were no longer allowed on the battlefield, even in closed litters. Nabia Abbott concludes that by the second and third centuries of Islam, "the seclusion and degradation of women had progressed beyond anything known in the first decades of Islam."[6] The arguments employed by contemporary religious authorities against women's participation in jihad originate in hadiths that were compiled at that time.

Women's Participation in Battle: Precedents and Holy Scriptures

'A'isha as woman did not set a pre-Islamic or Islamic precedent by participating directly in battle. In the *jahiliya* and in early Islamic times, women participated in tribal warfare on the Arabian peninsula.[7] Women were warrior-leaders heading armies, leaders of rebellions that included men, and nurses looking after the wounded on the battlefield.[8] Many women fought alongside the Prophet or against him. Hind Bint 'Utba, mother of Mu'awiya, is known for her bravery on the battlefield. With other women, she accompanied the Meccans on their expeditions against Medina in 625 and was one of the most ardent in urging the men to fight. According to some authors, she was condemned to death by the Prophet at the time of the capture of Mecca.[9] Following the Prophet's death, a woman by the name of Salma bint Malik led an armed rebellion against the Islamic state. Salma was killed only after "a hundred others" had fallen around her.[10] Even after the Battle of the Camel, women fought for both the fourth caliph 'Ali and his opponent Mu'awiya at Siffin. Only after Muslim conquests had led to an enormous influx of wealth and people, raising the socioeconomic status of the Arabs as well as the number of men able to fight the jihad, were veiling and seclusion extended from the Prophet's wives to all women with social standing. Since women were no longer needed to fight for Islam, they could now be relegated to the harem and banished from the battlefields.

Eighty of the Qur'an's 6,616 verses concern legal matters; not one of these addresses the place of women on the battlefield, whether in a military or a supportive role. There was, however, an oral record of what the Prophet had said and done as judge and administrator. As most of his companions had made note of what he did or said for their own guidance, their diligence later paved the way for codification of the Prophet's *sunna* (practice) when the jurist Muhammad ibn Idris Shafi (767–820 CE) ruled that all legal decisions not stemming directly from the Qur'an must be based on a tradition going back to the Prophet himself. In the first three centuries after the Prophet's death, some 2,700 of his acts and sayings were compiled in six canonical works, called *Al-Hadith* and accepted by Sunnis. The two considered most trustworthy are those of al-Bukhari and Muslim. Each saying that was accepted is said to be traceable in a direct line to someone who heard it from the Prophet or saw what the Prophet did. Putative hadiths that were perceived to conflict with the basic tenets of the Qur'an were excluded.[11] Shi'is valued especially those traditions that were traced through Imam 'Ali ibn Abi Talib and added their own collections to the Sunni *Al-Hadith.*[12]

It is said that 1,210 traditions were related on 'A'isha's authority, but barely 300 of these were retained by al-Bukhari and Muslim. Leila Ahmed observes that there is no record of the reactions of the Prophet's wives to the institutions of veiling and seclusion. She regards this silence remarkable when considering the eloquence of the Prophet's wives, especially that of 'A'isha, and concludes that those who did the recording also had the power of suppression.[13] The process of selection of hadiths was naturally influenced by the social values and politics in the period of codification. Since, at this time, women participated in public life less often, we should not expect to find many hadiths that mention, condone, or moreover advocate women's participation in battle.

The few hadiths addressing women's participation in battle may be grouped roughly into three categories. One category includes those hadiths that state that jihad is also the duty of the Muslim woman. The *Sahih al-Bukhari* includes the hadith "The invocation of men and women that Allah may let them participate in jihad and adorn them with martyrdom."[14] This hadith furthermore gives a woman direct access to martyrdom if she loses her life in the jihad. A hadith included in the *Sahih Muslim* tells of Umm Sulaim, who was ready to defend Islam with her dagger:

It has been narrated on the authority of Anas, one of the Prophet's companions, that on the Day of Hunain, Umm Sulaim took out a dagger she had in her possession. Abu Talha saw her and said: Messenger of Allah, this is Umm Sulaim. She is holding a dagger. The Messenger of Allah (may peace be upon him) asked (her): What for are you holding this dagger? She said: I took it up so that I may tear open the belly of a polytheist who comes near me. The Messenger of Allah (may peace be upon him) began to smile (at these words). She said: Messenger of Allah, kill all those people—other than us—whom thou hast declared to be free (on the day of the Conquest of Mecca). (They embraced Islam because) they were defeated at your hands (and as such their Islam is not dependable). The Messenger of Allah (may peace be upon him) said: Umm Sulaim, God is sufficient (against the mischief of the polytheists) and He will be kind to us (so you need not carry this dagger).[15]

Here, the Prophet does not deny Umm Sulaim's right to participate in jihad to defend Islam but tells her to put her life in God's hands. His answer is not so much directed at Umm Sulaim the woman as it is at Umm Sulaim the believer.

Another category includes those hadiths that allot women a more restricted role in battle; women do not perform the same tasks as men on the battlefield, and they do not receive the same share of the booty. These hadiths describe women fighting alongside the Prophet and taking care of the wounded. The following hadith by Muslim shows that women followed the Prophet to battle, engaged in fighting, and took care of the wounded but were not treated as equals when the booty was divided. Their share was at the will of the Prophet:

It has been narrated on the authority of Yazid b. Hurmuz that Najda wrote to Ibn Abbas [one of the Prophet's companions] inquiring of him: Tell me whether the Messenger of Allah (may peace be upon him) took women to participate with him in Jihad; (if he did), whether he allotted them a regular share from the booty. [Ibn Abbas writes back with his answers, he says] He did take them [women] to the battle and sometimes he fought along with them. They [women] would treat the wounded and were given a reward from the booty, but he [the Prophet] did not assign any regular share for them.[16]

Al-Bukhari's collection also includes hadiths that describe women's supportive role in battle:

Narrated Anas: On the day (of the battle) of Uhud when (some) people retreated and left the Prophet, I saw Aisha bint Abi Bakr and Umm Sulaim, with their robes tucked up so that the bangles around their ankles were visible, hurrying with their skins (in another narration it is said, "carrying the water skins on their backs"). Then they would pour the water in the mouths of the people, and return to fill the water skins again and come back again to pour water in the mouths of the people.[17]

Narrated by Ar-Rabi' bint Mu'aywudh: We used to take part in holy battles with the Prophet by providing the people with water and serving them and bringing the killed and the wounded back to Medina.[18]

This category of hadiths shows that women participated mostly in supporting roles on the battlefields. They would bring water to the fighters and take care of the wounded and dead.

Another category of hadiths includes those that could be interpreted as an injunction against women's participation in jihad. For example, the following two hadiths in *Sahih al-Bukhari,* attributed to 'A'isha, state:

Narrated Aisha, the mother of the faithful believers, I requested the Prophet to permit me to participate in jihad, but he said, "Your jihad is the performance of *hajj.*"

Narrated Aisha, the mother of faithful believers, The Prophet was asked by his wives about the jihad and he replied, "The best jihad (for you) is (the performance of) *hajj.*"[19]

These two hadiths refer, strictly speaking, only to the wives of the Prophet. It is they who are told by their husband that they should perform the hajj (pilgrimage to Mecca) instead of going to battle. The hajj may have been more suitable to their elevated position of "Mother of the Believers" than the jihad. However, since the Prophet's wives were taken as an example for all women by later Muslim authorities, the Prophet's injunction could be interpreted as applying to all women. Just as seclusion and veiling were initially only peculiar to the Prophet's wives and then spread to all Muslim women, going on a hajj instead of a jihad may have spread from the Prophet's wives to the rest of the female community.

Shi'i Islam and Women's Participation in Jihad

Imam Muhammad ibn 'Ali al-Shawkani (1759–1839 CE) in his *tafsir*[20] titled *Nayl al-Awtar* (The attainment of goals) comments on most of the hadiths by al-Bukhari and Muslim that are quoted above.[21] He concludes that the participation in jihad is not as essential for the female believer as it is for the male believer. He concedes, however, that women may participate in battle when there is an extreme necessity for it, and he explains that since women's participation is contingent upon necessity, women are not allotted any share in the booty. According to al-Shawkani, women should perform the duties assigned to them, such as dressing the wounds of the injured or carrying water for the soldiers, with the full decorum of a Muslim woman. His main concern, which permeates his whole commentary, is that conditions on the battlefield may wreak havoc on proper gender relations. For example, women are allowed to treat wounded men who are not related to them. He also worries about whether a man, in the case when no woman is present, should be permitted to wash the body of an unrelated dead woman from behind a screen, or whether he should bury her without washing her.[22] In this vein, al-Shawkani also interprets the hadith: "Narrated Aisha, the mother of faithful believers, The Prophet was asked by his wives about the jihad and he replied, 'The best jihad (for you) is (the performance of) *hajj.*'" The author concludes that for female believers the performance of the hajj is better than participation in jihad, because when performing the hajj they are properly covered and do not have to mingle with unrelated men.

To summarize, al-Shawkani allows women to perform supportive roles in battle under circumstances of extreme necessity. On the surface, his conclusion seems to contradict Hassan Ul-Ameene's entry in the *Islamic Shi'ite Encyclopaedia*. Here, Ul-Ameene states that Islam "makes it obligatory upon every able-bodied and fit person, man and woman, to undertake struggle insofar as wealth, property and one's self is concerned, and then, prepares the whole nation in such a way that they all should constitute an army to fight in the way of God, as and when the need should arise. Every individual in the society undertakes the defence of one weak point."[23] According to this definition, women must fight in the way of God when the need arises. But this definition of jihad does not assign specific tasks to women. The tasks of defending "one weak point" may vary from fighting on the front line to policing other women or to urging sons and fathers to become martyrs. Iranian women, as we shall see later, undertake all of these diverse tasks.

Women in the Military of the United Arab Emirates

Al-Shawkani states that only extreme necessity justifies women's presence on the battlefield. Saddam Hussein's military buildup and invasion of Kuwait sent shock waves to all Gulf states and may have constituted such an extreme necessity for the United Arab Emirates, a small and oil-rich federation of seven emirates. It supported Kuwait in the spring of 1990 in an attempt to harm the Iraqi economy by flooding the oil market and lowering the price of oil. In the 1991 Gulf War, the United Arab Emirates joined the anti-Iraq coalition led by the United States and contributed $5 billion to the war chest. But relying solely on financial contributions was not considered sufficient means to stave off powerful Iraq. The United Arab Emirates needed to increase its troops, which numbered a mere 50,000 men at that time. The foundation of a military school for women in 1990 was clearly an attempt to boost the size of the troops.

According to an article in *Sayidaty* in 1990, the year of Iraq's invasion of Kuwait, the president of the Emirates, Shaykh Zayd ibn Sultan al-Nahyan, agreed to a military school for women. Called *al-madrasa al-ʿaskariya al-niswiya* (military school for women), this is the first school in the Gulf region that trains female soldiers. Women receive instruction in the use of weapons and also in the execution of administrative tasks. According to *Sayidaty,* the primary reason for the school was not to train women to become active participants in the armed forces of the United Arab Emirates but to create a force that would police other women: "Because some women carry weapons, commit theft, smuggle or murder, violate the laws, and frighten the public with their disgusting crimes, there must be—on the other side—women who carry weapons to protect the people and society as well as the laws. From there came the idea of a female police force that restrains women who violate the laws and that defends the country."[24] This idea of women policing women is not new to Muslim countries. It has been realized in other Gulf states. For example, in Oman, female police officers deal only with female offenders; they also serve as customs and immigration officers dealing solely with women. This kind of female police force, by maintaining sex segregation, helps enforce Islamic law that forbids men to have physical contact with women if they are not the husband, brother, father, or son. Male officers indeed violate Islamic law when they arrest or search female offenders who are not related to them.[25] By allowing women to police other women, the United Arab Emirates solves this legal dilemma. But, moreover, by training female officers to police other women, male officers who have performed this service so far are now free to join the military forces and contribute to the defense of the United Arab Emirates.

Although the career opportunities for the graduates of this school are limited to policing other women, religious authorities in the United Arab Emirates—94 percent of the population is Sunni—still find it difficult to reconcile themselves with the idea of women appearing in public: "Some senior officers in the Emirates' army found it hard to credit the fine results the women recruits were achieving. Lieutenant Colonel Mohamed Nasser, the commander of the academy, had admitted from the beginning that he felt lukewarm about the whole idea of women warriors. 'If we had a bigger population, I'd rather see women stay at home,' he said."[26]

The colonel's lukewarm feelings about women warriors echo 'Ali's feelings about 'A'isha's going to war: "Fear Allah, O 'A'isha, and return to your dwelling and cover yourself with your veil." These feelings of the commander of the academy reveal the ambivalent stance of military and religious authorities on women's roles in the armed forces. Moreover, they hint at the socioreligious obstacles that had to be overcome in order to found this academy.

Shaykha Fatima, wife of Shaykh Zayd of the United Arab Emirates, is the woman who suggested the recruitment of women soldiers. She left the task of convincing the religious authorities to one of her female friends, Hessa al Khalidi, the Emirates' first female civil engineer. With Shaykh Zayd's approval, Hessa was assigned to solve the problem of female recruitment and reconcile the religious establishment to the inclusion of women in the military. Hessa, who is well versed in Islamic history, the Qur'ran, and hadiths, succeeded in opposing the arguments of Muslim authorities who hold that some established hadiths do not allow for women to be recruited as soldiers. She countered with hadiths that describe women fighting alongside the Prophet, and she employed historical precedents of female warriors.[27] Establishing the religious legitimacy of women's roles in the military was not the only obstacle. Another problem was the question of who would train the women. The qualified instructors were men, and men were not allowed by Islamic law to supervise unveiled women's physical fitness training. They were not allowed to enter women's barracks to enforce discipline; nor could they touch a woman in order to adjust her stance with a rifle.[28] To solve this problem, the Emirates asked the U.S. Army to send female trainers. The U.S. Army complied with this request.

For the most part, the graduates of this school police other women, and, thus, sex segregation is upheld. But the fact that these women were allowed to leave their homes and wear uniforms represents a major social change. In 1990, the Emirates were still one of the most conservative Muslim societies, and most women lived and still live in strict seclusion. Outside the home, a woman usually wears the long black *abaya* (loose outer garment) and a cloth veil over her face. The photos published in *Sayidaty* of women wearing uniforms are therefore even more astounding. In one photo (FIG. 5.1), each woman wears an ankle-length skirt, a long jacket covering the hips and wrists, and a cap over a black scarf that covers hair and neck. This uniform is within the code of Islamic dress. Even their military combat uniforms comply with the coverage required by religious authorities. The only exposed areas of the body are the face and hands. The women in these combat uniforms do not tuck their shirts inside their military pants, so as not to attract attention to the shape of their bodies. This military outfit is worn with a military cap. The black head veil is tucked

مدرسة خولة بنت الأزور

FIG. 5.1. Graduates of the first military school for women in the United Arab Emirates. *Sayidaty*, December 1993.

FIG. 5.2. Women of the United Arab Emirates in uniform. *Sayidaty,* December 1993.

inside the shirt and covers the opening of the front collar and the back of the neck (FIG. 5.2).

The role of women in the armed forces of the United Arab Emirates is thus one of compromise between military needs and religious demands: first, by taking on tasks whose performance by men violates Islamic law, female soldiers allow male compatriots to concentrate on defending the Emirates; second, women's fatigues, while functional, comply with the Islamic dress code for women. The black head veil as part of the women's uniform signifies a compromise between the dictates of religious law and the needs of a small oil-rich country. It also symbolizes women's limited access to public life in the United Arab Emirates.

Fighting for Iraq

Iraq is another country in the Gulf region that integrates women in its armed forces because of necessity. The war with Iran (1980–88), the invasion of Kuwait (1990), and the war with the U.S.–led coalition (1991) necessitated the recruitment of women into the armed forces of Iraq. Under a law passed in 1977, women could be commissioned as officers if they held a health-related university degree, and they could be appointed as warrant officers or noncommissioned officers in army medical institutes if they were qualified nurses. By 1980, women in the armed forces accounted for 29 percent of physicians, 46 percent of dentists, and 70 percent of pharmacists. During this period, more than 40,000 women had been enrolled. Although the vast majority of women in the armed forces held administrative or medical-related positions, an increasing number of women performed in combat functions after 1981. Women were serving in combat roles both in the air force and in the Air Defense Command in 1987. This integration of women into the military reflected the shortage of trained males. Women worked as law enforcement officers, in ministries, as doctors in hospitals, and on construction projects. This emancipation was sanctioned by the government, which expended a significant amount of propaganda publicizing the role of women in helping to win the war against Iran. The government further maintained that after the war, women would be encouraged to retain their newfound work roles. And indeed, Iraq's interim constitution, adopted in 1990, states in Article 19 (Equality) that "equal opportunities are guaranteed to all citizens, according to the law."

Iraq's shortage of men was not the only reason for mobilizing women. Iraq's type of secularism, postulated by the Ba'th Socialist Party, played a major role in women's participation in Iraq's wars and warrants further investigation. In 1959, Iraq had enacted a secular law on personal status that was based on the *shari'a,* statutes from other Muslim countries, and legal precedents established in Iraqi courts. An amendment was enacted in 1963 when the Iraqi Ba'th Party came to power. Although the Ba'th Party was a proponent of secularism, it did not hesitate to use religion as a mobilizing agent. During the war with Iran, prominent Ba'th Party members made a public show of attending religious observances. Saddam Hussein was often depicted in prayer in posters displayed throughout Iraq. Also, by spending large sums of money to refurbish mosques, the Ba'th Party kept Iraq's Shi'is, who constitute the majority of Muslims in Iraq, from supporting the Shi'is in Iran.[29] In addition to drawing Shi'i sympathies, during the war with Iran, the Ba'th with Saddam Hussein at its head had to find a rallying point that clearly united all Iraqis—Sunnis and Shi'is.

The platform of the Baʿth Socialist Party of Iraq, like that of other Baʿth parties in other Arab countries, championed Pan-Arabism, a doctrine that maintains that no matter where Arabs live they are part of a single community. The term *baʿth* translates as "resurrection" or "renaissance." Thus, generally speaking, the Baʿth parties tried to resurrect the glorious past of all Arabs. Initially, Saddam Hussein portrayed his war with Iran as a struggle of the Arab homeland against Persian expansionism. However, when important Arab states such as Syria, Algeria, and Libya sided with Iran, Saddam Hussein was forced to rethink his strategy. Eventually, he made the concept of Pan-Arabism subservient to the idea of Iraqi nationalism, which was now used as the prime force to motivate citizens to join the war effort. He no longer glorified the past of all Arabs but the past of Iraq. These efforts went as far as to glorify Babylonian heroes and the honorable noble Arab tribes. Iraq was now cast as the cradle of all civilizations.[30]

In order to consolidate its power base in Iraq's towns and villages, the Baʿth Party instituted the People's Army in 1970. In 1977, this militia had 50,000 members; and by 1987, it had an estimated 650,000 members, approaching the number of the regular armed forces. Although the People's Army was intended originally to give the Baʿth Party an active role in every town and village, it began in 1981 to support the regular armed forces. The official function of this paramilitary force was to act as backup to the regular forces in times of war, to promote national consciousness, and to consolidate national unity. The members were recruited from among both women and men, eighteen years of age and older. Members usually underwent two months of training after which they were paid from party funds. Recruits were instructed in the use of a rifle.[31]

Photos that appeared in the *New York Times International* on November 26, 1997, show women who belong to this paramilitary force (FIGS. 5.3 and 5.4). Figure 5.3 carries this caption:

Volunteers in Baghdad's Cause

Iraqi volunteer commandos, part of the First Women's Brigade, received their black military uniforms yesterday as they shouted patriotic songs at a camp in Baghdad. At the same time, United Nations inspectors went on searching for weapons that violate conditions imposed after the Persian Gulf War.[32]

Above: FIG. 5.3. Volunteers in Baghdad's cause. *New York Times International,* November 26, 1997. AP/Wide World Photos.

Left: FIG 5.4. Cheering volunteers. *New York Times International,* November 26, 1997. AP/Wide World Photos.

In both photos, the women carry no arms. An embroidered inscription visible on their uniforms reads *fauj lil majida,* which translates as "brigade belonging to the glorious one." This brigade belongs to glorious Iraq, and its function is to raise public feeling against the United States. This brigade represents a synthesis of national and religious elements. The name of the brigade gives testimony to its nationalist ideology. In addition to leading patriotic cheers, this brigade appeals to the religiously observant. The women wear black scarves covering the neck area, loose-fitting uniforms, and combat boots. Only one woman, who may not have received all parts of her uniform yet, wears high heels and no head scarf.

Since the mass media in Iraq are under the control of the government and since the government's Iraqi News Agency distributes news to the foreign press based in or passing through Iraq, we may assume that the publication of these photographs was encouraged by the government.[33] What message did the Iraqi government try to convey to the world and, more importantly, to the Iraqis? The message to the world is one of determination: All Iraqis are prepared to fight in the name of the "glorious one." The message to Iraqis is more complex. The photographs are intended to raise anti-American sentiments and, by creating an atmosphere of "us against them," to reinforce identification with an Iraq that is economically no longer able to provide for most of its citizens. In order to deliver this message effectively, the female messengers have to appeal to the widest possible audience, including those Muslims who insist on proper Islamic dress and conduct. The women in the photographs comply with the Islamic dress code; they wear loose-fitting uniforms and head scarves. Interestingly, in these two photos the head scarf becomes an emblem of a paradoxical Islamic secularism. As we shall see below, another conciliatory gesture toward observant Muslims is the fact that most women in the foreground are past child-bearing age.

Both BBC News and CNN reported that on January 18, 1998, Iraqi authorities called on all Iraqi men and women to volunteer for "popular training" the next month as part of the nation's efforts to confront what was described as a military threat from the United States. Saddam Hussein is quoted as saying on state television: "We should show an essential part of the people's determination under the leadership of the great Ba'th [party]

FIG. 5.5. An Iraqi woman with an assault rifle. *Al Majallah,* March 1998.

to fight in order that Iraq exists and remains as it should be." In response to Saddam Hussein's call to weapons, in March 1998, the Iraqi publication *Al Majallah* published a photograph (FIG. 5.5) that shows a group of women surrounding two old women, one of whom demonstrates how to load and unload an assault rifle.[34] Each of the trainers wears the traditional black head scarf of cotton gauze, a *futa* that covers the chin, and an abaya. Both are old, maybe in their sixties or even seventies, and obviously not in physical shape for active combat. What is the purpose of using middle-aged (FIGS. 5.3 and 5.4) and old women (FIG 5.5) to show Saddam Hussein's determination to stand up against the United States? Of course, showing the resolve of a most vulnerable but honorable section of Iraqi society amplifies the message. Using old women for propaganda purposes also may have been an attempt by the government to placate religious authorities. Properly attired and past child-bearing years, these women can be shown handling weapons without running the risk of insulting religious sensibilities. They are unlikely to cause fitna, chaos caused by women's sexuality. Their "mingling with unrelated men" on the battlefield, which was of great concern to al-Shawkani, will no longer have the potential to disrupt public order.

Zaynab's Sisters at the Service of the Islamic Republic of Iran

As mentioned in chapter 4, Iranian women may become komiteh members, and as such they are allowed to carry guns. The female komiteh members safeguard people's moral conduct in public by searching for women who are not properly veiled. This female task force is better known in Iran as Khaharan-e Zaynab, or Zaynab's sisters.[35] The Khaharan-e Zaynab are devout Muslims and, for the most part, young and educated.

A photo in *Mahjubah: The Magazine for Muslim Women* published in 1983 shows Zaynab's sisters wearing a more informal *hijab* composed of a long-sleeved, ankle-length, loose black outer gown and a black scarf wrapped tightly around the head (FIG. 5.6).[36] The scarf is tied under the chin and the loose end of it is brought over to the front to cover the area of the bosom. Two of the women hold semiautomatic rifles: one carries her rifle slung over her shoulder and has her right hand over the trigger; the other woman carries her rifle in the right hand. A red carnation is stuck into the muzzle of her rifle.

FIG. 5.6. Zaynab's sisters. *Mahjubah: The Magazine for Muslim Women,* April 1983.

مقاتلات ايرانيات في عرض عسكري بمناسبة ذكرى الحرب مع العراق

FIG. 5.7. Zaynab's sisters commemorating the eighth anniversary of the holy defense against Iraq. *Majallah,* 1997.

This photo was published on the cover of *Mahjubah* three years into the war with Iraq. What message does this magazine cover convey? The name of the magazine, which translates as "the veiled woman," posits that the Muslim woman wears the hijab.[37] Furthermore, picturing a veiled woman with her fingers on the trigger of an assault rifle bespeaks her readiness to defend her beliefs. Showing a veiled woman holding a rifle with a red carnation, a symbol of martyrdom, stuck down its barrel signifies that she is ready to die for her beliefs. The cover of the magazine conveys the determination of Zaynab's sisters "to fight in the way of God" and to defend a weak point.[38] Since Zaynab's sisters are not allowed to actively participate in combat, their defense of a weak point must therefore be directed at supporting those who are allowed to fight on the front lines. Thus, the cover tells Iranian women that they must support their sons, fathers, and brothers in their duty to fight the jihad for the Islamic Republic of Iran. The cover's message to the male combatants is that all Iranian women, including their mothers, daughters, and sisters, rely on them to defend Islam and Iran. Here, the hijab signals religious solidarity among the people of the Islamic Republic.

Another photo (FIG. 5.7), which appeared in a 1997 issue of the Saudi magazine *Majallah,* shows a parade of Zaynab's sisters commemorating the eighth anniversary of the "holy defense" against Iraq. The Khaharan-e

Zaynab in this photograph wear a formal kind of hijab consisting of three pieces: a large black *maghnae,* a long black outer gown, and an additional head-to-toe veil similar to the traditional chador. The women wear white gloves similar to those worn by soldiers in parades. Their red headbands with the inscription *ya Zahra* were also worn by Iranian soldiers fighting on the front lines against Iraq.[39] These parading women hold their semiautomatic rifles by the butt and the stock. A red carnation is stuck into the muzzle of every rifle. The color of both the headband and the carnation symbolizes blood, the blood spilled in martyrdom. Zaynab's sisters are willing to sacrifice themselves for the Prophet's daughter Fatima and become martyrs.[40]

Figure 5.7 shows the commemoration of eight years of holy defense, as the Persian writing in the background indicates: 'hasht sal-e difa'-e muqaddas." Its caption in Arabic reads "Iranian fighters in a military parade commemorating the war with Iraq." This photo was published in 1997 in *Majallah,* a Saudi magazine published in London, to complement an article underneath it titled "Khatami is upset about reports of nuclear weapons." The article explains that Iranian president Khatami was upset about a recent report in a British newspaper, which claimed that an Iranian national staying in Glasgow, Scotland, had tried to buy sophisticated computer equipment used in the process of enriching uranium. The article then states that Iran assures that its nuclear research follows merely peaceful objectives, contrary to reports in Western and Middle Eastern countries claiming that the Iranian government is trying to develop nuclear weapons.

Why did the publishers of *Majallah* choose this photograph of parading Khaharan-e Zaynab to illustrate their article about a possible nuclear threat from Iran? An answer may lie in the way in which the Saudi publishers perceive these veiled women carrying AK-47 assault rifles. To them, these women may look threatening in their determination to give their lives for the Islamic Republic of Iran. Of course, we have to remember that women were denied access to active combat during the war with Iraq and that the purpose of this photograph was to raise mass consciousness and to show the world Iran's determination to win the war. The fact that the publishers of *Majallah* use this photograph to illustrate an article about a possible nuclear threat from Iran gives testimony to the success of Iran's public image campaigns. This campaign may be one of the sources of the image of the Iranian woman as one who wears the hijab, carries an assault rifle, and, moreover, is zealous in her defense of Shi'i Islam and Iran. The hijab constitutes here an integral part of the image of Islamic fanaticism.

Mujahedin-e Khalq

Some Iranian women are actively involved in military combat. These are members of the Mujahedin-e Khalq (The people's combatants).[41] This party was founded secretly in 1965 by former members of the Liberation Movement of Iran (LMI), which had been formed in 1960 by Mehdi Bazargan.[42] It is the first political party formed on the basis of Islamic ideology. The organization drew its inspiration and ideological force from Ali Shariati and his anticlerical version of Shi'i Islam.[43] Taking a fierce anticlerical stance, the party called upon Muslims to create a classless society by struggling against imperialism, capitalism, and dictatorship. Its Marxist agenda became explicit when it accused the Shi'i clergy of "using the holy teachings as a 'public opiate.'"[44] The ideology of the Mujahedin-e Khalq was labeled by the Pahlavi regime as Islamic Marxism. The Mujahedin-e Khalq split into two groups in 1975: centrists who retained the name Mujahedin-e Khalq, and Tehran-based leftists who were now popularly called Paykar. Both groups were instrumental to the success of the revolution in February 1979. When the Mujahedin-e Khalq refused to surrender their arms to the Islamic government of Ayatollah Khomeini, they came into conflict with the new regime. By 1982, the party claimed to have killed more than 1,200 religious and political leaders of the regime; the Iranian government puts the number of executed Mujahedin at 4,000, but the party claims twice that number.[45] The Mujahedin leader, Masud Rajavi, moved the party's headquarters in 1986 from Paris to Baghdad and, in 1987, assisted by Iraq, formed an armed wing of the party, the National Liberation Army (NLA). In 1988, 7,000 NLA troops, supported by the Iraqi air force, seized towns sixty miles into Iran. About 4,500 NLA and Iraqi troops were killed in the Iranian counterattack. In retaliation, the Iranian government also executed hundreds of jailed party members.[46] In 1989, when Saddam Hussein tried to improve relations with Iran, he officially halted all anti-Iranian activities by the Mujahedin, including hostile broadcasts. In 1991, the NLA successfully fought off a large-scale incursion by a force of elite revolutionary guards.

FIG. 5.8a. Male revolutionary guards. *Majallah,* 1997.

An article in the April 1997 issue of *Time* estimates that the NLA has about 30,000 troops, fully armored and ready for battle. Rajavi continues to function from Baghdad, sharing his leadership with his wife, Miryam. The couple has succeeded in building one of the world's powerful rebel armies as well as "a sophisticated resistance movement, with offices around the world, plus five radio stations and a new satellite-television network that beam anti-*mullah* propaganda daily into Iranian homes."[47] The NLA claims to have launched more than a hundred cross-border operations against Iran in the past several years. The Mujahedin-e Khalq claim in a report in *Iran Times* that since 1993, Iranian agents have attacked the Mujahedin in Iraq seventy-seven times, including the latest attack in September 1999.[48]

The article in the April 1997 issue of *Time* estimates that women constitute 35 percent of the 30,000 NLA troops and 70 percent of NLA officers. An article in a 1997 issue of the Saudi magazine *Majallah* provides a visual introduction to the world of women combatants in the NLA.[49] The editors of *Majallah* arranged the warring factions in dramatic fashion: the photo on the left (FIG. 5.8a) depicts male revolutionary guards who face female NLA members depicted in a photo on the right (FIG. 5.8b). Unlike the

FIG. 5.8b. Female NLA members. *Majallah,* 1997.

women in the Iraqi armed forces, the NLA soldiers are young and seem well trained. They wear gray uniforms, hold up assault rifles, and, most strikingly, wear bright red head scarves. Since the concept of martyrdom is also an important concept in Mujahedin ideology, the red scarf, just as the red headband of Zaynab's sisters, may symbolize the Mujahedin's willingness to die for their cause. It is more likely, however, that the Mujahedin would want to set themselves visually apart from their enemy, the Iranian government and its proponents, Zaynab's sisters, who wear black veils. Moreover, red is the color of communism, which represents an integral part of Mujahedin ideology. The red head scarf, therefore, may express the Islamic Marxist ideology of the Mujahedin-e Khalq. By wearing head scarves, the women of the Mujahedin-e Khalq observe the Islamic dress code; by wearing red head scarves, these women signal compliance with Islamic Marxist ideology.

The Islamic ideology of the Mujahedin is quite different from that of the Islamic Republic of Iran. The Mujahedin take a new approach to the interpretation of the Qur'an and Shi'i teachings and refute the traditionalist monopoly on tafsir held by Iran's conservative clerics. The fact that the

NLA women are allowed to participate actively in combat and hold leadership positions within the NLA demonstrates the Mujahedin's deviation from the viewpoints of Iran's conservative clergy with regard to the status of women. The May 1988 issue of the party's official publication, *The Mujahed,* featured women whose functions range from NLA general command, brigade commander, foreign purchase manager, physician, and combatant, to chief news editor. In one photograph, women shoot from the trenches (FIG. 5.9); in another, two women hold prisoners after an attack on positions held by troops loyal to the Ayatollah (FIG. 5.10). In both of these photographs, the women wear bulletproof vests, ammunition belts, gray combat uniforms, and helmets over red head scarves. Clearly, these NLA fighters, unlike Zaynab's sisters and the Iraqi women soldiers, are on a more equal footing with their male counterparts.

The article in the April 1997 issue of *Time* states that the NLA women were "dressed in fatigues topped off with green scarves." This switch over the last few years from red to green scarf may be a conspicuous indicator of change in the ideology of the Mujahedin-e Khalq—a change from the red of Marxism to the green of Islam. In order for the Mujahedin-e Khalq to

FIG. 5.9. NLA soldiers shooting from the trenches. *The Mujahed,* May 1988.

FIG. 5.10. NLA soldiers hold prisoners. *The Mujahed,* May 1988.

maintain and increase its troops, it needs an agenda that appeals to possible financial backers and that, moreover, convinces young people in the Islamic Republic of Iran to leave their homes and join the ranks of the NLA. In their effort to overthrow the Shah, the joint forces of the Mujahedin-e Khalq and the Ayatollah Khomeini were funded by the Soviet Union— funding that has dried up with the breakup of the Soviet Union and the decline of communism.[50] The Mujahedin-e Khalq have also looked to the United States for funding, and, according to an editorial in the *Washington Post,* "many members of Congress, in their frustration over the administration's failed policy in Iran and the failure of Iranian democrats to rally their own forces, have chosen to support the Mujahedin because they have the best-oiled public relations machine in town."[51] Changing the color of the head scarf may be part of the Mujahedin's attempt at forging new alliances. Abandoning the color red may be construed as an attempt at soliciting support from the United States. Interestingly, in a 1999 Mujahedin rally in The Hague, some women demonstrators wore American baseball caps.[52]

Adopting the color green, the color of Islam, may be seen as an attempt to cater to the government of any Islamic state that wants to supplant the government of the Islamic Republic of Iran: at this time, the Mujahedin-e Khalq is supported by Saddam's Iraq and the Taliban in Afghanistan. The green head scarf also distinguishes the women of the NLA from the women of the Islamic Republic who wear the black hijab. Although the color green symbolizes Islam, it maintains distance from the black of mullah-ruled Iran. This distinction proves crucial for the recruitment of that segment of Iranian society that has arguably lost the most rights and opportunities under the present regime: young and educated women. In the sixteen-point platform of the Mujahedin-e Khalq, Miryam Rajavi clearly states the group's belief in the rule of Islam. According to her, this is not the Islam of the conservative mullahs but an Islam that eliminates gender-based discrimination.[53] As long as the women of Iran suffer repression and inequality, the Mujahedin-e Khalq may be able to fill its ranks with young women who have lost hope for a future in the Islamic Republic.

The ease with which the Mujahedin-e Khalq changes ideologies and forms new alliances, symbolized by the change in the color of the head scarf, warrants a caveat. The liberation of the Iranian woman requires a government based on democratic principles. Although the Rajavis refer to their future government as "Democratic Islamic Republic," there has been no evidence that the Mujahedin-e-Khalq strives for democracy or even tolerates democratic opposition. Thus, when the Iranian woman abandons the black veil in favor of a green head scarf, she may just be changing despots.

After the Battle

Did women benefit from their participation in jihad? 'A'isha's defeat in the Battle of the Camel forced her to retire to private life. Since her defeat was used by some historiographers to demonstrate the danger that female participation in public life can pose to the Islamic community, 'A'isha's participation may have contributed to women's seclusion from public life. The militarization of the women of the United Arab Emirates allows some female volunteers to leave the confines of their homes and traditional veils. However, since their task is mainly the policing of other women, these volunteers actively perpetuate sex segregation.

During the war with Iran, Saddam Hussein's government promised women that after the war they would be allowed to keep their newfound jobs. In the same breath, the government also announced its determination to increase the birthrate. We will probably never know how Saddam

Hussein's government envisioned keeping this promise while increasing the birthrate. Today, because of Iraq's choked economy, a result of the U.S.-led blockade, many women have lost their jobs and abandoned their education, and many more focus all their efforts on searching for enough food and clean water to ensure their families' survival.

The government of the Islamic Republic of Iran did not make promises to improve the status of Iranian women once the war with Iraq was over. The discontent of Iranian women with the mullah-led government still manifests itself on many fronts: their opposition to the law of hijab; their fight against the exclusion of women from certain university majors; their struggle against Islamic laws considered to be misogynist, such as the laws permitting polygyny, the legal age of marriage for girls to be nine, and forced marriage. Recent reports estimate that even if couples practice birth control and have no more than two children, Iran will face a population explosion of thirty-five to forty million more people in the next twenty to twenty-five years.[54] Under these circumstances, we may be justified to conclude that the economic future of Iranian women looks bleak.

Whether or not joining the Mujahedin-e Khalq is a viable alternative to living in Iran has yet to be proven. The women of the NLA seem to have equal access to power within the party, although one could argue that Miryam Rajavi's power stems from her marriage to Masud Rajavi. But these women live in an artificial socioeconomic environment: they are ready at all times to do battle, they live communally, they receive no pay, and they have taken a vow to remain celibate until Iran is freed.[55] Judging by the number of their troops as compared to those of the Islamic Republic of Iran, it is doubtful that the Mujahedin-e Khalq will succeed in its ambitions. An amnesty granted by the Islamic Republic of Iran would lead the women of the NLA back into the fold of a society that has learned to see them as traitors, as collaborators with the enemy Iraq.

6 Literary Dynamics of the Veil

From Iraq to India

As we have explored in the previous five chapters, the veil has been exploited by advertisers of Western products in the United States and in Saudi Arabia, by publishers of Western erotica, by filmmakers in the East and the West, by Iranian politicians and clergy, and by militaries and militias in countries such as the United Arab Emirates, Iran, and Iraq. The focus of this chapter is the dynamics of the veil in the writings of poets and authors from Iraq, India, Uzbekistan, and Iran: poems by the Iraqi author al-Hajj 'Abd al-Hussayn al-Azri; a short story by the Indian writer Yashpal; the lyrics of an Uzbeki song; the poems of the Iranian authors Iraj Mirza, Mirzadeh 'Eshqi, Nezam Vafa, Parvin E'tesami, Forugh Farrokhzad, and Ayatollah Khomeini; and the work of the Urdu poet Asadullah Khan Ghalib from Agra, India. These selections are not meant to represent national literatures, nor to be inclusive of all works that poeticize the veil. The selected writings are intended to present a cross section of the great diversity of works that address the veil or employ the veil as metaphor, metonym, or synecdoche. The overrepresentation of Iranian works reflects the great interest of Iranian poets in issues associated with veiling and unveiling.

The semantics of the veil can be divided into two main categories: those works that endorse the veil and those works that reject it. To the first category belong those writers who allot moral value to the veil. The second category comprises those authors who reject the veil, describing it as restraint, as cage, and as prison. As we shall see, the second category embraces several subcategories. For example, while in their poems both Parvin E'tesami and the Ayatollah Khomeini reject the veil, the reasons for their condemnation are dramatically different.

Voices of Endorsement

The Poetry of al-Hajj ʿAbd al-Hussayn al-Azri

The Iraqi poet al-Hajj ʿAbd al-Hussayn al-Azri (1880–1954) was one of the most ardent supporters of the veil. In his collection of poems titled *Diwan al-Hajj ʿAbd al-Hussayn al-Azri,* al-Azri expounds why he considers it necessary for Muslim women to veil.[1] Al-Azri's poetry is anchored in the context of the major sociopolitical upheavals of his time. The poet was born when the area of today's Iraq still belonged to the Ottoman Empire. In 1869, the reform-minded Midhat Pasha became governor of Baghdad, al-Azri's place of birth. Midhat wanted to modernize Iraq on the Western model and introduced social and legal reforms, under the auspices of the *tanzimat* movement. In his poetry, al-Azri complains about the modernizing reforms that the Ottoman administration imposed on Iraq. In 1908, a new ruling clique, the Young Turks (Turkia Al-Fata), took power in Istanbul. They aggressively pursued a "Turkification" and "centralization" policy that alienated many Iraqi intellectuals, among them al-Azri, who expresses his alienation in his poetry.

During World War I, Turkey became a German ally, and its empire collapsed when British forces invaded Mesopotamia in 1917 and occupied Baghdad. The country became a British mandate. Local unrest (*thawra*) resulted in an Iraqi uprising in 1920, and after costly attempts to quell it, the British government decided to draw up a new plan for the state of Iraq and to lay out an institutional framework for Iraqi government and politics.

The British supported tribal sheiks over the growing, urban-based nationalist movement and resorted to military force when British interests were threatened. Al-Azri comments on "the whip of the foreigner" in one of his poems.[2]

Ja'far Khalili writes in his introduction to the *Diwan* that al-Azri was one of the strongest opponents of unveiling.[3] According to Khalili, al-Azri also took a stand against those who wrote about the emancipation and liberation of women by means of unveiling; among those was the Egyptian Qasim Amin.[4] Al-Azri's attitude toward unveiling reflects his resentment of the tyranny of the Ottoman administration that tried to enforce Western-oriented reforms and his hatred of British imperialism. The poet saw unveiling as an act foreign to Islamic tradition and practice. He was alienated by the great changes that occurred during his lifetime, and he projected this alienation onto the veil. In his poetry, he expresses his fear for the honor of a society that allowed its women to unveil.

In the following line we can sense al-Azri's concern for those young Iraqi women who chose to join the ranks of unveiled women (*sufur*): "In the forest of lust what is a meek lamb to do if it encounters a wolf?"[5] Al-Azri advises the woman who removes her *hijab* to safeguard her beauty with shame: "If you are met by the recklessness of a young man, then act like a shell that protects the core, don't gaze in all directions. If you are asked a question, give a polite and short answer. As for banter [with men] there are boundaries. Be careful not to cross those boundaries! . . . Withstand the weight of piercing eyes, and pretend that those piercing eyes are not there!"[6] Al-Azri tells women, especially beautiful women, that if they choose to unveil, they have to be sure not to draw unnecessary attention to their person. They need to protect their body, their core, with a shell of dismissals and rebuffs. The poet advises the woman who decides to unveil to seek "symbolic shelter." He asks her to restrict her expression of emotions. She is to avoid direct eye contact, laughing or smiling in an unrestrained manner, carrying on casual or informal conversations, and speaking in a loud voice. If we put his advice for unveiled women in the context of his notion of sexual dynamics, we may wonder how a "meek lamb" can prevent a wolf from ravishing her just by ignoring him or by giving him short and polite answers.

Al-Azri insists on the control of human sexuality: "If human sexual desires are not controlled by moral consciousness, then what would control them? In effect, sexual desires would lead to immoral conduct. Controlling human sexuality is an accepted virtue and valuable advice. No one should ignore its value for respected women, especially if they are beautiful. Only in observing this advice will a woman gain respect from a man."[7] The poet puts the responsibility for controlling human sexuality squarely on women, especially beautiful women: if the wolf ravishes the meek lamb, it is the fault of the meek lamb that did not protect itself properly. Al-Azri's attitude suggests a blame-the-victim mentality. What is conspicuous in this poem is its ambiguity. It does not make it clear if the respectable woman, especially if she is beautiful, should control her own sexual desires or those of her male pursuers. Does the veil protect her from the sexual desires of men or from her own? This poem shows that al-Azri's opposition to unveiling is only partly a reaction to profound sociopolitical changes in Iraq. His attitude also stems from his concept of sexual dynamics. In al-Azri's *Weltanschauung,* the veil protects the meek lamb from the clutches of the wolf. Furthermore, al-Azri allots women a passive as well as an active role in sexual dynamics.[8] Although he uses the metonym of "meek lamb" for woman, he sees woman as a temptress when he advises her to control her sexual desires. The poet illustrates his ambiguity toward female sexuality in a poem titled *Al-hijab* (The veil). Here he addresses the veiled women of Baghdad:

You respected veiled ladies of Baghdad don't be tempted by the
    current of modernization.
And also don't be tempted or cheated by the imagination of poets,
    since this is the tool of their trade.
They claimed that your only cure is to be unveiled [sufur].
They don't understand that the source of all evil is the act of un-
    veiling.
Don't they realize that a young woman by her nature is like water
    that can't be without a container?
The beauty of a young woman is in her shame.
The beauty of shame is that which is clothed with shame.
Who can guarantee the safety of these unveiled young women from
    thoughts of impudence?
Who can stop a young man in full bloom from deceiving every
    beautiful virgin?

The veil is not an obstacle for a young woman to get an education,
   since knowledge is not dependent upon clothing.
Couldn't young women be educated without showing off in their
   clothes?
Couldn't they be educated without roaming unveiled among men,
   swaying their hips and breasts?
As if the betterment of a young woman were impossible unless she
   were unveiled!
As if her education were impossible unless she were displayed on a
   stage.[9]
As if this stage couldn't be run without displayed women.[10]
It is better to show on this stage the virtues rather than singing and
   dancing women.[11]
Be careful about your situation, don't try to be a pioneer!

Al-Azri further explains that

the Qur'an ordered the hijab and didn't ask Muslims to display virgins.
Why does the *ulema* interpret things which are obvious, whose aim
   is clear?
Why are you afraid of a cover which protects you from evil
   thoughts and evil hearts?
Why are you afraid of a veil that protects a woman's body and skin?
If you were to ask a man who is in the company of a lady to be
   honest, will he tell you that there is anything but lust and temp-
   tation in his heart?
Educate young women, increase the level of their morality so they
   will be good mothers.
Before you unveil them test their morality.
Morality is something scarce.
Why don't you put to the test the strong, if you are sure of the vir-
   tue of the weak?[12]

Al-Azri tells women to veil, because the veil protects the body. The veil
saves young women from thoughts of impudence. It stops a young man
whose heart is full of lust and temptation from deceiving beautiful virgins.
In these lines, al-Azri advocates veiling as protection for women. However,

in other lines, al-Azri supports veiling as protection against women. He is concerned that women will roam unveiled among men, swaying their hips and breasts. Implicit in his call for increasing the level of woman's morality before she is allowed to unveil is the misogynist stance that women are inherently immoral. In this poem, woman embodies the paradox of seduced temptress. American erotica that exploits the veil, as we have seen in chapter 2, presents similar versions of this paradox when it pictures the "virginal whore" and the "submissive dominatrix."

Al-Azri's opponent on the issue of veiling, Qasim Amin, elaborates on the paradox of the seduced temptress when he asks who is protected by female seclusion: "If what men fear is that women might succumb to their masculine attraction, why did they not institute veils for themselves? Did men think that their ability to fight temptation was weaker than women's? Are men considered less able than women to control themselves and resist their sexual impulses? Preventing women from showing themselves unveiled expresses men's fear of losing control over their minds, falling prey to *fitna* whenever they are confronted with a non-veiled woman."[13] Qasim Amin reverses al-Azri's binary oppositions of seducer/seduced, hunter/hunted, and strong/weak; he makes women the seducers, the hunters, and the strong. He concludes, although jokingly, that if men are the weaker sex, it is they who need protection. According to Qasim Amin, woman's veil protects man from woman. It prevents man from losing control when looking at the face and body of a woman.

Regardless of the ambiguity with which al-Azri describes the protective value of the veil, as woman's protection from man or man's protection from woman, he clearly and firmly puts woman in charge of governing human sexuality. She is responsible for her own sexual desires as well as the sexual desires she arouses in men. The only tool available to her to accomplish the great task of controlling human sexuality is her veil. Should she choose to unveil, her shame is her only defense against her sexual impulses and those of men.

A Short Story by Yashpal

The use of the veil for the prevention of social chaos, particularly in the realm of sexual matters, was one of al-Azri's pivotal concerns. This concern for social order is also central to Hindu societies. Whereas Muslims use the veil and seclusion to safeguard their women from men outside the family, Hindus use the same devices to enforce women's subordination to their in-laws and to order the domain of family and kinship. Thus, as Sylvia Vatuk explains in her article "Purdah Revisited," there are two different purdah systems in South Asia,[14] "one that deals with the relationships of women with outsiders (the Muslim system) and the other which controls women inside the family and kindred (the Hindu system)."[15] Vatuk points out that in South Asia the semantics of "purdah" are complex: the term "does not carry the same semantic content everywhere in South Asia, and local vo-cabularies typically have a variety of words to refer to different aspects of the complex behavior which we tend to lump together under the term 'purdah.'"[16] It is with this caveat in mind that I want to approach a short story titled "Purdah" by the Indian writer Yashpal (1903–76).

Yashpal was born in Firozpur, Punjab. His family was poor, because he, his mother, and his brother had to live on the meager wages his mother earned in the teaching profession. In his autobiography, Yashpal mentions that his fellow students treated him with contempt on account of his pov-erty. He explains that although this had made a profound impression on his mind, he didn't consider himself responsible for the "crime" of his pov-erty.[17] The theme of poverty as "crime" permeates many of his short sto-ries.

Respect and honor are also dominant themes in his writings. Yashpal fought constantly to gain respect and honor for his compatriots. He joined the Hindustan Socialist Republican Army (HSRA or HSPS), which tried to liberate the Punjab from the British yoke, by force if necessary. He explains that he loathed and resented the British, who had conquered, crushed, and enslaved India, and he describes the humiliation and degradation Indians had to endure at the hand of the British. He admits that he felt degraded just watching the common people salute the English and grovel before them. By joining the HSRA, Yashpal was able to challenge the imperious English ways.[18] For his revolutionary activities, Yashpal was sentenced by the British in 1932 to fourteen years at hard labor. During the years of his imprisonment, India moved toward self-government. In 1937, congress declared that all political prisoners would be released without discrimina-tion. Yashpal was released from jail in 1938 at the age of thirty-five. After his release, he stayed out of politics and instead wrote stories, essays, and more than fifty novels. With his writing he tried to achieve what he had once attempted to attain through revolutionary activity—a better life for India's poor and downtrodden.

The association of poverty with dishonor constitutes the leitmotif in Yashpal's short story "Purdah," written in Hindi like most of his work.[19] Here he depicts the life of a destitute Hindu family that lives at the mercy of a wealthy landlord. Chaudhry Peerbuksh owes the landlord money but is unable to pay, because he is just barely making ends meet with his small salary and a large and growing family. His family does not get enough food, because Chaudhry needs to save enough money to repay his debt, which is steadily increasing because of accrued interest. Each month, when the landlord is due to call on Chaudhry to pay, he agonizes over excuses to explain why he is again unable to meet his financial obligations. Finally, he concludes that his best approach may be to avoid the landlord altogether. Thus, every time the landlord is due to arrive, Chaudhry leaves his house to wander aimlessly in the market. The landlord becomes frustrated after he is told time and time again by Chaudhry's women (his wife and older daughters) to come back later because Chaudhry is not at home. Finally, the landlord demands his money from the women. Again they tell him that he must come back when Chaudhry is at home. Completely out of patience, the landlord rips the purdah off the doorway of the house, behind which Chaudhry's wife and children are hiding. To his surprise, he sees Chaudhry's family dressed in rags. The women are very embarrassed by the intruder's gaze and quickly try to cover their bodies with their hands and pieces of the torn purdah; their clothes were inadequate to shield them from his gaze. The landlord leaves saddened and ashamed. Chaudhry cannot bring himself to put up the purdah again because the respect for his family, which was symbolized by the purdah, has now been forever lost.[20]

In this short story, Yashpal criticizes the society that is unable to take care of its people, especially those who are educated. Chaudhry is the most educated member of the family, but his salary is so small that he is unable to take care of his wife and children. In addition, this story reveals the material inequality that exists not only between members of society as a whole but also between members of one and the same family. It shows the great disparity in the material conditions of life experienced by Chaudhry on one hand and his wife and children on the other. Since the landlord cannot tell by looking at Chaudhry how poor he is, we may conclude that Chaudhry is not wearing rags like the rest of his family. The purdah works to the detriment of Chaudhry's wife and children because it hides their destitution. It renders their needs invisible to the eyes of society. While the purdah protects Chaudhry's honor, it buries his family in poverty.

Chaudhry and his family have lost respect because the landlord saw the rags worn by Chaudhry's wife and children. He has become a witness to Chaudhry's inability to provide for his family. His failure to support his family is portrayed as shameful. Furthermore, his shame is also that of his wife and children. This short story presents a telling example of an attitude that shames the poor for their predicament by making the poor responsible for the "crime" of poverty. The purdah protects not only the honor of Chaudhry and his family but also the socioeconomic status quo. Changes that would improve the situation of women and children are unlikely to be effected when poverty is invisible.

Both al-Azri and Yashpal portray the protective property of the veil. Al-Azri praises the veil as a bulwark against social chaos caused by human sexual urges. He champions veiling because it upholds patriarchy with its lopsided gender-based sexual restrictions. According to Yashpal, the veil protects the honor of the poor and the economic interests of the wealthy. Without the veil, poverty becomes visible and the socioeconomic status quo is threatened. In this short story, the two objectives that mattered most to Yashpal seem to clash: Yashpal had dedicated his life to improve the situation of the poor and downtrodden, and to gain respect and honor for his compatriots. The plight of the poor, however, cannot be improved if they are respected but hidden behind the purdah. The purdah protects the honor of Chaudhry but aggravates the poverty of his wife and children. It protects patriarchy with its lopsided gender-based distribution of wealth. In the writings of both al-Azri and Yashpal, therefore, the veil protects women much less than it does the patriarchal status quo.

Voices of Rejection

The Parandja in an Uzbeki Song

The literary flexibility of the veil is demonstrated in an Uzbeki poem that provides the lyrics of an Uzbeki song. Here the parandja, a heavy head-to-ankle veil, is depicted as a symbol of oppression. It is not primarily a symbol of "backwardness," as Iran's Reza Shah had claimed in his unveiling orders. We saw in chapter 4 that Reza Shah was not interested in improving the status of the Iranian woman. He wanted to show, mainly to the West, that his country had the potential to become a modern state. In order to fathom how and why the Soviet propaganda machine politicized the veil as a symbol of women's oppression, we need to look briefly at the history of Uzbekistan.

The territory of modern-day Uzbekistan and its neighboring countries in Central Asia has seen many empires rise and fall. The Sogdians, the Macedonians, the Huns, the Mongolians, the Seljuks, the Timurids, and the Khanates of Samarkand, Bukhara, Khiva, and Khorezm all held sway here at one time or another. Samarkand and Bukhara lay astride the Silk Road from China to the West, the most valuable trading route of its day. The riches that were transported along this route were used to build magnificent mosques and *madrasas*. In the fourteenth century, Timur the Lame built new cities throughout the empire, which stretched from Moscow and Baghdad to Ankara in the west. After Timur's death, the empire crumbled, and Central Asia was split into warring Khanates. Russia had its eyes on these territories from the time that Peter the Great sent his first military mission to Khiva in 1717. In the 1930s, Moscow finally took control.

The history of Central Asia under Soviet rule is one of exploitation. Uzbekistan was used, as it had been under the czars, as a place of internal exile. Fearing the power of ethnic minorities, Stalin relocated thousands of people into Uzbekistan and the surrounding republics. Chechens, Germans, Koreans, Meshketi Turks, and Tatars were transported in cattle cars to Uzbekistan. Stalin wanted to weaken native populations by diluting them. Another manifestation of the Soviet strategy to weaken Uzbekistan was the creation of an Uzbeki economy that was totally dependent on Moscow. For example, Uzbekistan was turned into a cotton monoculture, and the cotton it produced was processed in Russia and the Ukraine. Still another aspect of this Soviet strategy, one that is most relevant to the topic of the veil, was Moscow's attempt to "sovietize" Central Asia by destroying traditional systems of belief and behavior likely to evoke a national identity. Islam was a major binding force among the people of Central Asia and stood in the way of "sovietization." Moscow's attack on Islam utilized slogans such as, "Islam is the opiate of the toiling masses, distracting them from the social struggle against the exploiting parasites," and "it [Islam] is an anti-scientific creed projecting the dream of paradise into an imaginary other world while Marxism is building a paradise on this earth."[21]

The veil was the most conspicuous sign of Islamic culture in Uzbekistan. Moscow's strategy of unveiling Uzbeki women in order to gain greater control over Uzbekistan has many parallels with France's strategy of unveiling Algerian women in order to conquer Algeria.[22] Both the French and the Soviets equated the veil with Islam and Islam with woman's oppression. Therefore, according to their view, women who discard the veil discard oppression. Once Uzbeki women were unveiled, all of Uzbeki society was thought to abandon the oppression believed to be inherent in Islam. Frantz Fanon summarizes this argument succinctly when he explains that France sought "to win over the women and the rest will follow."[23]

The Soviet unveiling campaign was called *khundjum*. The Uzbeki author Marfua Tokhtakhodzhaera quotes Zumrad Inusova, a woman who described the effect of khundjum on her own family:

> Even though Grandmother discarded the parandja, she wore a large white scarf with which she hid her face whenever she met [strange] men. But mother on the other hand only wore a parandja at her marriage, as was expected of a bride. . . . Till the end of her life Grandmother did not recognize Soviet rule. She considered it anti-Islam when we, her granddaughters, recited poems about Lenin and the Party and what we had been taught at school. So she told us about the Qur'an, the prophet, and the *ahadith*.[24]

During the khundjum campaign, the Soviet propaganda machine employed many slogans that targeted women's desire to improve their situation such as "without the active involvement of women themselves the struggle for their emancipation will be slowed down." Women were told that "in the land of the Soviets there is no place for oppression, slavery, and violence against women!"[25]

The khundjum movement eliminated the segregation of the sexes that is so prevalent in Muslim societies. Many Muslim men considered it sinful for their women to discard the parandja. They did not agree with communist ideals but were forced to send their wives and daughters to the communist women's meetings in the villages. Many of the women who were not comfortable with the idea of unveiling nevertheless stopped wearing the parandja, yet they never stepped outside their homes without some sort of a head cover. Among the villagers, unveiled women were considered immodest and indecent. Some unveiled women lost their lives at the hands of their own husbands, brothers, or fathers, for whom male honor was synonymous with female modesty. Muslim men accused women who appeared unveiled in public of being prostitutes. These accusations led to bitterness, misunderstanding, and resentment among the population. The Bolsheviks took over Uzbekistan in 1920, but Uzbeki men put up a fierce seven-year resistance to women's independence and changes in family laws. Eventually, Uzbeki men lost most of their unmitigated power over women. The women benefited greatly from the legal changes. From a Machiavellian point of view, Moscow benefited as well, because it had successfully met its goal of dissolving the traditional cultural bonds among members of a once cohesive Muslim community.

The following poem is a translation of the Uzbeki song mentioned earlier. It shows Moscow's efforts to equate the parandja with woman's oppression.

Inside the parandja
Inside the parandja it is dark, like night.
A parandja is dark, like night.
So as to see light with my own eyes,
I discard the parandja intentionally.
I don't care how much abuse I hear,
let me be battered and bruised—
but unveiled at the meeting.
I shall appear among my fellow villagers,
so as to be born anew,
to be able to see broad daylight.
So that I may shine, like all who work—
I have no other path.[26]

The parandja, which is black, prevents a woman from seeing the light. It engulfs her in darkness. It is the source of her oppression. In order to escape this oppression, a woman needs to discard the veil. The song warns her that it will not be easy to abandon the parandja, since those who do not want her to be liberated will batter and bruise her. It tells her that, if she wants to see the light of day, she needs to defy her fellow villagers. By going unveiled to her meeting (presumably the communist women's meeting), she will show her neighbors that there is only one path to liberation.

The song juxtaposes Soviet ideology and Islam. It exploits the dualism of light and darkness and tells each Uzbeki woman that she has to make a choice between Soviet ideology and Islam, between light and darkness, between freedom and continued oppression. This dualism of light and darkness is an integral part of Zoroastrian cosmology. It may not be far-fetched to assume that the Soviet propagandists borrowed this Zoroastrian dualism intentionally. Before the advent of Islam, Zoroastrianism had flourished in regions and countries close to Uzbekistan: Tajikistan, present-day Afghanistan, Iran, and Kurdistan. The Soviet propaganda machine may have utilized Zoroastrian cosmology as antidote to Islamic ideology.

The reference to "work" bears semantic significance. Women are told they need to unveil in order to "shine" at work. Unless they discard Islamic practice and tradition, Uzbeki women cannot be good Soviet workers. The conceptual interweaving of "light" with "work" completes the list of binary oppositions that structure this song. The veil is associated with the terms that represent the negative components of oppositions such as darkness/light and night/daylight. The opposition bad/good is implicit in terms such as "battered," "abused," and "bruised" versus "shine" and "born anew."

The khundjum movement was successful insofar as unveiling was concerned. Did the Soviet system liberate women? Did the woman who discarded her veil discard oppression? Women received equal rights and equal pay but lived in a system that exploited all its workers. Women now had to work hard outside the home to make the new Soviet industries and farms function, while at the same time they had to continue to do their traditional work inside the house. Many would argue that this is not liberation and that the Uzbeki woman had exchanged one oppressor for another.

Independence was thrust upon Uzbekistan after the disintegration of the Soviet Union in 1991, but, as of yet, there is little political freedom. Political parties are banned, including the Islamic Renaissance Party (IRP), which has made considerable headway in other former Soviet Central Asian republics. In 1996, a new law was passed that permitted the formation of political parties if they had no ethnic or religious basis. Has national independence improved the situation of the Uzbeki woman? Uzbekistan continues to be a secular country, although Muslim fundamentalism has gained in popularity in recent years. In her book *In Search of Islamic Feminism*, Elizabeth Warnock Fernea describes her experiences in and impressions of Uzbekistan.[27] She writes that she had not seen women wearing the parandja. Fernea's interviewees say that women receive equal pay for equal work and have access to free child care. The interviewee Marfua Tokhta-khodzhaera explains that Uzbeki women have three problems: poverty, ignorance, and too many children.[28] Other interviewees agree, saying that especially in the villages women are often malnourished and that, because contraceptives are not available, women have many abortions and many children.

Since the Soviets' use of the veil as a wedge issue to destroy the traditional, cohesive Islamic culture succeeded, women's lives have improved in some ways while remaining fairly miserable in others. For example, they receive equal pay for equal work but their workload has doubled. They have access to free child care but not to contraceptives. Both the Soviets and Iran's Reza Shah were successful in abolishing the veil but unsuccessful in improving the plight of women—an issue that likely was not even on their respective agendas.

The Poetry of Iraj Mirza

The famous Iranian poet Iraj Mirza (1874–1926) also champions unveiling. But does he reject the veil because he considers it a symbol of women's oppression? Is his poetry truly concerned with the status of the Iranian woman? As we have seen in the case of Uzbekistan, the Soviet unveiling campaign was not aimed primarily at liberating the Uzbeki woman from the clutches of Islam. Its aim was to destroy the traditional power structure of Muslim society, following the Machiavellian maxim of *divide et impera*. In other words, the unveiling campaign was aimed primarily at taking power away from Uzbeki men.

Iraj Mirza lived during Iran's constitutional revolutionary period (1905–11). His father was Sadr al-Shu'ara' Ghulam Hussayn Mirza, the grandson of Fath-Ali Shah, the Qajar monarch. Along with his regular course of training at the College of Arts (Dar al-Fonun) in Tabriz, Iraj Mirza studied logic and philosophy with the great master of his time, Ayatollah Ashtiyani. In addition to French, he studied Arabic, Russian, and Turkish. His style of poetry is unique in terms of its simplicity and its charm for the ordinary people. Iraj Mirza is among the class of poets known as satire poets. Because of the political oppression in Iran, he, like many other writers of his day, chose the medium of poetry to convey his unhappiness and to get his messages across. Ehsan Yarshater explains that "social satire, distinct from invective, has had limited scope in Persia, no doubt largely because of the oppressiveness of autocratic rulers and fanaticism of the religious establishment."[29]

Iraj Mirza is known as a satirist of high standing. He is also known for the simplicity of his poetic diction. In his verses, he uses the actual words of everyday speech and includes many colorful colloquial idioms. His son Khosrow Iraj explains that his father's tendency to use simple straightforward language may represent a reaction against the pompous diction of the classicists.[30] Yarshater explains that Iraj Mirza "normally focuses his satire on situational incongruity in order to reveal the weaknesses and ills of a society stricken with ignorance, superstition, and corrupt religious and secular leadership."[31]

The following is a translation of one of Iraj Mirza's poems, titled *Tasfire Zan* (Image of a woman):

On the door of a traveler's inn
A woman's face was drawn in ink

From a reliable source of news
The turban-wearers heard the news

"Woe to our faith," they said
"People saw a woman's face unveiled"

From inside the mosque in haste
To the front of the guesthouse they raced

Faith and order at the speed of light
Were disappearing when the believers arrived

One brought water, another dirt
With a veil of mud they covered the face

Honor, scarce gone with the wind
With a few fistfuls of mud was saved

Religious laws thus saved from danger
They returned to their homes to rest

With a careless mistake, the savage crowd
Like a roaring lion was jumping about

With her face unveiled, completely bare
Her chastity they tore apart

Her beautiful, alluring lips
Like a sugar candy they sucked and sucked

All of them, the men in town
To the sea of sin were drawn

The doors of paradise stood shut
The whole lot was hellward bound

The day of Judgment was at hand
Even the horn was blown at once

Birds from their nests, beasts from their lairs,
Even the stars in the sky went wild

Thus, before creator and created
The religious scholars remained exonerated

With saviors such as this bunch
Why are people still so cynical?[32]

Iraj Mirza mocks the turban-wearers (the clergy) and their shallow religious attitudes. He shows how those with religious authority had shaped the mentality of people to such an extreme and bizarre point that just the image of an unveiled woman is sufficient to create chaos in the city. In the verse, "With her face unveiled, completely bare, Her chastity they tore apart," the poet ridicules the turban-wearers for equating the veil with chastity. He makes fun of "all of them, the men in town" for losing their minds when confronted with the drawing of the face of an unveiled woman. Moreover, he derides the turban-wearers for covering her with a mud veil and thereby opening again the doors of paradise, which had stood shut for all the male residents of the town. The turban-wearers saved the men from going to hell.

What is striking in this poem is its androcentricity: all the men of the town are about to commit sin and are thus hellward bound; the turban-wearers saved them by rescuing religious laws. In this poem, woman is absent; only her picture, most probably drawn by a man, is present. The veil of mud serves to stem the sexual desires of the men of the town and to restore their honor. Here we have a male poet who uses the veil to criticize clerics, the religious laws enforced by these clerics, and the men who follow these clerics and their laws. In *Veils and Words: The Emerging Voices of Iranian Women Writers,* Farzaneh Milani uses this poem to illustrate her belief that constitutional revolutionary intellectuals such as Iraj Mirza blamed religious clerics solely for perpetuating the veil. Milani explains that these intellectuals "focused attention on the merely physical existence and uses of the veil" and "ignored or denied its cultural, social, and psychological complexity, its power to express and organize male/female relationships."[33] Milani's interpretation shows that Iraj Mirza does not concern himself with the oppression of women when he condemns the veil. According to him, the veil, as required by religious authorities, is indeed a symbol of oppression, but it is the oppression of those who obey the absurd dictates of the clergy.

One of his poems, titled "Dastane Zane Ba Hejab" (The story of the veiled woman), which is part of a 515-line work titled *Arefnameh,* represents another example of androcentric poetry.[34] Since this narrative poem spans more than one hundred verses, I have chosen to excerpt those lines that are most pertinent to our discussion of the semantics of the veil. Iraj Mirza's narrator explains the absurdity of the veil to his male compatriots by telling them about a woman who is more concerned about her veil than her virtue:

> Let me tell you a story,
> so you will understand the chador's effect on society.
> When I was young and simple,
> I was standing in the doorway [of my house].
> A woman passed by
> and I felt sexually excited.
> I saw her double chin[35] peeking through her *picheh.*[36]
> I saw a little part of her chin and lips;
> these seemed like a beautiful moon
> peeking through dark clouds.
> I went to her and greeted her.
> I told her that I have a message for her.
> The angel whom I faced was hesitant,
> wondering who is the messenger and who is the sender of the message.

The next few lines explain how the narrator persuaded the woman to come to his room and elaborate on the ruses he utilizes in his effort to seduce her:

> I softly told her, "Remove this picheh from your face!"
> Why is it that you must hide your face from me?
> Am I a cat and you a mouse?
> You and I both are human, we both are equal in creation:
> Say, hear, see, stand up, and sit down.
> You are just like me, my sweet love.
> The purpose of you being created with such beauty
> was for us to enjoy with our eyes.
> Women bring life to gardens.
> The beauty of a flower is not going to be less,
> if a poor bird looks at it.

Finally, the woman, who is still waiting for him to give her the message, becomes angry:

> Go to hell, I am not a whore
> that I can be without my veil in the presence of forbidden men.
> The aim of this whole thing was to see me unveiled?
> Shame on you!
> I would not have been blessed with a husband
> if I had shown my face to anyone except him.
> Get lost! You are so daring to talk to me like this.
> My brother-in-law longed to see my face,
> my husband did not allow it.
> I am not one of those women of Tehran.[37]
> I am not among those with whom you are familiar.
> Go and set this trap for the other birds [women].
> Offer such advice to your own sister and mother.
> When you realize that you can't reach the nest of the *angha*,[38]
> settle for the homely chicken.
> If you cut me into pieces,
> the veil will not be removed from my face.
> Don't you have any shame?
> Why is it that you are so stubborn?
> What nonsense are you talking about?
> Are you crazy? I think you are drunk.

What a trap have I fallen in today?
Things have changed in our time.
No sign of Islam is left [in our society].
Don't you know that staring is a sin?
We are so close to our graves,[39]
and you are telling me that Judgment Day is nothing but chaos?
And, what mullahs are saying is a lie?
Are you telling me that all the *mujtahids* are talking nonsense?[40]
Spend one day at the pulpit [in the mosque]!
Listen to the lecture of a cleric!
The first night of the grave when you are naked,
Nakir and Munkar will be visiting you.[41]
They will be beating your brain,
you will "wet" your own tomb stone.

After her tirade, the narrator explains how he apologized for his mistakes and continued in his quest to seduce her:

I did not mention the word *hijab,*
but started to squeeze her elbow slowly.
I was almost sure this time that, because of my behavior,
she will be roaring like a lioness,
she will be attacking me,
hitting me, and throwing me on the ground.
All the neighbors will be coming to the roof top [to see what is
    happening].
I should get ready to get hit by her shoes.
And, my body will be purple from her blows.
To my great surprise, I saw that beautiful moon face.
She is cursing, but not too much.
She showed not anger, but ardor.
She used a loud voice, but kindly.
All her outraged scolding tongue
was changed to "be polite, be wise."
All her heavy cursing was changed to
"Young man sit calmly!"
When I saw this, I told myself:
"Good, my path is open."

I reached for that beautiful woman
just like a mullah devouring a bowl of rice or a believer a dish of
   halva.[42]
I tossed her on the rug like a rose.
I rushed to her.
Both her hands were clutching her picheh,
while both my hands were clutching her muscles.
I told her, "Cover your face well,
so I can do my work under the veil."
With much effort I managed to spread her legs apart.
I opened up the doors of heaven to myself.

After the narrator describes her genitals and the graphic details of intercourse, which was made possible by applying force and blows, he assures us
that, during the sexual act, the woman's main concern was holding her veil
in place:

Since her face was the repository of innocence and purity,
she did not expose it throughout.
Her picheh was held in place with both her hands,
so nothing was visible.
After I tasted my sweet candy,
she left and disappeared into the street.

In the next lines, the narrator explains the moral of his poem:

The veil of an ignorant woman is like this.
The covered, shy woman is like this.
She did not mind engaging herself in intercourse,
but she minded having her face unveiled.
It is true that honor and shame are only in the eyes [visible on the
   surface].
When you close your eyes [not seeing the honor and shame], the
   rest is nonsense.
If they teach women well, inform her about morality.
She will be on top [with her knowledge she comes first].
If she has learned only the [surface] meaning of coverage,
it is much better for her to remain unveiled.
They [unveiled women] will be in public mingling with men and

improving their skills.

When a woman gets training in education,

she can devote her soul and spirit to see the light [of God].

In doing that [soul searching], she will never be tempted by any
trick and lose her purity.

Even if she falls in the sea, she will not be wet [she will be saved
from temptation in any situation].

She will shine like the sun shines on earth [she can influence every-
one].

Yet she herself will be protected from all [harmful] influences.[43]

The moral of this poem is that women are kept in such ignorance that they think veiling is synonymous with possessing honor. They do not know the true meaning of chastity, purity, and morality. According to the poet, the veil serves only to preserve women's lack of ethical awareness. The woman who must do without the coverage of the veil is forced to learn the real meaning of morality and shame. This poem criticizes religious clerics who teach that the veil itself embodies honor and shame and who never consider the woman under the veil. Iraj Mirza ridicules religious authorities by presenting the example of a properly veiled but shameless woman.

One may also read this poem as a tale of rape and an exercise in misogyny: the narrator sets out to seduce a beautiful woman. He sees woman as object to be used for his pleasure when he states that "the purpose of you being created with such beauty was for us to enjoy with our eyes." His intentions are clear from the very beginning: he was thinking of having sex with her. The narrator then lies to her and dupes her into coming to his house. At first he urges her verbally to have sex with him, but when he realizes that she will not comply willingly, he manages "with much effort" to force her legs open. The narrator then claims that the woman did not mind engaging in intercourse, but that she did mind having her face unveiled. As long as she stays veiled, she thinks that she retains her honor, according to the narrator. In short, the narrator lures the woman into his house, rapes her, and then blames her for the rape.

What is the meaning of the veil in this poem? According to the first interpretation of the poem, the veil symbolizes woman's ignorance as well as her lack of shame and honor. Once unveiled, woman has to be educated in matters of morality and shame. Although Iraj Mirza advocates unveiling and his contemporary al-Azri champions veiling, they agree that the unveiled woman has need of instruction in ethical behavior, for, as al-Azri claims, "morality is something scarce." There is a striking difference between the approaches these two poets take to the issue of unveiling. While al-Azri addresses women directly, Iraj Mirza appeals only to his male compatriots, thus demonstrating that he did not allot women an active role in the whole debate over unveiling. We may argue that Iraj Mirza exploited the issue of the veil to criticize the politics of the powerful clergy without calling down their wrath on his person. Reza Baraheni has pointed out that the social atmosphere in Iran is totally dominated by males and that women are often pawns in men's power games.[44] Baraheni's assessment also applies to Iraj Mirza's poetry: the veil was used as a pawn in Iraj Mirza's narrative power game with the clergy.

According to the second interpretation, the issue of unveiling becomes a pretense for rape and literary exhibitionism. The poet's didactic quest to discover if a veiled woman has honor turns into the narrator's rape of the veiled woman. When the narrator tells the woman to cover her face well, so he can do his work under the veil, the poet endows the veil with aphrodisiac powers. When the narrator describes the rape in graphic details, the poet rivets the attention of his male readers by appealing to their libidos.[45] When the narrator claims that the woman uses the veil to hide her immoral nature, the poet relinquishes his literary responsibility for the rape. It may not be too reckless a thought that Iraj Mirza exploited the issue of unveiling to write a pornographic tale of rape.

The Poetry of Mirzadeh 'Eshqi

Mirzadeh 'Eshqi (1894–1924), a contemporary of Iraj Mirza and a product of the constitutional revolutionary period (1905–11), also challenged the Iranian autocracy by calling for an end to social and political inequality. In order to silence him, the dictatorial regime killed him.[46] Like Iraj Mirza, he used women and the veil to express his discontent with the social, political, and religious status quo of his time:

> What are these unbecoming cloaks and veils?
> They are shrouds for the dead, not for those alive
> I say: "Death to those who bury women alive"
> If a few poets add their voices to mine
> A murmur of discontent will start
> With it women will unveil

They'll throw off their cloak of shame, be proud
Joy will return to lives
Otherwise, as long as women are in shrouds
Half the nation is not alive.[47]

Milani explains that during the constitutional revolutionary period (1905–11), Iran's poets and writers "attributed Iran's 'backwardness,' to use the prevalent term of the day, to women's condition and especially to their 'imprisonment' in veils."[48] To be sure, 'Eshqi makes a powerful argument for unveiling when he describes the veil as a "shroud" that buries women alive. But it is a demagogic and myopic argument, for, as Reza Shah's anti-veil offensive in 1936 later proved, discarding the veil ultimately amounted to no more than discarding a piece of cloth. It did not change the inferior status of the Iranian woman. In fact, it worked against her, placing her between the demands of the clergy and the traditional husband or father and the orders of Reza Shah. Unlike Iraj Mirza however, 'Eshqi does not just ridicule religious authorities: he calls for the death of those who bury women alive. He also urges other poets to support him in his quest to abolish the veil. Both 'Eshqi and Iraj Mirza address the male literary elite of Iran and not the Iranian woman who was, with few exceptions, illiterate.

A Poem by Nezam Vafa

The Iranian poet Nezam Vafa (1887–1964), a contemporary of Iraj Mirza and 'Eshqi, was also influenced by events of the constitutional revolutionary period (1905–1911). Vafa taught in Tehran and for a brief period had a post with the Ministry of Education. He published a magazine called *Vafa* (Faith), in which he introduced his own poetry and literary works. This poet, who is considered a liberal nationalist, also tried to come to terms with the issue of unveiling. In 1945, ten years after Reza Shah's unveiling order, one of his poems, "Hijab," was published in the magazine *Iran Shahab:*

Hijab
With the arrival of spring, the flower removes its *burqah.*[49]
Oh, beautiful woman, remove the *pardeh* from your face.[50]

Reveal your face, no one will lustfully gaze at you.
I swear by your innocence.

Life is full of beauty and love.
What is the purpose of this segregation except harm?

Enough of this silence, shame, sorrow, and pain!
Speak, listen, be happy, read, and laugh!

A woman who has spent her life under the veil of ignorance,
how can she raise intelligent children?

May God free you from the dark cage of your chador.
Beware, so you don't get trapped again!

The true hijab for a woman is her chastity and education,
not the *chador, niqab, picheh, ruband.*[51]

If you [addressing men] prefer a woman's face to be under the veil,
she will do what is not proper under her veil.

Nezam, don't look for sweet fruit in the cypress tree!
The tree of ignorance and closed minds should be uprooted.[52]

This poem offers sentiments and rationales with regard to unveiling and veiling that we have already encountered in the poems of al-Azri, Iraj Mirza, and 'Eshqi, as well as in the lyrics of the Uzbeki song. Vafa, however, disagrees with al-Azri about the protective function of the veil: while al-Azri warns woman, especially the beautiful woman, that if she discards her veil she will make herself vulnerable to male lust and impudence, Vafa assures the beautiful woman that if she reveals her face, "no one will lustfully gaze" at her. Vafa agrees with al-Azri that an educated woman is a moral and chaste woman. Not surprisingly, when one considers that an Arab proverb lays paradise at the feet of mothers, both al-Azri and Vafa champion woman's education in the name of motherhood: al-Azri argues that the educated woman will be a good mother; Vafa extends the argument further to imply that only the educated woman will raise intelligent children.

Al-Azri claims that hiding a woman behind a veil will protect society from her immoral desires; only when she is unveiled will she have the opportunity to roam among men, "swaying her hips and breasts." Iraj Mirza and Vafa argue that a veiled woman does "what is not proper under her veil." According to them, veiling is conducive to woman's immoral conduct. As we have seen in chapter 2, cartoons in *Playboy* and *Hustler* also exploit the theme of "sex under the veil."

In "Hijab," Vafa employs tropes to describe the disadvantages of veiling that we find in the Uzbeki lyrics and 'Eshqi's poem. When Vafa uses the metaphor of the dark cage of the chador, he echoes the dark/light and night/day dualism of the Uzbeki song: Vafa's flower that "removes its burqah" in spring is "able to see broad daylight" and is "born anew," just as occurs with the woman who discards her veil in the Uzbeki song. The comparison of a woman's life under the veil to life in a dark cage is pugnaciously expressed by 'Eshqi's "[D]eath to those who bury women alive." Both 'Eshqi and Vafa associate veiling with shame, sorrow, and pain and unveiling with joy and happiness. Unlike Iraj Mirza, 'Eshqi, and the author of the lyrics of the Uzbeki song, Vafa seems not to pursue a political agenda here. He expresses genuine concern for the plight of women in Iran, especially when he encourages them to discard their veils in order to "speak, listen, be happy, read, and laugh!" The fact that Vafa addresses women directly also bespeaks his interest in improving the situation of the Iranian woman for her sake alone.

The Poetry of Parvin E'tesami

Thus far we have listened to male voices endorsing or rejecting the veil. This is not mere coincidence, since in patriarchal systems men have appropriated the pen. Women, for the most part, have been the object of their musings. Addressing the masculine history of Iran and the silence of women throughout more than a thousand years of a rich written literary tradition, Milani explains that the genesis of women's literary tradition in Iran coincides with their attempts to unveil.[53] One of the feminine voices that addresses the issue of the veil is that of Parvin E'tesami. She was born in Tabriz in 1907 and attended the American High School for Girls. She was offered an invitation from the newly founded Pahlavi court to become private tutor to the queen. E'tesami declined. Her marriage in 1934 proved disappointing, and she was divorced after two and a half months. She died in 1941 of typhoid fever.[54]

Hamid Dabashi, writing about the legacy of Parvin E'tesami, maintains that there is a common consensus among leading scholars of Persian literary history that E'tesami was "one of the most eminent Persian poets in history and the most accomplished woman poet in the entire classical pantheon of the Iranian literary edifice."[55] E'tesami's accomplishments, especially her advocacy of women's rights, are even more impressive when we consider that her poetry was inspired, judged, and published in a social milieu that was dominated by men: her father, who was also her best friend, was primarily responsible for encouraging her poetic endeavors. Furthermore, her place in society depended on her father. It was mostly male literary critics who judged her poetry. Her father and older brother decided which of her works to publish and when. Her father would not permit the publication of any of her poems for fourteen years, after the publication of her first poems in 1921 until 1935 when her *Divan* was published. Even then, her father did not include a poem titled "The Tree of Hope" in that collection of her work. The literary critic Jalal Matini opines that E'tesami's views concerning women's freedom were so extreme at the time that her father "did not consider it expedient to have her poem 'The Tree of Hope' published in her *Divan,* prior to the decree of unveiling."[56] In this poem, E'tesami does no more than ask, "Why are women deprived of their rights?"[57] E'tesami's older brother had an exclusive monopoly on her *Divan* for nearly four decades before it became public property. Today, E'tesami's poetry must be submitted to the censors of the Islamic Republic of Iran before being reprinted: in the introduction to a recent Persian edition of her *Divan,* the editor Shahram Rajabzadeh refers to and provides page numbers for a poem titled "Zan dar Iran" (Iranian women).[58] This poem is not included in this edition, however, perhaps because it criticizes the chador.[59]

E'tesami's voice decrying women's oppression was clearly heard when, at the age of seventeen, she publicly addressed the plight of Iranian women. During the graduation ceremonies of the American Girls School in 1924, she delivered "an effective speech about the injustice done to Iranian women." In the poem "Zan dar Iran," E'tesami voices her concerns about the condition of women in Iran prior to Reza Shah's unveiling decree:

Iranian Women
Formerly a woman in Iran was almost non-Iranian.
All she did was struggle through dark and distressing days.

Her life she spent in isolation; she died in isolation.
What was she then if not a prisoner?

None ever lived centuries in darkness like her.
None was sacrificed on the altar of hypocrisy like her.

In the courts of justice no witnesses defended her.
To the schools of learning she was not admitted.

All her life her cries for justice remained unheeded.
This oppression occurred publicly; it was no secret.

Many men appeared disguised as her shepherd.
Within each a wolf was hiding instead.

In life's vast arena such was woman's destiny:
to be pushed and shoved into a corner.

The light of knowledge was kept from her eyes.
Her ignorance could not be laid to inferiority or sluggishness.

Could a woman weave with no spindle or thread?
Can anyone be a farmer with nothing to sow or to reap?

The field of knowledge yielded abundant fruit,
but women never had any share in this abundance.

A woman lived in a cage and died in a cage.
The name of this bird in the rose garden was never mentioned.

Imitation is the desert of women's perdition, the pitfall causing her
    troubles.
Clever is that woman who never treads that murky road.

Beauty depends on knowledge; bracelets of emeralds or
Badakhshan rubies do not indicate superiority.

All glamour of painted silks cannot match the simple beauty of a
    tunic.
Honor depends on merit, not on indulgence in vanities.

Shoes and clothes are made worthy by the person who wears them.
One's value does not rise and fall with high and low prices.

Simplicity, purity, and abstinence are the true gems.
Mined gems are not the only brilliant jewels.

What is the use of gold and ornaments if the woman is ignorant?

Gold and jewels will not cover up that blemish.

Only the robe of abstinence can mask one's faults.
The robe of conceit and passion is no better than nakedness.

A woman who is pure and dignified can never be humiliated.
That which is pure cannot be affected by the impurities of inconti-
nence.

Chastity is a treasure, the woman its guard, greed the wolf.
Woe if she knows not the rules of guarding the treasure.

The Devil never attends the table of piety as guest.
He knows that that is no place of feasting.

Walk on the straight path, because on crooked lanes
You find no provision or guidance, only remorse.

Hearts and eyes do need a veil, the veil of chastity.
A worn-out *chador* is not the basis of faith in Islam.[60]

Although al-Azri is a male poet writing in Arabic and E'tesami is a female poet writing in Persian, both poets not only describe sexual dynamics
based on the wolf metonym but focus on woman's purity and chastity.
When E'tesami explains that not a worn-out chador but chastity is the basis
of faith in Islam, she echoes Iraj Mirza. When she claims that educated
women who know about shame and honor no longer fall prey to the wolf's
cunning, she supports the claims of Iraj Mirza and al-Azri. When she compares woman's life to life in a cage, does she not share with Nezam Vafa the
metaphor of the dark cage of the chador? Does E'tesami's line "Her life she
spent in isolation; she died in isolation" not remind us of 'Eshqi's verse "as
long as women are in shrouds, half the nation is not alive"?

How does E'tesami's voice differ from the voices of al-Azri, Iraj Mirza,
'Eshqi, and Vafa? Some of her critics claim that her voice is not different
from the traditional male voice, that she did not use artistic innovations but
confined herself to the customary language and structures. She is accused
of remaining forever her father's daughter and of expressing in her poetry
his feelings and sentiments rather than her own. One of her critics, Reza
Baraheni, asserts that her poetry is manly and relies on age-old patriarchal
morality. According to Baraheni, the poet leaves the championing of
women's rights to men.[61] Another of her critics, Fereshteh Davaran, won-

ders if E'tesami was attracted to men and then mentions that she had the body of a man.[62]

There is no denying that there are many parallels between E'tesami's poetry and the poetry of male traditionalists. But there are also significant differences—differences that point to E'tesami's awareness of being a woman beleaguered by oppressive customs and traditions. E'tesami writes from inside the world of women, as a woman who may have had experience with the courts of justice in which no witnesses defended women, the schools of learning to which women were not admitted, and situations in which women's ignorance was blamed on their inherent inferiority or slug-gishness. When she writes that the bird in the cage was never mentioned in the rose garden, a reference to one of Iran's great literary works, Sa'di's *Golestan* (Rose garden), she castigates the Persian literary tradition for not including women's voices. We have to remember that E'tesami's poetic voice was one of the first female voices in Persian poetry. When she asks "Could woman weave with no spindle or thread?" we are reminded of Virginia Woolf asking for a room of her own in order to pursue her literary career. Another feature that sets her voice apart from male voices is her use of images that are part of the world of women in order to convey her message. As Milani puts it, "her repeated use of domestic images, her fre-quent references to pots and pans, beans and peas, thread and needle, and her sensitivity to and superb description of female bonds are clear indica-tion of her attempt to integrate as best she can a woman's point of view with poetry."[63]

The Poetry of Forugh Farrokhzad

E'tesami is often compared to Forugh Farrokhzad (1935–67), another great Iranian female poet. Strictly speaking, Farrokhzad did not have to deal with the issue of veiling, because at least officially the veil had been abol-ished by Reza Shah's unveiling order of 1936, the year after Farrokhzad was born. Yet her poetry is important to our discussion of the veil, because it illustrates that unveiling did not automatically lead to an elimination, or even alleviation, of the traditional restrictions that dominated the life of the Iranian woman. In her poems, Farrokhzad decries the sorrows of the Ira-nian woman who felt confined to a repressed life behind the curtain of tradition. She speaks for the young woman who wants to free herself of the prison of veiled chastity and forced modesty. Farrokhzad, unlike E'tesami, expressed her sensuality, desires, and anguish in her poems. At the age of nineteen, Farrokhzad composed "The Captive," which became the title poem of her first collection of verse published in 1955.

In his analysis of Farrokhzad's poetry and life, Michael Hillmann explains that it was poems such as "The Captive" that earned Farrokhzad the epithet of Iran's first feminine voice.[64] In this poem, she agonizes over her personal situation. The poet married when she was sixteen. At first her husband played the role of mentor, but soon she outgrew this patronal relationship and started to resent his tutelage. She also fell in love with another man. Her decision to divorce her husband was complicated by the fact that they had a child together. In the period before the 1967 Iranian Family Protection Act, children were always given into the custody of the father in divorce cases. Hillmann points out that even if Farrokhzad's divorce had taken place with the Family Protection Act in force, Farrokhzad would have lost custody of her son, because she was seeking a divorce without any legal complaint against her husband and because she had committed adultery.[65] In the poem "The Captive," a female speaker addresses her lover.

> I am thinking that in a moment of neglect,
> From out this silent prison I will fly,
> Laugh in the face of the man who jails me,
> And then begin life over by your side.

> If, O sky, I want one day to fly
> From out this silent prison, cold and stern,
> What shall I say to the child's weeping eyes?
> Forget about me, for I'm a captive bird.[66]

E'tesami uses the same imagery when she compares a woman's life in Iran to life in a cage: "A woman lived in a cage and died in a cage." Unlike E'tesami, however, Farrokhzad dares to blame the jailer for her imprisonment. Although E'tesami championed women's rights, she did not escape her cage, and she did not free herself of patriarchal constraints and paternal tutelage. Farrokhzad fled her jail, even though in doing so she had to make the biggest sacrifice any mother can make; that is, she had to leave her child behind. Her rebellion against traditional values and male patronage led her on a journey to selfhood. Farzaneh Milani points out that in her later work, Farrokhzad poeticizes gender dynamics that are no longer based on structures such as jailer/bird, oppressor/oppressed, or hunter/hunted. Many of Farrokhzad's later poems, according to Milani, lament the destructive effects that rigid gender roles have upon both men and women but at the same time depict a triumph over these effects and "celebrate the formation of new, and different physical and emotional bonds."[67] In those poems written shortly before her death, especially in her collection titled *A Rebirth,* Farrokhzad went beyond her individual world, her alienation and desperate search for lasting love, and introduced a kind of *personal* love poetry into the Persian tradition.[68] Forugh Farrokhzad had truly discarded her veil.

Veiled Anxieties

The Poetry of Asadullah Khan Ghalib

The celebrated Urdu poet Asadullah Khan Ghalib (1797–1869) from Agra, India, gives true testimony to the semantic flexibility of the veil. Mirza Ghalib, his *nom de plume,* is renowned for poems, letters, and prose pieces in Persian and Urdu.[69] He lived through the final dissolution of the Moghul Empire and the establishment of the British Raj. Though he was born into wealthy circumstances, his family lost all when his father and uncle, both well-paid mercenary leaders, were killed in military service. Orphaned and without financial resources, at the age of thirteen Ghalib entered into an arranged marriage with a girl from a well-to-do, educated family of nobles. According to his biographer and translator, Sayyid Fayyaz Mahmud, Ghalib felt a warm affection for his wife, "even though he called his married life an imprisonment and always passed off his domestic liabilities with a quip."[70] All his life, Ghalib had financial problems and even spent time in debtors' prison. In one of his poems, he addresses his imprisonment: "I want to begin with a word about my confinement in this prison. The pain in my heart has torn all veils of restraint and inhibition. I want to lament now."[71] In this verse, Ghalib liberated himself by "tearing the veil"; he escaped from the prison of restraints and inhibition. Although physically confined, Ghalib was able to set his mind free. The poet uses the veil as metonym for captivity. While poets such as E'tesami, 'Eshqi, and Vafa use the veil to describe women's imprisonment, Ghalib employs the veil to describe his own confinement within restraints and inhibitions.

Ghalib's poetry abounds with references to the veil. In many verses, he relies on the screening property of the veil. In these lines, Ghalib uses the Islamic convention of representing God as the eternal beloved or as eternal beauty and himself as the rejected suitor or pining lover. In the following excerpts from poems in Urdu, Ghalib uses the term *niqab* to describe his distance from the eternal beloved and from absolute beauty:[72]

> O Lover (of Truth) the beauty of the (Eternal) Beloved
> should be veiled [niqab] (you cannot see Absolute Beauty).
> The candle should have a lantern made of the
> wings of the dying moths![73]

> My great love has opened the strings holding the veil [niqab] over
> Eternal Beauty.
> Nothing stands now between me and the Ultimate Reality except
> my own sight (lack of sight).[74]

To create a sense of distance from the omnipresent god, Ghalib also uses the term *purdah:*

> Do not pass without a veil [purdah] through the valley where
> Majnun lived.[75]
> Here the veil [niqab] of every particle of sand hides a vibrating
> heart. (you will not be able to bear the intensity of love; do not
> therefore undertake the journey with a light heart).[76]

In the following poem, Ghalib implies that only wise men, men with vision, are qualified to see naked Reality, the Truth:

> The lack of vision of Men of Intellect (wisdom) veils [niqab] from
> them the sight of the Beloved!
> Their closed eyelids (absence of spiritual insight) act as a curtain
> [purdah] to conceal naked Reality (Truth).[77]

Ghalib uses the veil as a device to impose distance between mankind and an omnipresent, omnipotent, and omniscient god. Interestingly, we have seen in chapter 2 that American erotica also relies on this screening property of the veil in order to create a barrier between the model and the viewer. Thus, on a strictly linguistic level, Ghalib's verses do not contribute anything new to our discussion of the meanings of the veil. His verses do, however, add an extra dimension to our consideration of the semantics of the veil if we probe the mental structures that inform Ghalib's poetry.

Other great poets have used the veil in contexts where women are completely absent. For example, the fourteenth-century poet Hafez said:
"Happy the moment when from my face I cast the veil,"[78] and the mystical
poet Jalal ed-Din Rumi (d. 1273) said: "This is love: to fly heavenward, to
rend, every instant, a hundred veils."[79] Commenting on these verses,
Milani asks why the greatest of Iran's poets represent their own literary
anxiety, their struggle with love and words, in terms of woman's unveiling.
She hypothesizes that "perhaps the anxieties attached to the confrontation
of love and reality are displaced onto a woman's body and its nakedness.
Perhaps the veil, because of its symbolic potency, becomes a vessel in which
to place both the anxieties and the exhilarations of love and creativity."[80] Of
course, Milani is not the first to suggest that men are anxious about the
female body. Qasim Amin has explained that some men fear the female
body because they fear fitna—disorder or chaos provoked by sexual disorder and initiated by women.[81] Fatima Mernissi explains that "the Muslim
woman is endowed with a fatal attraction which erodes the male's will to
resist her and reduces him to a passive acquiescent role. He has no choice;
he can only give in to her attraction, whence her identification with *fitna,*
chaos, and with the anti-divine and anti-social forces of the universe."[82]

The *hadith* "When a man and a woman are isolated in the presence of
each other, Satan is bound to be their third companion" also expresses this
fear of a libido that shatters all social and religious boundaries.[83] In much of
Muslim discourse, unlike in Western discourse, it is primarily the woman
who is endowed with this earth-shattering sexual drive and who is therefore perceived as Satan.[84] Since the veil is the most visible sign of a woman,
it may be considered a synecdoche for male anxieties about the female
body. When projecting these anxieties about the physical reality of the female body into the metaphysical realm, when the female beloved becomes
the divine beloved, the veil becomes a synecdoche for male angst about
ontological issues.

Although Ghalib lived centuries after Hafiz and Rumi and in Muslim
India, he lived in a social and religious milieu that was similar to that of the
two medieval poets, especially with regard to women's seclusion and social
status. Therefore, we may justifiably apply Milani's hypothesis to Ghalib
and say that he used the veil as a vessel in which he placed his physical as
well as metaphysical anxieties. By taking into account the mental structures
upon which Ghalib's poetry is based, we may ascribe yet another meaning
to the veil, that is, a vessel of male existential angst.

The Poetry of Ayatollah Khomeini

Ayatollah Khomeini (1900?–1989) has also used the veil in a context that, at least on the linguistic level, does not relate to the female body. Although Khomeini is not considered a poet and has no standing among Iran's great poets, his writings in the areas of religion and philosophy served as the backbone of the revolution during his lifetime and functioned later to maintain support for his established theocracy. His work is available not only in Persian but in translation in various other languages. Among his lesser-known writings is a collection of poems not published during his lifetime. This collection, titled *Divane Imam, Sorudehaye Hazrate Imam Khomeini,* was introduced to the public through the efforts of his daughter, Fatemeh Tabatabaei.[85] This volume contains Khomeini's *irfan* (mystical writings).[86] The book's preface discusses how the classical Persian irfan poets such as Sa'di and Hafez influenced his work. The preface also claims that the writings of Khomeini have influenced in their turn the literary works of many contemporary Iranian writers and intellectuals.

In two of his poems, Khomeini uses the veil as metonym. The first poem is titled "Hijab" (Veil) and the second "Falsafeh" (Philosophy). Khomeini utilizes both of them to warn his daughter Fatemeh, who is a professor of philosophy, of the dangers inherent in her field of expertise:

The Hijab
Those who brag about the science of philosophy
are openly attacking other fields of studies
I am afraid that they end up wrapping themselves
in the great hijab [of philosophy]
become engaged with it, and lose themselves [their senses][87]

Falsafeh
Fati [nickname for Fatemeh] who is studying the science of phi-
    losophy
from *falsafeh* only knows *fa, la,* and *sin* [the consonants of the word
    falsafeh]
I hope that, with God's guidance,
she will be able to free herself from the hijab of philosophy.[88]

In these two poems, Khomeini attacks the science of philosophy and asks his daughter to free herself from the hijab of thought in which it has wrapped her. To simplify the history of falsafeh, between the ninth and the eleventh centuries Muslim thinkers such as Ibn Sina [Avicenna], al-Farabi, and al-Kindi utilized Hellenic thought in their quest for religious humanism and thus brought falsafeh to full bloom.[89] In the eleventh century, al-Ghazali brought an end to this blossoming of rational thought when he made supreme a theology that was the slave of dogma. In falsafeh, he perceived Gnostic trends, which he denounced because he considered them opposed to the Qur'anic spirit.[90] Today many Muslims, Sunnis as well as Shi'is, regard falsafeh as a Western science that is not applicable to Islamic thought, which stresses the science of *kalam,* the study of Islamic scriptures and ideas. According to Khomeini's poems, those who study falsafeh not only attack other fields of knowledge, such as the science of kalam, but lose themselves in tautological trivialities. The great hijab, that is falsafeh, becomes an obstacle that the true believer needs to overcome.

In the two poems quoted above, Khomeini rejects the veil that blurs the sight of the true believer. However, he endorses the veil that hides the body of the Muslim woman: in his rhetorical question, "Is it even possible for a person to be a Muslim and at the same time be a supporter of this disgraceful regulation regarding mandatory unveiling?"[91] Khomeini asserts his belief that the woman's veil represents a *sine qua non* of Islam. How can we reconcile these seemingly diametrically opposed meanings of the veil in Khomeini's *Weltanschauung?* If we again employ Milani's hypothesis that the veil functions as a vessel for male anxieties, we may assert that by using the veil in these two poems, Khomeini projected his anxieties about the female body onto philosophy. We may assume that, like Hafez, Rumi, and Ghalib, Khomeini used the veil as a vessel in which to place his existential angst.

Epilogue: Mathematics behind the Veil

The literary pervasiveness of the veil may be best illustrated by a book I found on the shelves of a science library. This book, titled *The Man Who Counted: A Collection of Mathematical Adventures* and written under the *nom de plume* Malba Tahan, features mathematical riddles some of which allot a prominent role to the veil.[92] Behind this pen name is the Brazilian mathematician Júlio César de Mello de Souza, who was born in 1895 in Queluz, Brazil, lived most of his life in Rio de Janeiro, and died in 1974. This author not only wrote his book about mathematical adventures in the manner of

The Thousand and One Nights but gave his pen name, Malba Tahan, credentials that would qualify him to write the tales found in *The Thousand and One Nights*. According to de Mello de Souza, Malba Tahan was born in Saudi Arabia in 1885, studied in Istanbul and Cairo, and traveled the world.

The narrator of *The Man Who Counted,* the same Malba Tahan, accompanies Beremiz Samir, a young Persian mathematician, on his journeys from the court in Baghdad to the prisons of Khorasan and to the maharaja of Lahore as well as to other interesting and exotic places. In many tales, Beremiz uses his mathematical skills to settle disputes, give wise advice, and overcome dangerous enemies. In a tale titled "In the Stars," the narrative plot hinges on the veil. Malba Tahan relates this romantic episode: Beremiz is invited to teach mathematics to seventeen-year-old Telassim, daughter of Sheik Iezid.[93] The sheik inquires of Beremiz: "My Daughter lives within the harem and has never set eyes on a man not of our family. She can attend her lesson in mathematics only from behind a thick curtain, with her face veiled, and with two family slaves in attendance. Given this condition, do you accept?"[94] Beremiz accepts these terms, thinking to himself that, of course, the reserve and modesty of a young girl have much more value than do algebraic formulas and must be preserved even if doing so makes his lessons more difficult to teach. He tells the sheik that "[i]t will be a pleasure to instruct your daughter, whom I do not know, and whose face I will never have the good fortune to admire. If Allah is willing, I can begin tomorrow."[95] Beremiz wonders if Telassim is beautiful and is assured that "she is as pretty as the fourth moon in the month of Ramadan, a real flower of Islam."[96] Beremiz gives Telassim two lessons in mathematics, and Telassim falls in love with him. She reveals her love when she gives her father a rug to be delivered to the young mathematician at a competition held at the court of the caliph. On this rug she has embroidered declarations of her affection for Beremiz in Kufic script, which he alone knows how to read; inside the rug she has also hidden a note saying "Courage. Trust in God. I pray for you." In true fairy-tale fashion, Beremiz also loves Telassim and asks the caliph for her hand in marriage after he has solved all seven riddles given to him by wise men. The caliph agrees under one condition: Beremiz has to figure out the eye color of five heavily veiled slave girls whom the caliph has just bought from a Mongol prince. Beremiz is told that two of the girls have brown eyes and three of the girls have blue eyes. He is also told that the blue-eyed girls are born liars, while the brown-eyed girls always tell the truth. Furthermore, Beremiz may question three of the five slaves, asking one question of each one. Beremiz takes up the challenge. He asks the first girl about the color of her eyes. She replies in a language that is unknown to Beremiz. He then asks a second girl what her companion has just replied. She tells him that her companion said that her eyes are blue. Beremiz then asks the third slave girl about the color of the eyes of the two slave girls he has just questioned. The third slave girl tells him that the first girl has brown eyes and the second blue eyes. Using logic, Beremiz concludes that the first girl has brown eyes; the second, blue eyes; the third, brown eyes; and the other two, whom he did not question, blue eyes.[97] His answers prove correct, and Beremiz gets his treasured Telassim. Of course, they live happily ever after.

Conclusion

The Semantic Versatility of the Veil

To delimit the meanings of the veil is indeed a challenging if not impossible task. The previous chapters reveal that the semantics of the veil depend on the specific cultural, historical, and religious contexts in which the veil is used. The representations of the veil in the popular Indian cinema and the Iranian cinema demonstrate that changing the cultural context effects diametrically opposed meanings: while the veil in the Hindi movie serves to draw the male gaze, the veil in the Iranian movie serves to deny the male gaze. The semantics of the veil also follow a historical trajectory: while Reza Shah of Iran saw the veil as a conspicuous sign of backwardness, Ayatollah Khomeini saw it as a sign of progress along the ideological path of Islam. Whereas Muslims use the veil and seclusion to safeguard women from men outside the family, Hindus use the same devices to enforce women's subordination to their in-laws.

But the semantics of the veil differ even within a specific cultural context. For example, American television ads for products such as IBM computers and Jeep Cherokees exploit the eroticism of the veil, while ads in women's magazines published in the United States for products such as perfume and cigarettes rely on the veil as a sign of women's oppression. Saudi advertisers ascribe family values to the veil when they sell toothpaste; they utilize the veil as a symbol of purity when selling Kotex sanitary napkins; and they endow the veil with romantic properties when selling expensive Concord watches. The image of the veil as a sign of modesty and respect as conveyed in the writings of Yashpal clashes with the erotic image of the veil pictured in popular Indian movies.

Furthermore, the meanings of the veil may change even within the pages of the same magazine, depending on whether photographs or cartoons are involved: while photographs of veiled women in *Playboy* and *Penthouse* aim at drawing the male gaze, cartoons of veiled women mock and ridicule Muslim society. The meaning of the veil when portrayed in a cartoon also depends on the overall state of political relations between the United States and the countries of the Middle East.

Recurring Images of the Veil

Certain meanings of the veil transcend cultural, religious, and historical boundaries. The veil is often ascribed an erotic meaning, although this usage has several subcategories corresponding to the specific context in which the veil appears. The photographers of *Playboy, Penthouse,* and *Hustler* exploit the eroticism of the veil in order to capture the male gaze. By veiling the model, the photographers evoke images from the tales of *The Thousand and One Nights,* in which women are eager to provide sexual pleasures. In some photographs, the veil is presented as Western fetish; in cartoons that aim to mock the Muslim, as Muslim fetish. The advertisers of IBM computers and Jeep Cherokees use the veil to sell products by depending on the eroticism and exoticism of the veiled woman to draw the interest of prospective buyers.

This erotic image of the veil is also promoted in the cinema. In the epic film *The Sheltering Sky,* movie director Bernardo Bertolucci relies on an erotic game of veiling and unveiling to captivate the audience. Although both American erotica and Bertolucci use the eroticism of the veil to appeal to their respective audiences, Bertolucci has to be more subtle in his depiction in order to avoid pornographic ratings. The makers of popular Indian movies also employ voyeuristic hide-and-seek games with the veil to draw the spectator's gaze while complying with Indian laws forbidding nudity in cinema. Indian filmmakers frequently send a veiled heroine into a downpour in order to show a wet veil clinging to her body and thereby accentuating its silhouette.

Since Indian films have a large female audience, movie makers have to appeal to the romantic inclinations of female moviegoers as well. Thus, they utilize the veil, praised in song lyrics and presented as the embodiment of cinematic aesthetics, to create an atmosphere that is conducive to romance. In addition to filmmakers, advertisers targeting Muslim women also endow the veil with romantic properties. Ads for expensive Swiss watches in *Sayidaty* feature a series of photographs documenting scenes from a courtship between a Bedouin woman wearing a black face veil and a handsome Bedouin man wearing a *kafiya* and *agal*. These ads are based on the assumption that female readers will want to identify with the heroine and thus become part of this romantic scenario. By buying the Concord watch they may be able to do just that.

The veil is often portrayed as a symbol of oppression, albeit not always as a symbol of women's oppression alone. Cartoons in American publications such as *Hustler, Penthouse,* and *Playboy* use the veil to mock the perceived backwardness and oppressiveness of Muslim customs and traditions in general. This change in meaning from symbol of eroticism to symbol of oppression constitutes the reaction of American erotica to the Iranian Revolution in 1979. Until that event occurred, the cartoonists of *Playboy* and *Penthouse* seemed to envy Muslims for those customs and traditions that appeared to propagate licentiousness and sexual abandon. With the advent of Ayatollah Khomeini's theocracy, the cartoonists condemned and blasphemed these same traditions and customs. This change in Western attitudes toward Islam may be best expressed in a *Playboy Report*. Playboy Enterprises paid for the publication of a translation into French (1979) and German (1980) of excerpts from the writings of Ayatollah Khomeini.[1] The Persian-to-French translator, Jean-Marie Xavière, explains in the introduction that because he did not want to bore Western readers by giving a complete translation of Khomeini's three works, *Valayat-e Faqih, Kashfol Asrar,* and *Tozih al-Masa'il,* he chose to translate only those sections that he believed would be of interest to them. Even as his introduction is permeated with racist slurs, his selection and arrangement of excerpts present an exercise in blasphemy and blatant racism: he chose to start a section titled "Divine laws that rule daily life" with excerpts on the art of urination and defecation. In the epilogue to the German translation, the translator Rolph Gaïl compares the significance of the *Playboy Report,* which has a green (the color of Islam) front cover and features a photograph of Ayatollah Khomeini's face, to Hitler's *Mein Kampf* and Mao's red bible. This apparent hostility toward Islam and Muslims underlies the cartoons in *Playboy, Penthouse,* and *Hustler* after 1979, and subsequent altercations between the United States and strongmen Muammar al-Qaddafi and Saddam Hussein led to its further intensification. Although American erotica is more crude and explicit in its caricatures of Muslims, American advertisers for Bijan perfume and Virginia Slims are no less racist in their depiction. Both try to sell their products by mocking the backwardness and oppressiveness of Muslim customs and traditions that the veil symbolizes. Both are interested in making money by perpetuating stereotypes about the Middle East, and neither is interested in portraying the reality of Muslim women's lives. Granted, both erotica and advertisements, in general, do not present reality but create images that appeal to the audience.

Using the veil as symbol of oppression is not limited to the United States. This understanding of the veil is not restricted by cultural or historical boundaries. Writing at the beginning of the twentieth century, Iranian poets such as Iraj Mirza and Mirzadeh 'Eshqi use the veil to depict the oppression of their male compatriots at the hands of a conservative and powerful clergy. An Uzbeki song composed by the Soviet propaganda machine decries the oppression of Uzbeki women under Islam, but Moscow was less interested in improving the status of Uzbeki women than in dissolving the cultural bonds among members of a once cohesive Muslim community. Ayatollah Khomeini and the Urdu poet Asadullah Khan Ghalib use the "confining" property of the veil to describe their own existential angst.

The Iranian poets Parvin E'tesami and Forugh Farrokhzad portray the veil as a symbol of women's oppression. In their poetry, they both describe women's imprisonment behind the veil. Recent years have seen a deluge of writings by Muslim and non-Muslim authors on the plight of the Muslim woman. Her life has been probed from economical, historical, political, religious, cultural, and gender perspectives. Muslim women, drawing a world audience, have also penned novellas, novels, and plays that depict the experiences of Muslim protagonists. The list of authors who deserve mention is long, but I will name only three in the context of this conclusion. One of the most prolific novelists and a feminist pioneer is the Egyptian Nawal El Saadawi. Her works have introduced many readers, including myself, to the world of Egyptian women and the customs and traditions that shape their lives. The Lebanese writer Hanan al-Shaykh portrays, in sensual strokes, women's reaction to polygyny. The Egyptian novelist Alifa Rifaat addresses the impact practices such as female circumcision have on women's emotional and sexual state.[2]

The Veil: A Force in and of Itself

The exploration of visual, political, and literary dynamics reveals that once the veil is assigned a certain meaning, it itself often acquires the power to dictate sexual, artistic, and political dynamics. Many Muslim cultures rely on the veil and women's segregation to prevent *fitna,* or chaos caused by women's sexuality. These conventions have repercussions that echo throughout the Muslim world. Some writers speculate that the veiling and secluding of women results in homosexuality. For example, in his analysis of *Arefnameh,* Paul Sprachman claims that Iraj Mirza launched in this work a "general attack on the pervasiveness of Persian pedophilia," blaming it on the strict segregation of the sexes.[3] In lines 79–88, Iraj Mirza states that as long as girls are veiled and boys are not, one cannot blame men for preferring boys. He further asserts that if girls were available, men would not sodomize boys. Clearly, it is not pedophilia that concerns Iraj Mirza but pederasty. In these lines, the poet greatly oversimplifies sexual dynamics between a man and a boy. Would the pederast really prefer girls over boys if girls were available to him? Does marriage and the resulting availability of women change the sexual preference of a pederast? This is not to say that sex segregation does not encourage sexual adventures between members of the same sex, men as well as women. Hanan al-Shaykh sets her novel *Women of Sand and Myrrh* in an Arab desert country where sex segregation is strictly enforced.[4] Her heroines provide each other with sexual pleasures. Here, "homosexuality," for lack of a more appropriate term, is a temporary necessity rather than a sexual preference.

The institution of veiling also has an impact on artistic expression, especially in the Iranian cinema. According to the censors of the Islamic Republic of Iran, wearing the *hijab* is synonymous with obeying Islamic laws that regulate the proper behavior of the female believer. The law of hijab forbids the cinematic depiction of women in the privacy of their home, where they would not veil. Iranian filmmakers have come up with ingenious ways to make motion pictures that comply with the law of hijab. The veil has created a cinematics of its own—a cinematics that focuses on aesthetics rather than on sexual dynamics.

The institutions of veiling and sex segregation have determined the extent and nature of women's role in war. Since strict segregation cannot be guaranteed in the heat of battle, women are almost never permitted to fight. Shi'i *mujtahids* deny women even a supportive role on the battlefield. They argue that according to Islamic injunctions, which regulate proper gender relations, women are not allowed to treat the wounds of *namahram* men or to wash their dead bodies. It is thus not surprising that the Islamic Republic of Iran, which enforces the law of hijab, does not allow women to join its armed forces. In the United Arab Emirates, women have limited access to certain branches of the armed forces; they are permitted to join the police and customs offices, where they are to deal with female offenders and travelers. In these capacities, they have to wear black head scarves under their caps and loose-fitting uniforms. In Saddam's armed forces, the majority of female soldiers hold administrative and medical-related positions, but an increasing number performed in combat functions after 1981. All Iraqi women soldiers wear loose-fitting uniforms and head scarves.

On the one hand, the veil is a simple garment that millions of women deal with in their daily lives as a matter of habit, without a second thought. They are raised to wear it; it is just another article of clothing. On the other hand, the veil is an enormously important symbol, as it carries thousands of years of religious, sexual, social, and political significance within its folds. Its original purpose, to separate respectable women from slaves, prostitutes, and women with low social status, has been blurred to a point at which it has different meanings to different people in different cultures, and even in the same culture. Some people think of the veil as erotic and romantic, others perceive it as a symbol of oppression, still others consider it a sign of piety, modesty, or purity. It has become so ubiquitous that everyone seems to have formed an opinion about it. The various connotations it has, the many emotions it arouses, testify to its continuing, perhaps even growing, significance in the modern world.

Notes

Introduction

1. *Hijab* is the Arabic as well as Persian word for veil. According to agreements between the Islamic Republic of Iran and international carriers, when entering Iranian air space, female passengers are reminded of the compulsory hijab observance in Iran. When applying for a visa to visit Iran, non-Iranian women are informed about the enforcement of the law of hijab. Visa applications for noncitizens of Iran require female applicants to wear the hijab for the photograph that must accompany every application. Iran Air, the property of the Iranian government, reserves the right of enforcing the law of hijab on board. This law is even extended to the areas of international airports from which Iran Air operates.

2. The customs officer knew that my flight originated in Frankfurt and that chocolate filled with liquor is a popular item at the duty-free shops in Frankfurt's airport.

3. For a discussion of this article, see chapter 4.

4. The chador is a full-length semicircular piece of cloth that is placed on the head and held in place with the right or left hand. It is usually black.

5. Keddie, *Women in Middle Eastern History*, 3.

6. Driver, *The Babylonian Laws*, 491–92.

7. I want to thank Ian Hanks for pointing me to Ovid's *Metamorphoses*.

8. Ovid, *Metamorphoses,* 94–98.

9. For more information on veiling practices in these empires, see El Guindi, *Veil,* 13–22.

10. Shaarawi, *Harem Years,* 7. Farzaneh Milani drew my attention to the fact that Qur'at Al Ain unveiled herself in Iran in 1848. For more information on Qur'at Al Ain, see Brown, *A Literary History of Persia,* vol. 4, 154, 197.

11. See, for example, William Langewiesche's *Sahara Unveiled;* Robert Arnett's *India Unveiled;* Asghar Ali Engineer's *Lifting the Veil: Communal Violence and Communal Harmony in Contemporary India;* Nicole and Hugh Pope's *Turkey Unveiled;* Anthony Sattin's *Lifting the Veil: British Society in Egypt, 1768–1956;* and Mehdi Khansari and Minouch Yavari's *The Persian Bazaar: Veiled Space of Desire.* Another category of books that include variations of "veil" in their titles is that which addresses Islam and its mystical interpretation, Sufism. See, for example, Neal Robinson's *Discovering the Qurʿan: A Contemporary Approach to a Veiled Text* and Frithjof Schuon's *Sufism: Veil and Quintessence.* For more examples, see El Guindi, *Veil,* 10–12.

Other books picture veiled women on the front cover but gloss over or completely fail to mention women's issues. For example, Hisham Sharabi's *Neopatriarchy* features four veiled women on its cover but allots only six pages to a section titled "Women and Neopatriarchy."

1. Veiled Images in Advertising

1. Seidenberg, "Advertising and Abuse of Drugs," 789–90. Also by the same author, see "Images of Health," 226–67.

2. Courtney and Whipple, *Sex Stereotyping,* 14.

3. Bassuk, in "The Rest Cure," gives an excellent account of medicine's struggle with female hysteria.

4. Courtney, *Sex Stereotyping,* 9.

5. According to the U.S. Census Bureau, the median household income in 1996 was $35,492.

6. According to the U.S. Census Bureau, women had an average income of $23,161 in 1996, while men had an average income of $32,144, a difference of 28 percent.

7. Schoemaker, *The Emergence of Folklore,* 61–62. Homeopathic or sympathetic magic along with contagious or touch magic studies are based on the original work of Sir James G. Frazer, a well-known nineteenth-century British anthropologist. For detailed information, see *The Golden Bough.*

8. Jean Kilbourne, an internationally known media critic and creator of the slide show "The Naked Truth: Advertising's Image of Women," shows a slide in which a woman's chest, scantily covered by a bra with one strap reconstructed, was used to advertise the ability of a brand of fishing line "to hold up" under anything.

9. John Foster Fraser as cited in Mabro, *Veiled Half-Truths,* 46.

10. For example, in Baltimore a survey revealed that 20 percent of the billboards in white communities advertised tobacco and alcohol, whereas 76 percent of the

billboards in African American neighborhoods advertised these products (M. Quinn, "Don't Aim That Pack at Us," *Time*, January 29, 1990).

11. This sect refuses to recognize the caste system or the supremacy of the Brahmanical priests. It forbids magic, idolatry, and pilgrimages.

12. American-Arab Anti-Discrimination Committee, 1989 Activity Report, 12.

13. Ibid., 1992 Activity Report, 14.

14. Ibid.

15. Recent advertisements in the *Los Angles Times* juxtaposed Muslim women in long chadors with bikini-clad beachgoers. The ads were part of a new campaign that tried to contrast images of Southern California with world events that the newspaper covered. Muslims and more than 200 *Times* editors and reporters signed a petition complaining that these ads were offensive. On April 20, 2000, the *Los Angeles Times* agreed to stop these ads.

16. Tuareg people are basically a Caucasoid people of Mediterranean type (some are mixed with other groups of sub-Saharan African peoples). There is no single group of unified Tuareg tribe, and when speaking of them as an entity it is only to make a reference to a group of people with common race, language, and custom as distinguished from their neighbors. Their language is of the Hamitic group, and it is closely related to the Berber of the Mediterranean. They are known as "les hommes bleus" for their fine robes of indigo-dyed (a natural blue dye) cotton and their blue veils falling from the bridge of the nose to below the chin showing little except hands, feet, and the area around the eyes. Even the small exposed sections of skin have a blue tinge, the result of the dye rubbing off the cloth. For more detailed information, see Murphy, "Social Distance and the Veil."

17. Because of popular demand, the ban on Coke and food cans was lifted in the 1980s.

18. These numbers are taken from a comprehensive study on Saudi households and their expenditure patterns, which was recently conducted by the Middle East Marketing Research Bureau working with the Mountjoy Research Centre in Durham in the United Kingdom.

19. Since many Saudi households employ domestic help, automated dishwashers may be considered superfluous.

20. See Barnet and Muller, *Global Reach*.

21. Dunn, "The Case Study Approach," 102–9. See also Ricks et al., "Pitfalls in Advertising Overseas," 47–51.

22. For more information on and an illustrated history of Kotex advertising, visit the Web site of Kimberly-Clark, http://www.kimberly-clark.com (October 10, 2000).

23. In *Blood, Bread, and Roses,* Grahn gives an excellent (and witty) account of the role menstruation played in the definition of culture and gender.

24. Ranke-Heinemann, *Eunuchs,* 22.

25. Ibid., 24.

26. Ascha, *La femme,* 26. For *hadiths* concerning menstruation, see "Kitab al-Haid" in Muslim's *Sahih,* 173–80.

27. Bouhdiba, *Sexuality in Islam,* 51.

28. Ascha, *La femme,* 49.

29. Ibn al-Jawzi, *Ahkam al-Nisa',* 33. In *The Veil and the Male Elite,* Mernissi discusses how and why the polluting essence of femaleness became the subject of many hadiths; see especially 70–75.

30. Malti-Douglas, *Woman's Body,* 121.

31. Abu-Lughod, *Veiled Sentiments,* 137–38.

32. I found this particular ad in *Elle* (May 1998): 43.

33. See Wolf's *The Beauty Myth* for a discussion of women's magazines and their representation of female sexuality.

34. Mernissi, *Beyond the Veil,* 41.

35. Malti-Douglas, *Woman's Body,* 106.

36. Al-Tirmidhi, *Sahih,* 8–10.

37. Mernissi, *Beyond the Veil,* 45.

38. According to a report by the U.S. Census Bureau titled "Children Ever Born by Parity, Race, Age, Marital Status and Nativity of Women: April 1990," in 1990, the average number of children born to white women was about 1.8, compared with 2.1 children for African American women, 2.3 children for American Indian or Aleut women, and 2.7 children for Eskimo women.

39. Urban Saudis hold the Bedouins of the desert in high esteem. Bedouin women, often married more than once, have in many cases more freedom than their sisters in the towns. Bedouins stress genealogies and kinship. For a concise history of the Bedouins and their present political situation in Saudi Arabia, see *Encyclopaedia of Islam,* vol. 1, 872–74.

40. These lines are taken from a poem by al-Mutanabbi titled "Shame Kept My Tears Away," in Pound, *Arabic and Persian Poems,* 46.

41. Williamson, *Decoding Advertisements,* 43.

42. Government officials in Saudi Arabia take quite seriously their task of keeping out what they consider "Western decadence," especially if this decadence from foreign countries is received by satellite dishes. There are many instances of satellite "executioners" randomly shooting at displayed satellite dishes on the roofs of houses in cities throughout Saudi Arabia. These people are locally known as the "satellite police."

2. Veiled Images in American Erotica

1. Mediamark Research Inc., "Magazine Audience Estimates," estimates that in 1998 12 percent of *Penthouse* and 17 percent of *Playboy* readers were adult women. *Penthouse* online had a 4 percent female readership.

2. Mediamark Research Inc., "Spring 1998 Median Age."

3. For the purpose of this study, I have used the term "Middle East" in its wider geographical sense, including the core region (Iran, the Fertile Crescent, the Arabian Peninsula, and Egypt) and peripheral regions (Sudan, Arab North Africa, Turkey, and Cyprus).

4. The University of Texas at Austin's library collection of these magazines is incomplete, which impeded the thoroughness of this study. The university, for example, does not hold any issues of *Playboy* that date before 1962. (Since older issues of *Playboy* are collector's items, it is very difficult to locate any of these older issues in libraries.) Nevertheless, this incompleteness should not detract from my findings about the stereotypes of the veil that are presented in these three magazines.

5. *Consumer Magazine and Agri-Media Source*, published monthly by Standard Rate and Data Services.

6. Mediamark Research Inc., "Magazine Audience Estimates."

7. The popularity of pornographic magazines is probably dropping these days, since there are so many online sex sites from which to choose.

8. Transcript, 128–57.

9. The magazines under discussion present pornographic as well as erotic images of veiled women. While erotic writings and pictures suggest indirectly and figuratively employing sexual metaphors and metonyms, pornographic writings and pictures rely on graphic depictions of human nudity and sexual acts.

10. *The Thousand and One Nights* is also referred to as *Arabian Nights Entertainments*. This collection of Oriental stories of uncertain date and authorship has captured the imagination of Western readers. The first European translation of the *Nights* was made by Antoine Galland in the early eighteenth century. The Arab text was first published in full at Calcutta, in four volumes (1839–42). The source for most later translations, however, was the so-called Vulgate text, an Egyptian recension published at Bulaq, Cairo, in 1835. Richard Burton's version, *The Book of the Thousand Nights and a Night,* based on John Payne's little-known full English translation, has become the best-known English translation.

11. See Dehoï, *L'érotisme des Milles et une Nuits,* 86–183.

12. We may want to refer to the sexuality portrayed in the tales of *The Thousand and One Nights* as "Oriental" sexuality in order to clearly distinguish it from the reality of Middle Eastern/Muslim sexuality. *Playboy, Penthouse,* and *Hustler* are, of course, not the first publications to exploit the harem motif. A large body of writings deals exclusively with the fantastic eroticized images of the seraglio, in particular those of the sultan, i.e., the imperial harems. See, for example, Michel Baudier, *Histoire générale du serrail* (1924), and Ottaviano Bon, *The Grand Signor's Seraglio,* 1650.

13. Bouhdiba gives a list of manuals in his work *Sexuality in Islam,* 140–58. See also Walton's introduction to Nefzawi, *The Perfumed Garden of the Shaykh Nefzawi.*

14. Nefzawi, *The Perfumed Garden,* 127–56.

15. Ibid., 36.

16. For example, E. W. Lane gives a mutilated and bowdlerized version of *The Arabian Nights.* He meticulously expurgated the Arabic original. In the Liseux edition of *The Perfumed Garden,* the chapter on pederasty has been omitted. Sir Richard Burton's translation of *The Perfumed Garden* leaves out a short story about bestiality

and also several names for genitals because, as Alan Hull Walton points out, they are "too coarsely humorous, and, in the case of the female, unpleasantly odoriferous" (47).

17. American erotica is not, of course, the first to focus on the sexual mores of Middle Easterners. Translations and interpretations of *The Thousand and One Nights* and *The Perfumed Garden* spawned a new genre of Western literature. This new genre claimed to be scholarly in nature and was justified as works of science dealing with "sex" in the Orient. Europeans had found a way to indulge in the pleasures of the Orient that was beyond the constraints and taboos of European repression. Among such "scientific scholarly" works are Bernhard Stern's *Medicine, Superstition, and Sex Life in Turkey* (1903) and *The Scented Garden: Anthropology of the Sex Life in the Levant* (1934). The tales of *The Thousand and One Nights* provided ample material on which Western authors could draw in order to create erotic tales taking place somewhere in the Orient. They offered a blueprint for Western "Oriental" erotica by portraying the sexual mores of the "Oriental" savage—strange and "shocking" by Western standards but immensely fascinating and entertaining.

18. Pickthall, *The Meaning of the Glorious Koran,* 405–6.

19. For a detailed discussion of this argument, see Daniel, *A Book on Islam.* See especially chapter 5, in which there is a discussion of Islamic paradise, as well as issues of divorce and polygamy. Such issues are used as hard evidence to support the assertion that Islam is a "sensuous religion." On the "Sexual Ethos," see *The Cambridge Encyclopedia of the Middle East,* 215.

20. On the creation of these fixed images, see Alloula, *The Colonial Harem,* 3–5; see also Mabro, *Veiled Half-Truths.*

21. In *Images of Women,* Graham-Brown gives an excellent example of European misconceptions about the harem. She relates the encounter of Grace Ellison, an Englishwoman who visited Istanbul at the turn of the twentieth century, with a British newspaper. Ellison had submitted a photograph of a Turkish family to the London paper. The photograph was returned to Ellison along with the following comment by the newspaper editor: "The British public would not accept this as a picture of a Turkish harem" (80). The photograph showed European furniture, which was commonly used in affluent Turkish households but which, as the newspaper editor knew, did not conform with the image British society had formed of "authentic" Turkish harems.

22. Flaubert, *Sentimental Education,* vol. 2, 327.

23. Stekel, *Sexual Aberrations,* 82.

24. See Steele, *Fetish,* for an illustrated exploration of fetishism in contemporary fashion.

25. Dennis, "Ethnopornography," 23.

26. Ibid., 22.

27. Sorayama displayed more than fifty of his original posters at his first U.S. show at the Tamars Bane gallery in Los Angeles in 1994. His prints and posters were

also made available for sale. Some of his illustrated poster work was made into a calendar and made available for purchase through mail order.

28. See Steele, *Fetish,* for the use of high boots in sadomasochism, especially 33–38.

29. Hill & Knowlton (H&K), the world's largest public relations firm at that time, represented "Citizens for a Free Kuwait" (CFK). CFK received $11.9 million from the Kuwaiti government, which went to H&K in the form of fees. The task of H&K and its front, the CFK, was a formidable one. It had to tell the American public that a longtime U.S. ally was in fact a monster who had killed about 150,000 Iranians, in addition to at least 13,000 of his own citizens. It also had to persuade the American public that Kuwait was a struggling democracy and not a super-rich state ruled by an oligarchy that had brutally suppressed the country's democratic movement. H&K lived up to this task. In addition to massive media campaigns, CFK published a booklet about Iraqi atrocities titled *The Rape of Kuwait,* which was featured on television talk shows and in the *Wall Street Journal.* According to an article in the *Progressive* by Arthur E. Rowse titled "Flacking for the Emir" (May 1991, 21–22), the Kuwaiti embassy bought 200,000 copies of the booklet for distribution to American troops. CFK also prepared the media kit of the testimony of the fifteen-year-old Kuwaiti girl Nayirah, who accused Iraqi soldiers of taking 312 babies out of their incubators in a Kuwaiti hospital and leaving them on the cold floor to die. This story was repeated over and over. It was even told by President Bush. Her testimony may have had the most decisive impact on public opinion. Later, it was learned that Nayirah was a member of the Kuwaiti royal family and that she had told an outrageous lie.

30. Hiro, *Dictionary of the Middle East,* 117.

31. For example, Saudi Arabia received an impressive $1.725 billion in export revenues in 1968 but an astronomical $39.230 billion in 1974. See Richard F. Nyrop, *Area Handbook for Saudi Arabia,* 3rd ed. (Washington: U.S. Government Printing Office, 1977), 280.

32. Cartoons having features generally unique to the children's world of entertainment are described as "child magnets." An estimated 27 percent of *Playboy,* 33 percent of *Penthouse,* and 47 percent of *Hustler* cartoons and illustrations can be identified as "child magnets." Cartoons showing flying carpets fulfill the criterion of "child magnet." For more information, see the guide by the U.S. Department of Justice, *Images of Children, Crime, and Violence in Playboy, Penthouse, and Hustler.* This guide was prepared under Grant No. 84-JN-AX-K007 from the Office of Juvenile Justice and Delinquency Prevention, Office of Justice Assistance, Research and Statistics, U.S. Department of Justice (1985). The principal investigator was Judith A. Reisman.

33. Said explains in *Covering Islam* how the Western media disregard the reality of Middle Eastern cultures and languages. He explains that during the first days of the Iranian hostage crisis, about three hundred reporters were in Tehran, and not a

single Persian speaker was among them. As a result, almost all the reports coming from Iran were essentially the same (xii). There is generally much confusion about Middle Eastern nomenclature in the Western media. For the purpose of this analysis, it suffices to mention that only 20 percent of all Muslims are Arabs. The largest number of Muslims, 150 million, are Indonesians. Twenty million Chinese, 55 million Russians, 100 million Indians, 95 million Pakistanis, and 90 million Bangladeshis are also Muslims. Islam embraces in its fold more than 4,000 ethnic groups. Furthermore, not all Arabs are Muslims; and although most Iranians are Muslims, they are not Arabs.

34. Al-Tirmidhi, *Sahih*, 8–10.

35. Female circumcision is a controversial topic that has drawn international attention and criticism both from the West and from within many societies in which it is practiced. Misconceptions abound about the different forms of female circumcision, about its medical ramifications, and about the religious, social, and cultural issues involved. The practice of female circumcision was recorded in the pharaonic kingships of ancient Egypt. Herodotus mentioned the existence of female circumcision seven hundred years before Christ was born. The researchers Harold Barclay and C. G. Seligman believe that an extreme form of circumcision/excision (infibulation) was practiced in Sudan before the advent of Islam. For more information on female circumcision, see Foster, "On the Trail of a Taboo," 244–50; Ghadially, "All for Izzat," 17–20; Gordon, "Female Circumcision," 3–14; and Lightfoot-Klein, *Prisoners of Ritual*.

36. Kahf, *Western Representations*.

3. The Cinematics of the Veil

1. In the past decade, Iranian films have won nearly 300 awards at international festivals. In 1998 alone, the Iranian cinema won 60 international awards and prizes.

2. Akrami, "The Blighted Spring," 131–44.

3. Issa, "Re-Orienting Our Views."

4. In 1995, Jafar Panahi's *The White Balloon,* scripted by Abbas Kiarostami, won the Camera d'Or at Cannes and Best Foreign Film from the New York Film Critics Circle, and it became the first Iranian film to gain broad art-house distribution in the United States.

5. In 1999, Majid Majidi's *Children of Heaven* won the Montreal World Film Festival Grand Prix of the Americas Award and the Air Canada People's Award and was nominated for an Academy Award in the category of best foreign film.

6. Naficy, "Veiled Vision," 138.

7. Ibid., 132.

8. Ibid., 133.

9. Khoei, *Tozih al Masa'il*, 423.

10. Behbahani, *Resale Jame' al Masa'il*, 495.

11. Mulvey, "Visual Pleasure and Narrative Cinema," 28.

12. Naficy, "Veiled Vision," 142.

13. Ibid.

14. Quoted by Naficy in "Veiled Vision," 141.

15. Mernissi, *Beyond the Veil,* as quoted by Malti-Douglas, *Woman's Body,* 43–44.

16. Al-Ghazali, *Ihya' 'Ulum al-Din,* 28.

17. Ibid.

18. Ali, *The Holy Qur'an,* vol. 24, 30–31.

19. Naficy, "Veiled Vision," 131.

20. Forugh Farrokhzad directed the documentary *The House Is Black.*

21. Naficy provides a list of woman directors and their films in "Veiled Vision," 134.

22. The *ghuunghat* is a form of veil worn by the Hindu and Sikh traditional female population in India.

23. India has more than 100 languages and more than 2,000 dialects. The Indian constitution recognizes only 15 major languages, with Hindi spoken by about 40 percent of the Indian population. The fact that many Indians understand Hindi is partly due to the popularity of the Hindi film.

24. Gokulsing, *Indian Popular Cinema,* 137.

25. Fuglesang, *Veils and Videos,* 163–66.

26. India has one billion people.

27. For more information on the practice of veiling among Hindus, see Vatuk, "Purdah Revisited," 54–78.

28. For example, in the movie *Nikaah* (The wedding), a song is titled "Chaharaa chupaa liyaa hai kisii ne hijaab me.n" (Look! Someone has hidden her face behind the *hijab*). Another song in this film, "Man bhaavan ke ghar jaae gorii" (The fair lady goes to her beloved's house), is a wedding song that praises the bride's beautiful veil. For other songs about the veil, visit the online archive of Hindi movie songs. Shankar, "Archive of Hindi Movie Songs."

29. *Mere Huzoor* in this context means "My lady." This movie stars Raaj Kumar, Mala Sinha, and Jetinndra and is directed by Vinod Kumar. The music is by Shankar Jai Krishan.

30. *Naqaab* is the Hindi word for the Arabic *niqab.*

31. I am thankful to Tanweer Aslam for translating this poem into English.

32. Mulvey, "Visual Pleasure and Narrative Cinema," 114.

33. Neale, *Genre,* 33.

34. This movie is directed by Manmohan Desai and stars Amitabh Bachchan (Anthony), Vinod Khanna (Amar), Rishi Kapoor (Akbar), Pran, and Nirupa Roy.

35. The anglicized version of "pardaa" is *purdah.*

36. Akbar refers to himself as "Akabar" for assonance.

37. I am thankful to Tanweer Aslam for translating this poem.

38. *Bharat Mata* (Mother India) has English as well as Arabic subtitles. It stars Nargis, Raaj Kumar, Kanhaiyalal, Sunil Dutt, and Rajendra Kumar and is directed

by Mehboob Khan. Its music is by Naushad. This movie won many awards in its day and was nominated for an Academy Award for best foreign film. During its shooting, Dutt saved Nargis from a fire and soon after that they were married.

39. I am thankful to Vandana Agarawal for the translation of this poem from Hindi into English.

40. There are many Hindi songs in which the female singer describes her vantage point behind the veil. For example, in the song "Ghuunghat kii aa. D se dilavar kaa" (From the corners of the bride's veil), from the movie *Hum hain raahi pyar ke* (We are travelers on the path of love) (1993), the bride explains that, by looking from the corners of her veil, she is able to get a first glimpse of her husband at their wedding.

41. The Hindi title *Chowdhveen ka chaand* can also be translated as *Like the beautiful full moon.* The film stars Waheeda Rehman as Jameelah. I want to thank Tanweer Aslam for explaining sensitive cultural aspects of this story to me.

42. This is a popular Urdu love song. It was written by Shakeel Badaayuni, a well-known poet of the Indian film industry, and sung by the much-adored Indian singer Mohammed Rafi. Ravi Shankar plays the music. I am thankful to Tanweer Aslam for translating this song.

43. A *dupatta* is a large scarf.

44. For a discussion of cross-dressing in the Iranian passion play, see Chelkowski, *Ta'ziyeh.*

45. This movie is directed by John Madden. It stars Joseph Fiennes, Gwyneth Paltrow, Geoffrey Rush, Colin Firth, and Judi Dench.

46. This movie is directed by Bernardo Bertolucci and produced by Jeremy Thomas. The screenplay is by Mark Peploe and Bertolucci. It stars Debra Winger (Kit Moresby), John Malkovich (Port), Campbell Scott (George), and Eric Vu-An (Belqassim) and is narrated by Paul Bowles.

47. The Tuareg are the largest group of nomads living in the Sahara. More than 300,000 Tuareg live in the desert, chiefly in Algeria, Mali, and Niger. The Tuareg are Muslims and are related to the Berbers of Northern Africa; they speak Tamershak, a Berber language. They are sometimes called the Blue Men of the Desert, because they often wear indigo-dyed robes that leave a blue color on their skin. The men wear turbans for protection against sandstorms and the sun. They wrap the turbans around their heads and across their faces to form a veil so that only their eyes can be seen. The Tuareg have converted to Islam, but their beliefs have many traditional religious elements. Women in Tuareg society have more freedom than women in other Muslim societies. Social status is dependent on matrilineal descent. The society is strongly hierarchic, divided into nobles, vassals, and serfs, and descendants of slaves have problems breaking free from their inherited social status. See *World Book Encyclopedia,* vol. 19. See also Murphy, "Social Distance and the Veil," 290–314.

48. Ebert, "Ebert: The Sheltering Sky," and Hicks, "Movie Review: The Sheltering Sky."

49. Ebert, "Ebert: The Sheltering Sky."

50. Bowles, *The Sheltering Sky*, 301.

51. Ibid., 284.

52. Ibid.

53. Hicks, "Movie Review."

4. Iranian Politics and the Hijab

1. See *Khoshonat va Farhang* and *Vaqe'e Kashfe Hejab*.

2. *Vaqe'e Kashfe Hejab*, 21–22.

3. *Khoshonat va Farhang*, 123. The signature of the lieutenant colonel is illegible. His name may have been "Nosrat."

4. See Moghissi's *Populism* for an excellent account of the history of women's movements in Iran.

5. *Mut'a* is a usufruct marriage contracted for a specified time and exclusively for the purpose of sexual pleasure. See Wehr, *Arabic-English Dictionary*. Temporary marriage is also known in Persian as *sigheh* (short contract).

6. Esfandiari, *Reconstructed Lives*, 4.

7. Motahari, *Mas'aleh-ye Hejab*.

8. Ibid., 91–93.

9. Moghissi, *Populism*, 65.

10. Shariati, *Fatima Is Fatima*, 46.

11. Constitution of the Islamic Republic of Iran.

12. Addendum 1.02, ratified on 18/05/1362H [1983]. See *Simaye Hijab*, 17.

13. Ibid., addendum 4, ratified on 08/12/1365H [1986].

14. The Persian word "bad" also means "bad" in English.

15. For a discussion of the appropriate Islamic dress for women, see Shirazi-Mahajan, "A Dramaturgical Approach," 35–51.

16. Saddam Hussein (reportedly upon the request of the Shah) had expelled Khomeini in 1977 from An Najaf in Iraq, where he had lived in exile for thirteen years.

17. As soon as Khomeini had come to power, a revolutionary court passed death sentences on four of the Shah's generals, military and police officers, SAVAK agents, cabinet members, Majlis deputies, and officials of the Shah's regime. These executions led to the disintegration of the once invincible Imperial Iranian Army. The mullahs who were now leading Iran's armed forces had little or no military experience.

18. Iranians refer to this waterway as Arvand Roud.

19. Omid, "Islamic Stance on Art," 77.

20. On my visit to the shrine of Hazrate Ma'suma, the sister of the eighth Shi'i imam, in the holy city of Qum, I observed signs at the entry to the shrine's compound saying: "Wearing a *rupush* and *ruusari* (loose outer gown and head scarf) is not considered proper *hijab*, sisters must wear our traditional chador in order to enter the holy shrine's compound." Next to this fairly large sign were ablution fountains and washroom facilities for women pilgrims to change into the proper

form of hijab. When I entered the tomb's grounds, where a special *du'a* (a prayer specifically composed for Hazrate Ma'suma) would be recited in a very respectful manner and a *fatiha* (first *sura* of the Qur'an) would be said for her soul, I saw the same warning sign sitting on top of her beautifully carved tomb. Interestingly, since only women are allowed to go inside the room where her tomb is located, there would be no need for women to cover up in such meticulous fashion.

21. Since pictures of humans could not be used on posters, stamps, billboards, etc., graphic arts flourished in Iran. High-quality graphic works showing war and religious subjects, produced by both unknown and well-known graphic artists, were heavily promoted by the government. For an excellent account, see *A Decade with the Graphists of the Islamic Revolution, 1979–1989.*

22. For an analysis of Fatima's legacy, see Spellberg, *Politics, Gender, and the Islamic Past,* especially 156–61.

23. In 1988, Iran openly accused the United States of helping Iraqi forces in their heavy air attacks in the Gulf. The United States also undertook independent actions against Iran: in the fall of 1987 and spring of 1988, the United States attacked several Iranian oil platforms and sank some Iranian gunboats. These attacks were contrary to the principles of the U.N. charter and the principle of neutrality in the war.

24. It is noteworthy that, although Shi'is have lived in Iran since the earliest days of Islam, historians believe that most Iranians were Sunnis until the seventeenth century. The Safavid dynasty made Shi'a Islam the official state religion in the sixteenth century and aggressively proselytized on its behalf.

25. The Iranian government referred to the Iran-Iraq war as "imposed" war (*jange tahmili*): Iran had to defend its religion and territory against the invader.

26. Workman, *The Social Origins of the Iran-Iraq War,* 124.

27. Ibid., 124.

28. The *shahada* is the first pillar of Islam. Its recitation is the first duty of every Muslim. The complete text of the *shahada* is: "I testify that there is no god but Allah and that Muhammad is the Messenger of Allah."

29. Moghissi, *Populism,* 60–61.

30. This poster is included in *A Decade with the Graphists of the Islamic Revolution, 1979–1989.*

31. Although Iranian women were not allowed to participate actively in the war, female *komiteh* members were allowed to carry guns on their patrols of bad hijab.

32. I obtained this poster in Iran in the summer of 1995 (my translation).

33. We may assume that most of the graffiti is condoned, if not written, by members of the Hizbollah.

34. For a discussion of the Muslim concept of active female sexuality, see Mernissi, *Beyond the Veil,* 27–45.

35. Baraheni, *The Crowned Cannibals,* 47.

36. A report in *Iran Times* (October 1, 1999) indicates that some clerics are willing to give women equal access to political and religious power. Yousef Sanei, who is an influential cleric and teacher at the prestigious theological school in Qum, opines

that women should be allowed to hold any position of power in the Islamic Republic, including that of president and ayatollah.

5. Militarizing the Veil

1. In *Politics, Gender, and the Islamic Past,* Spellberg provides an excellent analysis of the impact of these sources on the shaping of ʿAʾisha's historical persona.

2. *Encyclopaedia of Islam,* vol. 2, 415.

3. Ahmed, "Advent," 690.

4. Ibn Shahrashub, *Manaqib Al Abi Talib,* 148.

5. Ali, *Qurʾan,* 33:29.

6. Abbott, "Women and the State in Early Islam," 106–26, 115, 123.

7. *Jahiliya* means "age of ignorance." It refers to pre-Islamic times.

8. Ahmed, "Advent," 691.

9. *Encyclopaedia of Islam,* vol. 3, 455.

10. Ahmed, "Advent," 687.

11. *Hadiths* consist of two parts: the *isnad,* or chain of named, originally oral, transmitters; and the *matn,* the core content of the report.

12. The Shiʿi collections were compiled by Abu Jaʿfar Muhammad al-Kulini (d. 939 CE), Abu Jaʿfar Muhammad al-Kummi (d. 991 CE), and Abu Jaʿfar Muhammad al-Tusi (d. 1068 CE).

13. Ahmed, "Advent," 684.

14. Al-Bukhari, *Sahih,* vol. 4, 38.

15. Muslim, *Sahih,* vol. 3, 1001.

16. Ibid., 1002.

17. Al-Bukhari, *Sahih,* 86.

18. Ibid., 87.

19. Ibid., 85.

20. *Tafsir* is the interpretation of and commentary on the Qurʾan and *hadiths.*

21. Al-Shawkani, *Nayl al-Awtar,* vol. 9, 141–42.

22. According to Islamic law, the whole body of a dead person must be washed. This ritual ablution is called *ghusl.*

23. Ul-Ameene, *Islamic Shiʿite Encyclopaedia,* vol. 2, 72.

24. *Sayidaty,* no. 6 (1990): 6 (my translation).

25. In the Gulf states, the tasks assigned to women can be administrative, supervisory, or health industry and defense related. The type of tasks, as well as the type of training received, varies from Gulf state to Gulf state.

26. Brooks, *Nine Parts of Desire,* 113.

27. Ibid., 109.

28. Ibid., 111.

29. Ninety-five percent of Iraqis are Muslims; 60 percent are Shiʿi, and 35 percent are Sunni. Sunnis control the Baʿth Party.

30. See, for example, Baram, "Culture in the Service of *Wataniyya,*" 265–313. See also Baram, "Mesopotamian Identity in Baʿthi Iraq."

31. Chapin-Metz, *Iraq.*

32. *New York Times International,* Wednesday, November 26, 1997.

33. Chapin-Metz, *Iraq.*

34. Al-*Majallah* (March 1998): 9.

35. This is a reference to Her Holiness Zaynab, who was the daughter of Imam 'Ali, and Her Holiness Fatima, who was the daughter of the Prophet Muhammad. Zaynab was also the sister of Hussein and Hassan.

36. *Mahjubah: The Magazine for Muslim Women* is published by the Islamic Thought Foundation in Tehran and distributed throughout the world. Recently, it changed its name to *Mahjubah: The Islamic Magazine for Family.*

37. *Mahjubah* translates literally as "the woman who wears the *hijab.*"

38. Ul-Ameene, *Islamic Shi'ite Encyclopaedia,* 72.

39. This is a reference to Fatima, daughter of the Prophet Muhammad; she is also known as Zahra, or as Fatima Zahra.

40. Zaynab's brother Imam Hussein is called the Great Martyr. Interestingly, in December 1978, the onset of the Ashura festival, which centered on his martyrdom, irrevocably turned the tide against the secular regime of Mohammed Reza Shah Pahlavi.

41. The official title of this Iranian political party is Sazman-e Mujahedin-e Khalq-e Iran (Iranian people's combatants organization). This party is also known as the Mujahedin-e Khalq Organization (MEK or MKO), the People's Mujahedin of Iran (PMOI), and the National Council of Resistance (NCR). The militant wing of the Mujahedin-e Khalq is called the National Liberation Army (NLA).

42. Daneshvar, *Revolution,* 88.

43. Abrahamian, *Radical Islam,* 92.

44. Daneshvar, *Revolution,* 90.

45. Hiro, *Dictionary of the Middle East,* 205.

46. Ibid., 206.

47. Serrill, "Armed Women of Iran."

48. *Iran Times,* vol. 29, no. 27 (September 17, 1999), 14.

49. This issue of *Majallah* (no. 918) appeared in 1997, although the photograph of parading NLA women was probably taken years earlier, when the NLA was fully mobilized.

50. The goal of the former Soviet Union in funding the Mujahedin and the Ayatollah Khomeini was to topple the Shah and thus supplant U.S. influence in Iran.

51. Timmerman, "Easing Sanctions."

52. *Iran Times,* vol. 29, no. 27 (September 17, 1999), 14.

53. Brief on Iran, Representative Office of the National Council of Resistance of Iran, no. 378, March 27, 1996.

54. *Neshat* 5, vol. 1, no. 96 (July 4, 1999). According to statistics in this issue, more than 54 percent of Iranians are under the age of twenty, and 70 percent are under the age of thirty. Twenty million of the 70 percent are between the ages of ten and

twenty, ten million are between the ages of one and ten. About fifteen million between the ages of thirty and thirty-five are not yet married.

55. Serrill, "Armed Women of Iran."

6. Literary Dynamics of the Veil

1. Jasim and Shukr, *Diwan*.

2. Ibid., 15.

3. Ibid., 20–21.

4. The Egyptian Qasim Amin (1865–1908) published *Tahrir al-Mar'a* (Woman's history) (1899) and *Al-Mar'a al-Jadidah* (The new woman) (1901). In his books and articles, Amin has argued that originally Islam acted to improve the condition of women and that a return to the true precepts of Islam, in addition to improvements in education and legal and social rights, would accord woman her proper position in Muslim society.

5. Jasim and Shukr, *Diwan,* 20. I am thankful to my respected late father, Mahmood Shirazi, and to my respected uncle, Aboul Qasim Shirazi, for their help and much patience in translating the original text from Arabic into English.

6. Ibid., 21.

7. Ibid.

8. For a discussion of active versus passive female sexuality, see Mernissi, *Beyond the Veil,* 30–45.

9. In this particular context, a woman displayed refers to an available woman, to someone who is as available as a prostitute.

10. This reference to stage means public.

11. Women singers and dancers have the same status as prostitutes.

12. Jasim and Shukr, *Diwan,* 30–31.

13. Amin, *The Liberation of Women,* 65, as quoted by Mernissi, *Beyond the Veil,* 31. See Badran, *Feminists, Islam, and Nation,* and Baron, *The Women's Awakening in Egypt,* for critical assessments of Qasim Amin's role in the Egyptian feminist movement.

14. *Purdah* is an anglicization of the Hindi *pardaa,* literally "curtain."

15. Vatuk, "Purdah Revisited," 54–78.

16. Ibid., 58.

17. Friend, *Yashpal,* 10.

18. Ibid., 4–5.

19. Yashpal, "Purdah."

20. I am thankful to my dear friend Mrs. Kumkum Jain for translating this short story from Hindi into English.

21. Kappeler et al., *Muslim Communities,* 304.

22. For an account of French attempts to destroy traditional Algerian society, see Fanon, *A Dying Colonialism,* 35–67.

23. Ibid, 37.

24. Tokhtakhodzhaera, *Slogans of Communism,* 46.

25. Ibid., 57.

26. Ibid., 66.

27. Fernea, *In Search of Islamic Feminism*, 1–61.

28. Ibid., 61.

29. Yarshater, *Persian Literature*, 29.

30. Iraj Mirza's son Khosrow Iraj wrote the introduction to *Iraj Mirza's Poetry*.

31. Yarshater, *Persian Literature*, 29.

32. Iraj Mirza, *Iraj Mirza*, 177, as quoted by Milani, *Veils*, 30.

33. Milani, *Veils*, 30.

34. Iraj Mirza, "Dastane Zane Ba Hejab," 37–48. This poem is part of the *Arefnameh* (Book of Aref). The name of this book may allude to Ferdowsi's epic work *Shahnameh* (Book of kings). In the *Arefnameh*, the narrator vents his anger at the pederast Aref for declining his hospitality. The choice of the name Aref may also not be a coincidence: Iraj Mirza, who had studied Arabic, would have been aware that "'arif" means "the one who knows." For an artistic translation of half of this poem, see Sprachman, *Suppressed Persian*, 83–90.

35. A double chin is a mark of beauty and a reference to a well-fed and elite woman in premodern Iran.

36. A *picheh* is a black veil that covers the face. It is an old-fashioned form of the hijab and was common during the nineteenth and early part of the twentieth centuries in Iran. Both the picheh and the chador were abolished as part of Reza Shah's unveiling campaign.

37. The women of Tehran and other major cities in Iran were known to be more Westernized and liberal in their ways than the women living in smaller towns and rural areas.

38. The Arabian *angha* in the form of a griffin is said to have been created by God to destroy the wild beast in Palestine.

39. A literal translation of this line is "our distance to [our] graves is just measured like the four fingers put together." This idiom is used to express the ephemeral nature of "earthly" life.

40. *Mujtahid* denotes, in contemporary usage, one who possesses the aptitude to form his own judgment on questions concerning the *shari'a*, using personal effort (*ijtihad*) in the interpretation of the fundamental principles of the *shari'a*. For more information, see *Encyclopaedia of Islam*, vol. 7, 295–96.

41. Nakir and Munkar are the names of the two angels who examine and, if necessary, punish the dead in their tombs. The infidels and the faithful, the righteous as well as the sinners, are liable to an examination in the tomb. The dead are set upright in their tombs and must state their opinion regarding the Prophet Muhammad. The righteous faithful will answer that he is the Apostle of Allah; thereupon they will be left alone till the Day of Resurrection. The sinners and the infidels, on the other hand, will have no satisfactory answer to give them and the angels will beat them severely, until Allah is satisfied. According to some authorities, they will be beaten until the Day of Resurrection, except on Fridays. The Qur'an alludes to the punishment in the tomb but does not state this clearly.

42. This is a reference to the sweetness of "delights," to something that can be gained without much effort. Public opinion in Iran holds that the clergy are able to obtain the good things in life without putting forth much effort or work. Both rice and *halva* were considered food for elites at this time. Halva is a sweet dish that contains butter, sugar, saffron, and flour. It is considered to be an expensive dish because of its ingredients.

43. Iraj Mirza, *Divane*, 37–48 (my translation).

44. Baraheni, *The Crowned Cannibals*, 47.

45. Iraj Mirza's *Divane* also includes a poem titled "Kariest Gozashtast va Saboest Shekastast" (Don't cry over spoiled milk), 20–26, in which the narrator describes in graphic details the rape of a young boy.

46. See Ghanoonparvar's *Prophets of Doom* for an in-depth analysis of the interaction between modern Iranian literature and Iranian politics. See especially chapter 6, "Literary Ambiguity," 149–77.

47. Mirzade-ye 'Eshqi, *Koliyat-e Mosavar-e 'Eshqi*. 218, as quoted by Milani, *Veils*, 29.

48. Ibid.

49. A *burqah* is a face veil. It is usually black and is similar to the face veil worn by Saudi women.

50. The *pardeh* is the Persian equivalent of the Hindi *pardaa*. See also note 14.

51. The term *ruband* consists of the morphemes "ru," meaning "face," and "band," meaning "band, tie." A *ruband* is a face veil.

52. Vafa, "Hijab," 28 (my translation).

53. Milani, *Veils*, 1–2.

54. E'tesami, *A Nightingale's Lament*.

55. Moayyad, *Once a Dewdrop*, 48.

56. Ibid.

57. Ibid., 18.

58. Rajabzadeh, *Divane Parvine E'tesami*.

59. I have found this particular poem in an earlier edition.

60. E'tesami, *A Nightingale's Lament*, 107–9.

61. Baraheni, *Tarikhe Mozakkar*, 102.

62. Moayyad, *Once a Dewdrop*, 84.

63. Milani, *Veils*, 150.

64. Hillmann, *A Lonely Woman*.

65. Ibid., 23.

66. Farrokhzad, *Another Birth*, 9.

67. Milani, "Forugh Farrokhzad," 145.

68. Farrokhzad, *A Rebirth*, x.

69. Urdu is an Indo-Aryan language that originated in the region between the Ganges and Jamuna rivers near Delhi. It is now the official language of Pakistan and numbers close to fifty million speakers. It is the primary language of the Muslims of both Pakistan and northern India. While the grammar of Urdu follows basic Hindi grammar, the vocabulary is drawn from Hindi, Persian, Arabic, and Turkish. Thus,

Urdu is rich in terms of words and expressions. It is written in the Persian-Arabic script, and, with a few major exceptions, the literature in Urdu is the work of Muslim writers who take their themes from the life of the Indian subcontinent.

70. Mahmud, *Ghalib,* 76.

71. Ibid., 91–92.

72. The *niqab,* worn by conservative South Asian Muslims, resembles the black face veil worn by Saudi women.

73. Mahmud, *Ghalib,* 186.

74. Ibid., 190.

75. Majnun, whose real name is Qayes, loved a woman named Layla. Because he could not be with her, he chose to live among the wild animals, away from civilization. He became known as "Majnun," which means "crazy" in Arabic. The story of Layla and Majnun is a well-known Arabic love story.

76. Mahmud, *Ghalib,* 198.

77. Ibid., 249.

78. Hafez, *Divan,* 864.

79. As quoted by Talat S. Halman in Yarshater, *Persian Literature,* 200.

80. Milani, *Veils,* 7.

81. Mernissi, *Beyond the Veil,* 31.

82. Ibid., 41.

83. Al-Tirmidhi, *Sahih,* 120–21.

84. For a discussion of Western reactions to woman's body and its functions, especially those expressed by Freud, see Kristeva, *The Powers of Horror.*

85. Khomeini, *Divane Imam.*

86. *Irfan* are mystical writings that contain multiple layers of meanings and provide an arena for various interpretations.

87. Ibid., 209 (my translation).

88. Ibid. (my translation).

89. *Falsafa* in Arabic.

90. For a more detailed discussion of the history of *falsafeh/falsafa,* see *Encyclopaedia of Islam,* vol. 2, 769–75.

91. *Simaye Zan dar Kalame Khumayni,* 43.

92. Tahan, *The Man Who Counted.*

93. Ibid., 55.

94. Ibid., 57.

95. Ibid., 58.

96. Ibid., 155.

97. Malba Tahan explains the logic behind Beremiz' questions on p. 240. Briefly, the first girl must have *said* that she has brown eyes, because if she has brown eyes she has to tell the truth and if she has blue eyes she has to lie and say that her eyes are brown. Now knowing what the first girl's answer was, Beremiz can determine that the second girl is lying when she claims that the first girl has said that she has blue eyes. Knowing that the second girl is a blue-eyed liar, Beremiz has to establish

if the first girl is a blue-eyed liar as well. Thus, he asks the third slave girl about the color of the eyes of the first and second slave girls. If the third girl says that the eye color of the second girl is blue, which Beremiz has established, he could conclude that the third girl told the truth and thus must have brown eyes. Knowing that the third girl told the truth, Beremiz concludes that her eyes are brown. Now he has found the two brown-eyed girls and deduces that the eyes of the other two girls, whom he was not allowed to question, must be blue.

Conclusion

1. *Playboy Report, Ayatollah Khomeini.* I want to thank Renate Wise for drawing my attention to this *Playboy* publication.

2. Any biographical dictionary of Middle Eastern women novelists who depict women's plight in the Muslim world would include Evelyne Accad (Lebanon), Etel Adnan (Lebanon), Samira Almana (Iraq), Layla Ba'labakki (Lebanon), Simin Daneshvar (Iran), Sahar Khalifeh (Israel), Fatima Mernissi (Morocco), Ghadah al-Samman (Lebanon), Ahdaf Soueif (Egypt), and many more.

3. Sprachman, *Suppressed Persian,* 77.

4. Al-Shaykh, *Women of Sand and Myrrh.*

Glossary

agal Arabic, a cord wound around the head to hold the *kafiya* in place.

angha Arabic, the *angha* in the form of a griffin is said to have been created by god to destroy the wild beast in Palestine.

Ashura a Shi'i religious festival observed on the tenth day of Muharram of the Muslim calendar commemorating the martyrdom of Hussein, the grandson of Prophet Muhammad.

aya Arabic, a verse in the Qur'an.

bad hejab Persian, a term used in the Islamic Republic of Iran to designate those women who wear a "bad" *hijab,* an unacceptable or improper form of the veil.

chador Persian, literally, "tent." *Chador* is a form of *hijab,* consisting of a full-length semicircular piece of material. It is placed on top of the head and covers the entire body. It is held in place with one hand at all times. Sometimes a corner of it is pulled over the face to cover part of the mouth.

dupatta Hindi, a large scarf.

falsafa Arabic, philosophy.

falsafeh Persian, philosophy.

fatiha Arabic, the opening chapter of the Qur'an, recited in the daily prayers.

fatwa Arabic (plural: *fatawa*), a formal legal opinion of a religious authority.

fiqh Arabic, Islamic jurisprudence.

fitna Arabic, its many meanings include temptation, trial, infatuation, civil strife, riot, sedition. It is often used to denote chaos caused by women's sexuality.

galabiya colloquial Egyptian, from Arabic *jallabiya,* also called *djellaba(h),* a long, loose outer garment worn in Arab countries.

ghusl Arabic, a major ritual ablution, that is, a washing of the whole body (Islamic law).

ghuunghat Hindi, a form of veiling prevalent among traditional Hindu and Sikh women.

hadith Arabic, accepted accounts of what the Prophet Muhammad said and did.

halva Arabic, a sweet dish containing butter, sugar, saffron, and flour.

haram Arabic, actions forbidden by Islamic law.

hejabe behtar Persian, a term designating a "superior" form of *hijab* in Iran. The traditional Iranian *chador* is often considered a better and superior form of *hijab,* as opposed to the more modern form of Islamic dress that consists of an outerwear gown (*rupush*) and a large scarf (*rusari*).

hijab Arabic and Persian, veil.

imam Shi'i religious leader who is believed to have the special guidance of God to enact his will on earth.

irfan Persian, mystical writings that contain multiple layers of meanings and provide an arena for various interpretations.

Islam Arabic, literally, "submission to the will of God."

isnad Arabic, chain of named transmitters of traditional accounts (*hadiths*) of the life of Prophet Muhammad.

jahiliya Arabic, literally, "the age of ignorance." It refers to the time before the advent of Islam.

jihad Arabic, often translated as "holy war," "struggle," or "striving." It refers to an overt action on behalf of Islam.

kafiya Arabic, a headdress worn by Arabs as protection against dust and heat; it is a large square of cotton cloth, draped and folded, and held in place by the *agal.*

madrasa Arabic, school.

mahram Arabic, something forbidden, taboo; being in a degree of consanguinity precluding marriage (Islamic law).

Majlis House of Representatives in Iran.

matn Arabic, subject or content matter of a *hadith*. The *matn* follows the *isnad*.

Mujahedin-e Khalq Iranian political party with the official name Sazman-e Mujahedin-e Khalq-e Iran (Iranian people's combatants' organization). This party is also known as Mujahedin-e Khalq Organization (MEK or MKO), the People's Mujahedin of Iran (PMOI), and the National Council of Resistance (NCR). The militant wing of the Mujahedin-e Khalq is called the National Liberation Army (NLA).

mujtahid Arabic, a legist who has the authority to practice *ijtihad,* the interpretation of the *shariah*.

Nakir and Munkar Two angels who examine the righteousness of the deceased and, if necessary, punish them in their tombs on the first night they are there.

namahram Persian, those who are not in a degree of consanguinity precluding marriage (Islamic law).

naqaab Hindi for the Arabic *niqab,* a form of face veil.

nikaah Arabic, a Muslim wedding.

parandja Uzbek, the veil that Muslim women used to wear in Uzbekistan.

pardaa Hindi, anglicized "purdah." This term originates in Persian, where it literally means "curtain"; in Urdu, *pardaa* refers to segregation as well as to the veil worn by a Muslim woman.

picheh Persian, a black face veil. A *picheh* is an old-fashioned form of *hijab* that was common during the nineteenth and early twentieth centuries in Iran.

purdah The anglicized version of the Hindi *pardaa*.

qasida Arabic, an ancient Arabic poem that has, as a rule, a rigid tripartite structure. It is a laudatory, elegiac, or satiric poem that is found in Arabic, Persian, and many related Oriental literatures. For more information, see Merriam-Webster's *Encyclopedia of Literature* (Springfield, Mass.: Merriam-Webster, 1995), 919.

Qur'an Arabic, literally, "recitation." The Qur'an has 114 *suras,* or chapters, and Muslims revere it as the word of God.

rupush Persian, outer wear. In the Islamic Republic of Iran, the *rupush* is the outer gown worn as a part of the Islamic dress code. It fits loosely, has long sleeves, and reaches below the knee.

rusari Persian for "worn over the head." It is a large scarf worn over the head and is usually worn with the *rupush*. The *rusari* is considered a modern form of Islamic dress in the Islamic Republic of Iran.

SAVAK Iranian internal security forces that were active during the reign of Mohammed Reza Shah Pahlavi.

shahada Arabic, doctrinal formula of the Muslim creed: "There is no god but God, and Muhammad is His Prophet."

shahid Arabic, martyr.

shariʿa Arabic, Islamic law.

Shiʿa Arabic, the branch of Muslims who recognize ʿAli, the Prophet's first cousin and son-in-law, as his rightful successor.

Shiʿi Arabic, follower of the Shiʿa.

sigheh Persian for *mutʿa,* or temporary marriage.

sunna Arabic, literally, "usage sanctioned by tradition." Accepted accounts of the Prophet's behavior and sayings constitute the *sunna* of Islam. The *sunna* is a main source of Islamic law.

Sunnis Arabic, "people of the path of the prophet." Sunnis are the largest sect within Islam. They regard the first four caliphs—Abu Bakr, ʿUmar, ʿUthman, and ʿAli—"rightly guided."

sura Arabic, chapter in the Qurʾan.

tafsir Arabic, commentary on and interpretation of the Qurʾan.

Taliban Persian plural for the Arabic word *talib* (student). The Taliban rule Afghanistan.

Tuareg a Caucasoid people of Mediterranean type (some are mixed with other groups of sub-Saharan African peoples). Their language is of the Hamitic group and is closely related to Berber.

ʿ*ulama* Arabic, a body of educated scholars who have the authority to adjudicate questions related to Islamic law and theology.

Urdu an Indo-Aryan language that originated in the region between the Ganges and Jamuna rivers near Delhi. Urdu is the official language of Pakistan.

Bibliography

Abbott, Nabia. "Women and the State in Early Islam." *Journal of Near Eastern Studies* 1 (1942): 106–27.

Abrahamian, Ervand. *Radical Islam: The Iranian Mojahedeen*. London: I. B. Tauris, 1986.

Abu-Lughod, Lila. *Veiled Sentiments: Honor and Poetry in a Bedouin Society*. Berkeley: University of California Press, 1986.

Ahmed, Leila. "Women and the Advent of Islam." *Signs* 11, no. 4 (1986): 665–91.

Akrami, Jamsheed. "The Blighted Spring: Iranian Cinema and Politics in the 1970s." In *Film and Politics in the Third World*, ed. John D. H. Downing. New York: Praeger, 1987.

Ali, Yusuf. *The Holy Qur'an: Text, Translation, and Commentary*. Brentwood, Md.: Amana, 1983.

Alloula, Malek. *The Colonial Harem*. Minneapolis: University of Minnesota Press, 1986.

ul-Ameene, Hassan. *Islamic Shi'ite Encyclopaedia*. Beirut: SLIM Press, 1970.

American-Arab Anti-Discrimination Committee. *Activity Report*. 1989.

———. *Activity Report*. 1992.

Amin, Qasim. *The Liberation of Women*. Cairo: n.p., 1928.

Ascha, Ghassan. *Du statut inférieur de la femme en Islam* (Woman's inferior status in Islam). Paris: L'Harmattan, 1989.

Badran, Margot. *Feminists, Islam, and Nation: Gender and the Making of Modern Egypt*. Princeton: Princeton University Press, 1995.

Baraheni, Reza. *The Crowned Cannibals: Writing of Repression in Iran*. New York: Vintage Books, 1977.

——. *Tarikhe Mozakkar* (Masculine history). Tehran: Elmi, n.d.

Baram, Amazia. "Culture in the Service of Wataniyya: The Treatment of Mesopotamian-Inspired Art in Ba'thi Iraq." In *Studies in Islamic Society*, ed. Gabriel R. Warburg and Gad G. Gilbar. Haifa: Haifa University Press, 1984.

——. "Mesopotamian Identity in Ba'thi Iraq." *Middle Eastern Studies* (October 1983).

Barnet, Richard, and Ronald E. Muller. *Global Reach: The Power of Multinational Corporations*. New York: Simon and Schuster, 1974.

Baron, Beth. *The Women's Awakening in Egypt: Culture, Society, and the Press*. New Haven: Yale University Press, 1994.

Bassuk, Ellen L. "The Rest Cure: Repetition or Resolution of Victorian Women's Conflicts?" In *The Female Body in Western Culture: Contemporary Perspectives*, ed. Susan Rubin Suleiman, 139–51. Cambridge: Harvard University Press, 1985.

Behbahani, Hajj Sayyad Ali. *Resale Jame" al Masa'il* (The complete book of clarifications of questions). N.p., n.d.

Bouhdiba, Abdelwahab. *Sexuality in Islam*. Trans. A. Sheridan. London: Routledge and Kegan Paul, 1985.

Bowles, Paul. *The Sheltering Sky*. New York: Belgrave Press, 1949.

Brief on Iran, Representative Office of the National Council of Resistance of Iran, no. 378 (March 27, 1996).

Brooks, Geraldine. *Nine Parts of Desire: The Hidden World of Islamic Women*. New York: Anchor Books, 1995.

Brown, Edward G. *A Literary History of Persia*. Cambridge: Cambridge University Press, 1930.

al-Bukhari. *Sahih al-Bukhari*. Trans. Muhammad Muhsin Khan. Al-Medina Al-Munauwara: Islamic University, n.d.

Cambridge Encyclopedia of the Middle East and North Africa. Cambridge: Cambridge University Press, 1988.

Chapin-Metz, Helen, ed. *Iraq: A Country Study*. Federal Research Division, Library of Congress. May 1988. http://lcweb2.loc.gov/frd/cs/iqtoc.html (November 7, 1999).

Chelkowski, Peter J. *Ta'ziyeh: Ritual and Drama in Iran*. New York: New York University Press, 1979.

Constitution of the Islamic Republic of Iran. Trans. Hamid Algar. Berkeley, Calif.: Mizan Press, 1980.

Courtney, Alice E., and Thomas W. Whipple. *Sex Stereotyping in Advertising*. Lexington, Mass.: Lexington Books, 1983.

Daneshvar, Parviz. *Revolution in Iran*. New York: St. Martin's Press, 1996.

Daniel, Norman. *A Book on Islam and the West: The Making of an Image.* Edinburgh: Edinburgh University Press, 1960.

A Decade with the Graphists of the Islamic Revolution, 1979–1989. Tehran: Art Center of the Islamic Propagation Organization, 1989.

Dehoï, Enver F. *L'érotisme des Milles et une Nuits* (The eroticism of *The Thousand and One Nights*). Paris: J.-J. Pauvert, 1961.

Dennis, Kelly. "Ethnopornography: Veiling the Dark Continent." *History of Photography* 18, no. 1 (1994).

Driver, G. R., and John C. Miles, eds. *The Babylonian Laws.* Oxford: Clarendon Press, 1952.

Dunn, Watson S. "The Case Study Approach in Cross-Cultural Environment of International Marketing." *Columbia Journal of World Business* 12 (Winter 1977).

Ebert, Roger. "Ebert: The Sheltering Sky." *Chicago Sun-Times* (November 1, 1991). http://www.suntimes.com/ebert/ebert_reviews/1991/01/629310.html (June 3, 2000).

El Guindi, Fadwa. *Veil: Modesty, Privacy and Resistance.* Oxford: Berg, 1999.

Encyclopaedia of Islam. 2d ed. Ed. H.A.R. Gibb et al. Leiden: E. J. Brill, 1960–.

Esfandiari, Haleh. *Reconstructed Lives, Women and Iran's Islamic Revolution.* Baltimore: Johns Hopkins University Press, 1997.

'Eshqi, Mirzade-ye. *Koliyat-e Mosavar-e 'Eshqi* (Illustrated works of 'Eshqi), ed. Ali Akbar Moshir-Salimi. Tehran: Sepehr, 1978.

E'tesami, Parvin. *A Nightingale's Lament.* Trans. Heshmat Moayyad and A. Margaret Arent Madelung. Lexington, Ky.: Mazda Publishers, 1985.

Fanon, Frantz. *A Dying Colonialism.* New York: Grove Press, 1967.

Farrokhzad, Forugh. *Another Birth.* Trans. Hasan Javadi and Susan Sallée. Emeryville, Calif.: Albanu Press, 1981.

——— [Farrokhzaad, Foroogh]. *A Rebirth.* Trans. David Martin. Costa Mesa, Calif.: Mazda Publishers, 1997.

Fernea, Elizabeth Warnock. *In Search of Islamic Feminism: One Woman's Global Journey.* New York: Anchor Books, 1998.

Flaubert, Gustave. *Sentimental Education; or the History of a Young Man.* 2 vols. Akron: St. Dunstan Society, 1904.

Foster, Charles. "On the Trail of a Taboo: Female Circumcision in the Islamic World." *Contemporary Review* 264, no. 1640 (1994): 244–50.

Frazer, Sir James G. *The Golden Bough: The Roots of Religion and Folklore.* New York: Avenel, 1981.

Friend, Corinne. *Yashpal Looks Back: Selections from an Autobiography.* New Delhi: Vikas, 1981.

Fuglesang, Minou. *Veils and Videos: Female Youth Culture on the Kenyan Coast.* Stockholm: Department of Social Anthropology, Stockholm University, 1994.

Ghadially, Rehana. "All for Izzat: The Practice of Female Circumcision among Bohra Muslims." *Manushi* 66 (1991): 17–20.

Ghanoonparvar, M. R. *Prophets of Doom: Literature as a Socio-Political Phenomenon in Iran*. Lanham, Md.: University Press of America, 1984.

al-Ghazali, Abu Hamid. *Ihya' 'Ulum al-Din* (The revivification of religious sciences). 5 vols. Beirut: Dar al-Qalam, n.d.

Gokulsing, Moti K., and Wimal Dissanayake, eds. *Indian Popular Cinema: A Narrative of Cultural Change*. London: Trentham Books, 1998.

Goodwin, Jan. *Price of Honor: Muslim Women Lift the Veil of Silence on the Islamic World*. Reprint. New York: Penguin USA, 1995.

Gordon, Daniel. "Female Circumcision and Genital Operations in Egypt and the Sudan: A Dilemma for Medical Anthropology." *Medical Anthropology Quarterly* 5, no. 1 (1986): 3–14.

Graham-Brown, Sarah. *Images of Women*. New York: Columbia University Press, 1988.

Grahn, Judy. *Blood, Bread, and Roses: How Menstruation Created the World*. Boston: Beacon, 1993.

Hafez, Shams ed-Din Mohammed. *Divan*. Ed. Parviz Natel Khanlari. Tehran: Kharazmi, 1980.

Hicks, Chris. "Movie Review: The Sheltering Sky." *Deseret News* (November 1, 1991). http://deseretnews.com/movies/view/1,1257,1644,00.html (June 3, 2000).

Hillmann, Michael C. *A Lonely Woman: Forugh Farrokhzad and Her Poetry*. Washington, D.C.: Three Continents Press and Mage Publishers, 1987.

Hiro, Dilip. *Dictionary of the Middle East*. New York: St. Martin's Press, 1996.

Ibn al-Jawzi. *Ahkam al-Nisa'* (The opinions of women). Beirut: Dar al-Kutub al-'Ilmiyya, 1985.

Ibn Shahrashub. *Manaqib Al Abi Talib* (The virtues of Al Abi Talib). Cairo: Matba'at al-Kubra al-Aminiyya, 1904.

Iraj Mirza. "Dastane Zane Ba Hejab" (The story of the veiled woman). In *Iraj Mirza, Divane Iraj Mirza*. Tehran: Bongahe Matbu'atiye Takhte Jamshid, n.d.

———. *Iraj Mirza*. Ed. Mohammad Ja'far Mahjub. Tehran: Andisheh, 1974.

Iraj Mirza's Poetry. Bethesda, Md.: Ibex Publishers, 1992.

Issa, Rose. "'Re-Orienting Our Views': A Rediscovery of Iran through Its Cinema and Women Filmmakers." http://www.nima3.com/IranMedia2/women.htm (June 3, 2000).

Jasim, Maki al-Said, and Shakir Hadi Shukr. *Diwan al-Hajj "Abd al-Hussayn al-Azri*. Baghdad: n.p., n.d.

Kahf, Mohja. *Western Representations of the Muslim Woman*. Austin: University of Texas Press, 1999.

Kamali, Mohammad Hashim. *Principles of Islamic Jurisprudence*. Rev. ed. Cambridge: Islamic Texts Society, 1989, 1991.

Kappeler, Andreas, Gerhard Simon, and Georg Brunner, eds. *Muslim Communities*

Reemerge: Historical Perspectives on Nationality, Politics, and Opposition in the Former Soviet Union and Yugoslavia. Durham: Duke University Press, 1989.

Keddie, Nikki R., and Beth Baron, eds. *Women in Middle Eastern History: Shifting Boundaries in Sex and Gender.* New Haven: Yale University Press, 1991.

Khoei, Mosavi. *Tozih al Masa'il* (Clarification of questions). Tehran: Intesharate Gha'm, n.d.

Khomeini, Ayatollah. *Divane Imam, Sorudehaye Hazrate Imam Khomeini*. 2d ed. Tehran: Mo'assese Tanzim va Nashre Ashare Imam Khomeini, 1372 H.SH.

Khoshonat va Farhang: Asnade Mahramanehe Kashfe Hejab (1313–1322) (Violence and culture: Confidential records about the abolition of the hijab, 1313–1322 H.SH.). Tehran: Department of Research Publication and Education, 1990.

Kristeva, Julia. *The Powers of Horror: An Essay on Abjection*. New York: Columbia University Press, 1982.

Lightfoot-Klein, Hanny. *Prisoners of Ritual: An Odyssey into Female Genital Circumcision in Africa*. London: Haworth Press, 1989.

Mabro, Judy. *Veiled Half-Truths: Western Travellers' Perceptions of Middle Eastern Women*. New York: I. B. Tauris, 1991.

Mahmud, Sayyid Fayyaz. *Ghalib: A Critical Introduction*. Delhi, India: Adam Publishers, 1993.

Malti-Douglas, Fedwa. *Woman's Body, Woman's Word: Gender and Discourse in Arabo-Islamic Writing*. Princeton: Princeton University Press, 1991.

Mediamark Research Inc. "Magazine Audience Estimates, Spring 1999." http://www.mediamark.com/cfdocs/MRI/pp_S99a.htm (November 4, 1999).

———. "Spring 1998 Median Age, Household Income and Individual Employment Income." http://www.mediamark.com/Pages/techguide/tg_s98_age_hhi.htm (November 4, 1999).

Mernissi, Fatima. *Beyond the Veil: Male-Female Dynamics in Modern Muslim Society.* Rev. ed. Bloomington: Indiana University Press, 1987.

———. *The Veil and the Male Elite: A Feminist Interpretation of Women's Rights in Islam*. Trans. Mary Jo Lakeland. Reading: Addison-Wesley, 1994.

Milani, Farzaneh. "Forugh Farrokhzad: A Feminist Perspective." In *Bride of Acacias: Selected Poems of Forugh Farrokhzad*, ed. Ehsan Yarshater. Delmar, N.Y.: Caravan Books, 1982.

———. *Veils and Words: The Emerging Voices of Iranian Women Writers*. Syracuse: Syracuse University Press, 1992.

Minces, Juliette. *Veiled: Women in Islam*. Translated by A. M. Berrett. Blue Crane Books, 1993.

Moayyad, Heshmat, ed. *Once a Dewdrop: Essays on the Poetry of Parvin E'tesami*. Costa Mesa, Calif.: Mazda Publishers, 1994.

Moghissi, Haideh. *Populism and Feminism in Iran*. New York: St. Martin's Press, 1994.

Motahari, Morteza. *Mas'aleh-ye Hejab* (The question of the veil). Tehran: Sadra Publication, 1374 H.SH.

Mulvey, Laura. "Visual Pleasure and Narrative Cinema." In *Contemporary Film Theory*, ed. Antony Easthope. London: Longman, 1993.

Murphy, Robert F. "Social Distance and the Veil [Tuareg]." In *Peoples and Cultures of the Middle East: An Anthropological Reader*, ed. Louise E. Sweet, 290–314. New York: Natural History Press, 1970.

Muslim, Ibn Hajjaj al-Qushayri. *Sahih Muslim*. Trans. Abdul Hamid Siddiqi. Lahore: Ashraf Press, 1976.

Naficy, Hamid. "Veiled Vision/Powerful Presence: Women in Post-Revolutionary Iranian Cinema." In *In the Eye of the Storm: Women in Post-Revolutionary Iran*, ed. Mahnaz Afkhami and Erika Friedl, 131–50. Syracuse: Syracuse University Press, 1993.

Neale, Stephen. *Genre*. London: BFI, 1980.

Nefzawi. *The Perfumed Garden of the Shaykh Nefzawi*. Trans. Sir Richard F. Burton. Cambridge: Cambridge University Press, 1969.

Omid, Nikfarjam. "Islamic Stance on Art." *Echo of Islam* 148 (1996).

Ovid. *Metamorphoses*. Trans. Mary M. Innes. London: Penguin Books, 1955.

Pickthall, Mohammed Marmaduke. *The Meaning of the Glorious Koran*. New York: New American Library, n.d.

Playboy Report, Ayatollah Khomeini, Meine Worte: Weisheiten, Warnungen, Weisungen (Playboy Report, Ayatollah Khomeini. My words: Wise sayings, warnings, and instructions). Trans. Jean-Marie Xavière (Persian to French) and Rolph Gaïl (French to German). Munich: Moewig Verlag, 1980.

Pound, Omar S. *Arabic and Persian Poems*. New York: New Directions, 1970.

Rajabzadeh, Shahram, ed. *Divane Parvine E'tesami*. Tehran: Entesharat-e Ghadyani, 1373 H.SH. [1996].

Ranke-Heinemann, Uta. *Eunuchs for the Kingdom of Heaven: Women, Sexuality, and the Catholic Church*. Trans. Peter Heinegg. New York: Doubleday, 1990.

Ricks, David, Arpan Jeffrey, and Marilyn Fu. "Pitfalls in Advertising Overseas." *Journal of Advertising Research* 14, no. 6 (1974).

Rose, Issa. "'Re-orienting Our Views': A Rediscovery of Iran through Its Cinema and Women Filmmakers." http://www.nima3.com/IranMedia2/women.htm (June 3, 2000).

Said, Edward W. *Covering Islam: How the Media and the Experts Determine How We See the Rest of the World*. New York: Pantheon, 1981.

Schoemaker, George H., ed. *The Emergence of Folklore in Everyday Life*. Bloomington: Trickster Press, 1990.

Seidenberg, Robert. "Advertising and Abuse of Drugs." *New England Journal of Medicine* 284, no. 14 (1972).

———. "Images of Health, Illness, and Women in Drug Advertising." *Journal of Drug Issues* 4 (Summer 1974).

Serrill, Michael S. "Armed Women of Iran." *Time,* vol. 149, no. 16 (April 21, 1997).

Shaarawi, Huda. *Harem Years: The Memoirs of an Egyptian Feminist.* Translated and introduced by Margot Badran. London: Virago, 1986.

Shankar, Anurag. "Archive of Hindi Movie Songs." Kabra, Navin, maint. http://www.cs.wisc.edu/~navin/india/songs/isongs/11/1174.html (June 3, 2000).

Shariati, Ali. *Fatima Is Fatima.* Trans. Laleh Bakhtiar. Tehran: Shariati Foundation, n.d.

al-Shawkani, Muhammad ibn Ali. *Nayl al-Awtar* (The attainment of goals). Cairo: Maktaba al-Qahira, 1978.

al-Shaykh, Hanan. *Women of Sand and Myrrh.* Trans. Catherine Cobham. London: Quartet Books, 1989.

Shirazi, Faegheh. "Islamic Religion and Women's Dress Code: The Islamic Republic of Iran." In *Undressing Religion: Commitment and Conversion from a Cross-Cultural Perspective,* ed. Linda B. Arthur, 113–30. Oxford: Oxford University Press, 2000.

Shirazi-Mahajan, Faegheh. "A Dramaturgical Approach to Hijab in Post-Revolutionary Iran." *Journal for Critical Studies of the Middle East* 7 (1995): 35–51.

Simaye Hijab (Face of the veil). Tehran: Ma'avenate Mobareze ba mafasede ijtima'iye naja, 1373 H.SH.

Simaye Zan dar Kalame Khumayni (Images of women in the speeches of Khomeini). 4th ed. Tehran: n.p., 1991.

Spellberg, D. A. *Politics, Gender, and the Islamic Past: The Legacy of 'A'isha Bint Abi Bakr.* New York: Columbia University Press, 1994.

Sprachman, Paul. *Suppressed Persian: An Anthology of Forbidden Literature.* Costa Mesa, Calif.: Mazda Publishers, 1995.

Steele, Valerie. *Fetish: Fashion, Sex, and Power.* New York, Oxford: Oxford University Press, 1996.

Stekel, Wilhelm. *Sexual Aberrations: The Phenomenon of Fetishism in Relation to Sex.* Trans. Samuel Parker. New York: Liveright, 1971.

Tahan, Malba. *The Man Who Counted: A Collection of Mathematical Adventures.* Trans. Leslie Clark and Alastair Reid. New York: Norton, 1993.

Timmerman, Kenneth R. "Easing Sanctions Will Not Help Democratic Movement in Iran." *Washington Post.* November 3, 1998: A18.

al-Tirmidhi. *Sahih al-Tirmidhi.* 9 vols. Cairo: al-Matba'at al-Sawi, 1934.

Tokhtakhodzhaera, Marfua. *Between the Slogans of Communism and the Laws of Islam.* Lahore: Shirakat Gah Women's Resource, 1992.

Vafa, Nezam. "Hijab." *Iran Shahab: Name-e Mahayane-e Fanni va Ijtemai* (Iran Shahab: A monthly publication of technical and social issues), no. 14 (1945). Tehran: Bongahe Ta'avani Shahab.

Vaqe'e Kashfe Hejab, Asnade Montasher Nashodehe Kashfe Hejab dar Asre Reza Khan (Reality of unveiling: Unpublished document from the time of Reza Khan). Tehran: Agency of Cultural Documents of the Islamic Revolution, 1990.

Vatuk, Sylvia. "Purdah Revisited: A Comparison of Hindu and Muslim Interpretations of the Cultural Meaning of Purdah in South Asia." In *Separate Worlds: Studies of Purdah in South Asia*. Ed. Gail Minault and Hanna Papanek. Delhi: Chanakya Publications, 1982.

Wehr, Hans. *Arabic-English Dictionary*. Ithaca: Spoken Language Services, 1976.

Williamson, Judith. *Decoding Advertisements*. London: Marion Boyars, 1973.

Wolf, Naomi. *The Beauty Myth*. New York: Morrow, 1991.

Workman, W. T. *The Social Origins of the Iran-Iraq War*. Boulder, Colo.: Lynne Rienner, 1994.

World Book Encyclopedia. Vol. 19. Chicago: World Book, 1991.

Yarshater, Ehsan, ed. *Persian Literature*. New York: Columbia University Press, 1988.

Yashpal. "Purdah." *Yashpal, Pratinidhi Kahaniyam* (Symbolic representations of aspects of life). New Delhi: Rajkamal Prakashan, 1987.

Index

—as a symbol: of civilization, 107; of independence, 93; of Islamic secularism, 126; of oppression, 58, 177, 178; of terrorism, 58
Versace, Gianni, 46
Virginia Slims, 15–18, 178
Vogue, 18
voyeurism, 75, 78, 82

Walton, Alan Hull, 42
Washington Post, 135
West, the, 43, 52, 62, 138, 147; clothes in, 30, 89; consumers in, 38, 42, 60, 83; culture of, 28, 64, 89, 108, 170; media in, 16, 28, 40, 55, 88, 187n.33; movies in, 67, 83; values of, 92, 93, 108; women in, 18, 38, 53
Western stereotypes: of Islam, 177; of Middle Eastern women, 11, 12, 16, 17, 21, 39; of Middle Eastern sexuality, 42, 44, 45, 46, 47, 50, 51, 70
Whipple, Thomas W., 11
White Revolution, 91
Wikan, Uuni, 6
Williamson, Judith, 36
Winger, Debra, 84

wives of the Prophet, 111–17 *passim*
Woman's Day, 95, 100
women, images of, 11, 30, 95, 103, 131; in battle, 114, 115, 116, 117, 120, 124, 134, 180; improperly dressed, 62, 107, 108, 140, 172; namahram, 68; policing women, 119, 120, 121, 128, 136, 192n.31; purity of, 70, 72, 165; rights of, 163, 167; self-determination, 70; as temptress, 143, 170
women's organizations, 91, 119
Woolf, Virginia, 166
World Trade Center, 49
World War I, 139

Xavière, Jean-Marie, 177

Yarshater, Ehsan, 151, 152
Yashpal, 4, 138, 144–46, 176
Yazid, 96
Young Turks, 139

Zaynab's sisters. *See Khaharan-e Zaynab*
Zoroastrianism, 150
al-Zubayr, 112, 113

Faegheh Shirazi is assistant professor of Middle Eastern languages and cultures, Islamic Studies Program, at the University of Texas at Austin. She specializes in textiles and material cultures as they relate to social and cultural practices of Muslim women in contemporary Islamic societies.